Sidney Weintraub
University of Pennsylvania

Capitalism's Inflation and Unemployment Crisis:

Beyond Monetarism and Keynesianism

Addison-Wesley Publishing Company

Reading, Massachusetts
Menlo Park, California • London
Amsterdam • Don Mills, Ontario • Sydney

This book is in the ADDISON-WESLEY SERIES IN ECONOMICS

Permission to quote Professor Milton Friedman was granted by the author and the American Economic Association. The passage by Professor Peter Wiles from the *Economic Journal* appears by consent of the Cambridge University Press as publisher. Quotations from J. M. Keynes have been approved by Harcourt, Brace Jovanovich, Inc., New York, and Macmillan, London and Basingstoke.

By the Same Author

Price Theory (1949)

Income and Employment Analysis (1951)

An Approach to the Theory of Income Distribution (1958)

Forest Service Price and Appraisal Policies (1958)

A General Theory of the Price Level (1959)

Classical Keynesianism, Monetary Theory, and the Price Level (1961)

Some Aspects of Wage Theory and Policy (1963)

Intermediate Price Theory (1964)

Growth Without Inflation in India (1965)

A Keynesian Theory of Employment Growth and Income Distribution (1966)

Keynes and the Monetarists, and Other Essays (1973)

Income Inequality (Editor, 1973)

Incomes Policy for Full Employment Without Inflation in Canada (1976)

Modern Economic Thought (Editor, 1976)

Preface

Economists stand in the dock for the tribulations of our economy. The instabilities of the market economy show only scant signs of receding, and less evidence of vanishing. Inherently, the chronic dismal state of affairs is a reflection of errant conventional analysis. Orthodoxy, in a shocking display of stoicism by luminaries and an awesome complacency by disciples, has become superbly irrelevant. Conjectural models, and ritualistic policies in the practical domain, are esoterically cultivated to nourish the unemployment morass and the inflation disorder, either singly or in tandem. Approximately a decade has elapsed since the stagflation-slumpflation virus infected the affluent market economies. Still, hush-a-byes of monetary caressing and fiscal stroking make the staked-out rounds, with little progress in serious discussion of institutional innovation to end the unruly deadlock.

My own deviation from orthodoxy is of long standing, stemming from a conviction that what the consensus taught could not happen might—and did—happen. Years ago I concluded that the small 1957–1958 stagflation emitted a warning of rupture in our theory, an episode crying to alert us to deficiencies in monetary and Keynesian demand-management responses to a wayward price trip accompanying a pernicious job drop. Largely, the diagnosis met studied evasion (or diatribes), though the price-level formula was adopted in several econometric models. Policy implications, except for the *Guideposts* in the Kennedy era, commanded a wary ambivalence, suggesting that the generality of the price-level formulation was imperfectly assessed. The result has been a theoretical and policy hodgepodge even among those demonstrating sympathy for the analytic principle. To be sure, in almost all quarters a fairly universal skepticism over the feasibility of price and wage controls emerged—an attitude which I share.

It has taken the economic debacle since 1968 to confirm (to my mind) the validity of the basic thesis. More support for the unorthodox theory can be mus-

319467

tered today, albeit with intermittent Phillips curve–fiscal demand management backsliding after rhetorical nods to money-income pressures. At the operational level, the Nixon-Ford economic policies hardly conferred high marks on monetary practitioners so certain of the glow of victory in the aftermath of the 1968 political transition. On the theoretical side, several gaping holes in Monetarism have been exposed, leading to some awkward permutations in the once confident models. Nonetheless, it is not astonishing that Monetarists cling to a defunct policy: to err is human—but for promulgators to abandon a doctrine is unworldly. Political officials, however, are less persuaded than they once were of the virtues of programmed central bank rules being sufficient to assure stabilization. Deeper correctives, however, have been shunned: jaded by the appalling waste of President Johnson's Great Society projects, which were supposed to usher in the millenium, the grievous Vietnam wounds, and the bumbling of British socialism, legislators have been reluctant to embark on new initiatives. Too, labor groups would have to be disabused of money-wage confusions: politicians are not eager to alienate a voting constituency, even though an educational venture rather than real injury would be entailed. Monetarism has made it a more respectable pastime "to flay the Fed," the central bank, rather than to tackle the onerous money-income distortion.

Small wonder then that our economy suffered a long sinking spell which, by transmission and emulation, has cast a global economic pall. Prominent professional voices, reiterating that salvation beckoned in a retreat to the old-time Monetarist religion, rationalized inaction and washed constructive debate from professional view: pages of leading economic journals can be thumbed in vain for detailed ventilation of specific proposals for Incomes Policy. Entries have been sedulously monitored by Monetarist referees for doctrinal purity; even thoughts of Incomes Policy have been abjectly condemned as a form of heresy, and confused in some inner contentment by stale denunciations of the obscenities of price and wage controls. Meanwhile, minor refrains on "inflationary expectations" have been puffed up and blown to choral status, as if chanting makes inflation go, or as if wishes can disperse the price surge regardless of the income winds.

Against the Monetarist legions committed to a singular simple idea of steady money-supply growth, tenderly mounted as a wispy spire on top of a massive foundation to ward off inflation, some residual Keynesian contingents (who once dominated the literature) still espouse demand-management programs to restore full employment. Many, in some perversion of Keynes, even derided inflationary concerns as a vestigial red herring. Their model emphasis on demand in real terms is too often hopelessly entangled with market demand in money terms through a failure to penetrate the price-level and money-wage nexus. In soft-pedalling the ramified distress of inflation the school has spent its former credibility. The recent breach by Nobel laureate Sir John Hicks, whose apparatus conferred logical sanctuary on the doctrine, may loosen the theoretical log-jam that has obstructed wider Keynesian participation in policy debate. Unfortunately, the percolation process is likely to be a slow drip, judging from lags in textbook dissemination.

While I have frequently lamented the strange detours of Keynesianism from Keynes, and their policy import, I am indebted to Dr. André Raynauld, Chairman of the *Economic Council of Canada,* for an invitation to submit my views on measures to eradicate the stagflation woes of our times. Obviously, these experiences are scarcely a unique Canadian property: in practically every mature, affluent, politically stable (and many not so stable) economy the double-trouble prevails.

Canada (on October 13, 1975) adopted a three-year timetable of (fairly porous) price and wage controls designed to tighten the inflation lid in successive stages. The program is unlikely to bolt the price level securely at the expiry of the latest experiment in a checkered bureaucratic control history. The administered restraints are still another exhibit of ephemeral patching and hankering for the coercive arm of central government. Predictably, the measures are destined to vanish through some illusion of lasting success, which will lead to their dismantlement, or as suffocation over bureaucratic harassment impels a clamor for their dismemberment. Controls inevitably compromise the market system by meddling in too many private daily transactions, with baneful inroads on production, labor hire, and purchase decisions. Something more flexible, enduring, and less vexatious is required by way of a policy for a decade (or longer) rather than for an acute emergency spell.

I like to believe that I have offered a constructive alternative, on which others may improve, so that Western market economies can achieve the proper goals of abundant job opportunities alongside a flat price track. Like all good legislation dealing with nonviolent human behavior, the proposal relies on a combination of incentive-deterrent stimuli to influence conduct. While the ideas are rooted in the tax mechanism, the aim is *not* tax collection, no more so than with posted auto speed limits: the objective is a sane road rule. Individuals could still violate the legal mandates—but at a penalty price to deter steep transgressions except under premeditated circumstances. In analogy with speed limits, only money sanctions are imposed, in lieu of criminal charges, incarceration, or fits of moral opprobrium. The provisions are compatible with a market economy in which transactions and production decisions are guided by the price-cost calculus, and tax breaks or burdens. The tax aspect of the proposal, to repeat, is to deflect mischievous inflationary behavior, and not to swell Treasury coffers.

The adoption of a Tax-Based Incomes Policy (TIP), in a form resembling the original Wallich-Weintraub plan, can be a constructive innovation for promoting a stable market economy. The original TIP plan is modified (strengthened, I think) through TIP-CAP (developed in Chapter 6). Since TIP was first set down the few theoretical discussions have been uniformly favorable concerning its income restraining features. Economists, however, have not immersed themselves in the subject of money-incomes restraint, having become lulled in the view that monetary policy, with or without demand management, would suffice, or opting generally for refuge in less controversial studies with less formidable economic practitioners and personalities.

I thank Professors Douglas Vickers, Lawrence Seidman, and Eileen Applebaum for reading an earlier version. Eileen Applebaum persuaded me to adhere to a format more nearly resembling the *Economic Council* report, with comment on alternative theories largely deferred till the close.* Thus the first three parts

---

*   *Incomes Policy for Full Employment Without Inflation* (Ottawa: Economic Council of Canada), March 1976.

render my own position rather directly, unhampered by a critique and digression on other views that ordinarily leave students shell-shocked under the economists' interminable "war of words."

Keynes expressed a faith in the ultimate triumph of ideas over vested interests. While my own efforts are directed toward revitalizing the market economy, any long-time dissenter who has tried to rebut economists of eloquence and repute finds progress measured in inches while miles remain to be traveled. There is some mild solace in Karl Marx's dictum: "Every beginning is difficult, holds in all sciences." Marx saw the opposition to new ideas solidified behind a protective wall for relative income retention. Relative income motivations are not, however, the dominant factors obstructing dialogue on the stagflation issue: on this subject ideas have imprisoned the faithful.

Jevons, a revolutionary of a markedly different stripe than Marx, foresaw the noxious influence of intellectual authority, in his day zealous in preserving the labor-cost theory of value. His message is again timely: his final passages call for "sedition" in science, or critical sifting of authoritative father figures as being preferable to "a despotic calm" which "is usually the triumph of error." In dissociating himself from "that able but wrong-headed man, David Ricardo," he wrote:

... it is impossible that one who has any regard for truth can long avoid protesting against doctrines which seem to him most erroneous. There is ever a tendency of the most hurtful kind to allow opinions to crystallize into creeds. (W. Stanley Jevons, Theory of Political Economy, *5th ed.)*

Monetarist and standard Keynesian interpretations have, in our time, led to an economic fiasco "of the most hurtful kind." This thought must give purpose to any work dedicated to a better economic future. The supporting analysis can alter our perception of the behavioral characteristics and operating mechanics of our economic system, inviting overhaul of some tendentious orthodox models and obsolete policy recipes.

S.W.

Philadelphia, Pennsylvania
August 1977

Abbreviations and Symbols Frequently Used

$A = Q/N$ = average (gross) real output of labor
EOE = equation of exchange
GBP = gross business product
GE = general equilibrium
GEM = general equilibrium model
GNI = gross national income
GNP = gross national product
GT = *General Theory of Employment Interest and Money*
k = average markup of prices over unit labor costs (PQ/wN)
KaM = *Keynes and the Monetarists, and Other Essays*
$L = N + U$ = labor force
M = money supply
$M^d = L$ = money demand
MA = monetary authority (or Fed or central bank)
MPT = marginal productivity theory
N = total employment
N_c = consumer sector employment
N_f = full employment
NI = national income
NQTM = new quantity theory of money

OQTM = old quantity theory of money
P = price level
P_c = consumer price level (CPI)
P_cQ_c = market value of consumer output
PQ = GBP (in some contexts, GNP)
Q = real output
Q_c = real consumer output
QT = Quantity Theory
QTM = Quantity Theory of Money
$U = L - N$
U = unemployment
U' = unemployment rate (U/L)
V = money velocity
w = average money wage
$W = wN$ = wage bill
w/A = unit labor costs (ULC)
WCM = wage-cost markup equation
Y = GBP $(= PQ)$

$\Delta P, \Delta Q, \Delta N, \Delta M$ = increments in P, Q, N, M, etc.
σ = expectational variable
$\omega = (1/k)$ = wage share (wN/PQ)

Contents

PART 1
THE STAGFLATION SETTING   1

Introduction: The Reality and the Ideal   1

ONE
The Inflation and Unemployment
Ordeal   5

The Keynesian and Monetarist Dialogue   7
The "Slows": Lincoln and His Generals   11
The Price and Unemployment Record   17
The Destroy-to-Revive Fantasy   20

TWO
The Costs of Inflation
and Unemployment   21

The Costs of Unemployment   21
The Inflation Impacts   27
Mischievous Potency of Inflation   33
Anticipated Inflation   35
Inflation as a Brain-Drain   37

Contents

PART 2
THE THEORETICAL STRUCTURE 39

*Introduction: The Money Wage
and Money Price Level Connection* 39

THREE
The WCM Theory: the Double-Edged Demand and Cost Blades 43

*The General Price Level in the Closed
Economy* 44
The Consumer Price Level 48
Money Wages in a Time Setting 53
Profit Inflation and Income Inflation 54
Historical Trends in WCM Components 55
The Price Level in the Open Economy 56
Not Why, But How 62

FOUR
Money In a Money-Wage Economy 65

The Macrodemand for Money 66
The Potency of the Money Supply 69
Money in a WCM Model 75
The Monetarist "Hole-in-the-Middle" 77
The Steady-Money-Growth Rule 84
*Money Wages: From Silence to
Expectations* 88
Central Bankers: A Maligned Lot? 89

FIVE
Money Wages: Phenomena in Search of a Theory 91

An Exogenous-Endogenous Dialogue 92
A "Compleat" Endogenous Wage Function 95
The Neoclassical Derived-Demand Theory 95
A Potpourri of Money-Wage Misadventures 102
*The Missing Theory and Some Misplaced
Class Struggle* 109
The Misplaced Class Struggle 110

PART 3
INFLATION REMEDIES: INCOME GEARING 113

*Introduction: The Debut of Incomes
Policy* 113

SIX
A Tax-Based Incomes Policy:
TIP-CAP 121

Ingredients of a Solution 123
A Corporate Tax on Excessive Wage Settlements: TIP 126
Shifting the TIP Surtax 136
Unions and Collective Bargaining 137
Some Technicalities and Omissions 140
Supplements to Facilitate TIP Compliance 141
The Administrative Feasibility of TIP 142

SEVEN
Profit Margins and Personal Income:
TIP-M and TIP-P 145

Tax Benefits for Lowering Profit Margins 145
Using the Personal Income Tax Lever 147
Alternative Incomes Policy Proposals 151
Payroll Tax Cuts and Wage Restraint 152

EIGHT
A Summing Up: Controls,
Indexation, and TIP 154

Price and Wage Controls 154
Indexation and Corrections 157
Little to Lose, and Much to Gain 160
Resolving the Crisis 162

PART 4
OTHER INFLATION THEMES 165

Introduction: Some Omitted Analyses 165

NINE
More on Money 167

*The Money-Wage Standard: The Pivotal w
Price* 168
The EOE and WCM as Predictive Theories 172
Monetary Policy Under Full Employment 175
The Open Economy 176
Lags: A Less Intimidating Perception 177
*Natural Unemployment, Money Transmission,
and Wage "Catch-Up"* 178
Expectations of Inflation 183
The Demand for Money 185

Contents

TEN
Keynes and the Keynesian Detours   194

Keynes and Keynesians   195
Keynesian 45-Degree Models   200
The IS-LM Model   205
Phillips Curve Keynesianism   207
Fiscalism: Functional Finance   210
The Keynesian Inflation Irrelevance   211
A Note on Aggregate Demand and Aggregate Supply   212

ELEVEN
Monopoly Malevolence   216

The Monopoly Inflation Shadow   217
Monopoly as a Noninflation Issue   226

TWELVE
Government Profligacy   227

Acquittal or Probation?   237

To *Rareté* Models of Courage

Joan Robinson: Sifting Theory	*André Raynauld:* Facing Facts
J. K. Galbraith: Expunging Myths	*A. P. Lerner:* Eschewing Dogma

Cost inflation at a high rate has produced a "general crisis of capitalism," and the stability of Communist prices shines like a good deed in a naughty world; yet economic theory has nothing to say. This article is born of shame. It attacks by implication many famous names, having first vulgarised their doctrines. But there is reason behind this vulgarisation. First, the writer is hardly capable of more, being no expert on the economics of capitalism. But in so serious a collapse of theory the fool has a duty to rush in where the fallen angels persistently refuse to tread. Secondly, the vulgarisation accurately represents basic thought and gut reaction. It certainly misrepresents thought at its growing points, and omits all the qualifications made by experts. But it is not through growth or qualification of the existing body of theory that cost inflation can be incorporated. It is time to re-examine the base, and acquire new gut reactions.

Peter Wiles, "Cost Inflation and the State of Economic Theory," *Economic Journal* (June 1973).

PART 1

The Stagflation Setting

Introduction: The Reality and the Ideal

The infirmities of capitalism have become chronic and virulent. During the last decade the affluent market economies have suffered simultaneous tremors of unemployment and fevers of inflation. If capitalism is to remain a viable economic system, it must be able to extricate itself from this dual crisis and provide abundant job opportunities and a stable price environment to facilitate rational intertemporal expenditure and savings decisions.

The times have been traumatic for too many people, with the systemic debilitation testing the patience of champions of the market order. A choice must be made. On the one hand, we can acquiesce in cosmetic doctoring of past policies which permit the ordeal to continue on both job and price fronts. The likelihood is that this will lead to a long recuperation at best and a sinking spell at worst, swelling the ranks of the foes of the market order as the system struggles to restore itself during feeble interludes of remission from its dual malaise. On the other hand, we can make some institutional reforms in order to eliminate the double blight. It goes without saying, whatever modifications are made in the system will have to be compatible with the democratic ideal. But those who are committed to freedom, and who apprehend the inherent strengths of noninterventionist decentralized systems, have been chary about devising ways for preserving the virtues while eliminating the defects. By now it should be apparent that some innovative action is required.

Restoration, not dethronement, of the market order is the focus of the work that follows. This is a tract not for statism but for enhancing the market order. Totalitarian economies are not our ideal for emulation. Nevertheless, some important institutional revision will have to be ventured in order to relieve the system of its now chronic distress.

There is considerable misunderstanding in diagnosing the crisis, and the confusion was compounded during the 1976 presidential campaign. The Republican nominees, on the defensive concerning their price and jobs record, stressed that the country was at peace and attributed the prosperity enjoyed during previous Democratic administrations to the Korean and Vietnamese Wars. The standard refrain was that the severe postwar inflation during the Republican incumbency was actually a (long) delayed response to the Democrats' reckless attempt to provide both "guns and butter." Yet, ironically, in suggesting that "peace" was the cause of the job recession, the unreflective free-market zealots became unwitting propagandists for Marxist doctrine! It is a Marxist theme that war, or lavish military outlays, rescues the market economy from its periodic employment lapses. To be sure, wars lessen the unemployment drag by draining off personnel into the armed forces, and by a massive accompanying scale of expenditures for the military hardware. But anyone observing the American scene quickly senses the vast unfulfilled dream; there is much work to be done in housing, health, transportation, pollution, energy, and aesthetics. To treat many of these needs would not necessarily entail massive governmental expenditure; there are myriad ways to assist the private sector to improve the quality of life—its ultimate mission. It is a confession of intellectual bankruptcy for a "conservative" to conclude that war is capitalism's only route to full employment. Too often it seems that the market economy must first be saved from some of its impassioned friends!

More serious than the uninformed apologetics is the deeper stalemate that has developed with respect to the twin issue of price and job disorders. One camp, more sensitive to the creation of jobs, has been bereft of ideas on how to cope with inflation. Too often these advocates have blinked their eyes and declared that the spiralling price record is a mirage or that, if it does occur, it scarcely matters; they advise that we "live with it." Yet this half-vision of the economy will never usher in abundant job opportunities unless it is supplemented by a compatible strategy to suppress inflation. Conversely, the opposite camp is more adamant about subduing the inflation rate, even at the cost of increasing unemployment. There are, to be sure, vague soundings that "ultimately" price stabilization will restore full employment. But most of this can be classed as wistful rhetoric, lacking in particulars to prevent the economy from floundering even more deeply into unemployment on the mere promise of a dubious price surcease.

In general, these positions reflect the prominent Keynesian and Monetarist schools. They have had enormous influence on economic thought and public policy. Yet neither school has been helpful in isolating the stagflation virus nor in devising policies to correct the grave flaws that have strained democracy itself. Without a new theoretical perspective, economic analysis is likely to remain irrelevant to our age.* Meanwhile, our economy is likely to struggle along short of its optimal performance while too many undergo personal privation.

It should be possible to erect a sounder theory of the ongoing market crisis from elements already present in the analysis. It is also incumbent for economists to detail stabilization measures that are harmonious with the market system. These will require shedding the security blanket of things as they are and reaching out to consider how the system might operate more benignly with modest evolutionary revision. Compared to the more technological problem of finding new energy sources, the inflation and unemployment ordeal compels institutional modification.

In Turkey, it is said, the color of the fez on the outside of the head was once changed to provoke novel ideas inside the head. Analogously, we shall have to revise our relentless assault on the laws of arithmetic by way of money incomes. Our mindless overkill in monetary policy to counter inflation may be no more effective than the seven maids with seven brooms desperately sweeping back the seven seas.

---

*   Cf. Joan Robinson, "The Second Crisis of Economic Theory," *American Economic Review* (May 1972).

CHAPTER ONE

The Inflation and Unemployment Ordeal

In 1848 Frédéric Bastiat wrote:

What a profoundly afflicting spectacle France presents to us!

It would be difficult to say if anarchy has passed from ideas to facts, or from facts to ideas, but it is certain that it pervades all, and abounds everywhere.

The poor rise up against the rich, men without fortune or profession against property; the populace against the bourgeoisie; labour against capital; agriculture against manufactures; the country against the town; the provinces against the metropolis; the denizens against the stranger.*

Bastiat was a notorious apologist for *laissez-faire* doctrines. He was obsessed with the harmonious working of the economic order, believing that if only the market were let alone conflicts could smoothly be resolved in an equilibrium orderliness. Alive today, he would note that many of the ancient antagonisms still persist and that many market and democratic systems are reeling, some even tottering.

The contemporary malaise of the free world economies can be traced to two big ills: an overdose of inflation and excessive unemployment. These ailments aggravate all the old and lesser failings. Inflation and unemployment constitute the ongoing crises of market economies; practically all democratic societies are afflicted, denied immunity despite the varying applications of government intervention and welfare statism. The twin ordeal has affected elections in the United States, the United Kingdom, Canada, France, and Aus-

---

* Frédéric Bastiat, *Harmonies of Political Economy* (London: John Murray, 1860), p. 34.

tralia. In Italy, India, Portugal, and Spain, the economic disorders threaten old and new democratic processes. Democracy and the market economy are never short of foes: some are well-intentioned; many are uninformed; most are simply frustrated. Unless the mixed-market economies are able to mitigate the price and job ills, the Western world will be incessantly turbulent and threatened by demagogues promising a quick fix in exchange for a relinquishment of democratic safeguards.

Thus the stakes in the inflation and unemployment waiting game are high. A correct diagnosis and effective remedial tactics are vital if we are to preserve a free-market society that will be progressively able to cope with the perplexing problems of our age, once relieved of the perennial concern with jobs and the inequities inflicted by inflation. While the analysis to be developed and the policies to be espoused repudiate the dominant brands of economic orthodoxy, which are at the bottom of the painful experience and which have consigned the system to languish in the economic quicksands, new foundations for a stable economy can be erected by drawing on available strands of economic thought, organized in a new pattern.

At the policy stage, rather than hand-wringing and pleas for patience in the face of the interminable double trouble in prices and jobs, a concrete plan for short- and long-term economic restoration is tendered; others may well improve on the agenda once the source of the mischievous disorder is discerned. None of the programs jeopardize the market economy. On the contrary, they are wholly compatible with the democratic market order that prevails in the Western world (including Japan and Australia). Their objective is to break the inflation-unemployment shackles; they are intended not to hamper the price mechanism, but to assist its functioning in the manner envisaged in the optimistic minds-eye of orthodox equilibrium theorists contemplating the wholesome ends of a fully stable economy.

Salvaging the market economy, not displacing it, is the aim. Some institutional reform is, of course, imperative and inevitable. But the revisions can cohabit with the market system, and not collide with it. Incomes Policy, or Incomes Gearing, as we shall come to call it, can supplement the macroeconomic monetary and fiscal stabilization techniques wielded in all modern economies; Incomes Policy can buttress the conventional instruments in accomplishing their objectives.

Every age presents problems which test the resolve of democratic societies. In the 1930s they faced the distress of wholesale unemployment, with its spillover into repressive Nazism and Fascism in Europe, and the reformist New Deal—with all its errors and blemishes—in the United States. Analytically, it was to the job despondency that Keynes addressed his grand theory for coping with the flaw he detected in the market economy. Keynes took the giant, percipient step of exposing the shortcomings in the doctrine of automatic full employment under government *laissez-faire*. In the 1940s the democratic societies faced war, and then the postwar conversion and restoration.

War-time full employment through government expenditure was, in a way, a laboratory test of Keynes' ideas on the relation between effective market demand and full employment. The same set of demand-management ideas was carried over to shoal up the 1950s normalcy, with an addendum in growth theory (by Harrod and Domar) whittled from pieces found in Keynes. Growth aspects dominated the Kennedy-Johnson years, until the Vietnam convulsion wreaked a political tumult that edged the economic problem from center stage.

Inflation and unemployment are old sores, though their *simultaneous* appearance is a queer and confounding modern tandem: it is their juxtaposition that now challenges our resolve. Unless these instabilities are erased, we will be unlikely to settle the many complex and significant new issues, such as the terms of *detente* under the nuclear threat, the energy shortfall and oil blackmail, environment and ecology, pollution and effluents, health care, crime, urban chaos, and the quality of life generally. Political attention and thought will remain riveted on inflation and unemployment, and distracted from the fresh and proliferating conundrums. Temporizing with the job and price dilemma of the past, the future will slip away.

The Keynesian and Monetarist Dialogue

Over the last decade a surrealistic and quixotic debate on economic policy has raged between economists tagged (with shades of independence) as Keynesians and Monetarists. The dialogue has been incessant, even as it has wandered into wonderland. Starting out as warring camps with opposing ornamental models and ideologies, with each side professing scientific acumen, the controversy drifted into a fracas over "half-a-loaf" of economic performance, with the Keynesians clamoring for higher employment and the Monetarists urging lower inflation. If we continue to apply the prescribed measures, the economy is likely to continue to wallow in both inflation and unemployment —the double concatenation of "stagflation" and "slumpflation" blues.

The boom-bust cycles

The names "stagflation" and "slumpflation" were invented to describe the new disorder; in Chapter 4 we shall define the terms more carefully. Stagflation, in essence, typifies the simultaneous experience of inflation-unemployment with moderate production restraint; this has largely marked the United States, Germany, France, Canada, Australia, and other countries since about 1970. Slumpflation, on the other hand, carries receding output, inevitably compelling severe unemployment jumps, as in the United Kingdom in 1974–1975 and the United States for part of the period. Of the two, slumpflation is the more dismal spectacle.

Until recently, the cyclical economy experienced simultaneously *higher* prices, *decreased* unemployment, and *greater* output in the recovery and boom phase of the business cycle.* In the recession and depression stages, there occurred falling prices, higher unemployment, and lower production levels. In measuring the business cycle, one could invoke the price wave or the output path: both tended to display the same directional tendencies though, of course, amplitudes would differ. Conversely, while it would not be a precise mirror image, the unemployment rate would thrash about in a contrary pattern. To set ideas, the older business cycle might be pictured schematically, as in Fig. 1.1.

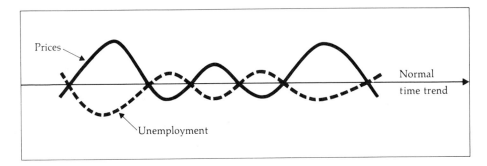

Figure 1.1

Prices and unemployment thus traversed reciprocal cycles, one up and the other down.† This is in marked contrast to the recent *simultaneous* surge of *both* prices and unemployment. In the 1930s, anyone who expressed alarm over inflation occurring in the midst of the Great Depression would have been derided as an illogical crank, possibly inclined to violence. The real task then was seen to be that of securing price "reflation," or consciously restoring prices—inflating them—to reverse the *unemployment* calamity.

Stagflation belonged to the unthinkable. Occasionally, it might be mentioned as a pathological condition endemic to backward economies, such as the comic (to us) "banana" republics, pock-marked by revolution and riven by dictators, bandits, property expropriation, printing-press money, and political spoil-sports. Yet the embarrassing scenario of backward societies now impairs the functioning of politically mature, affluent economies.

---

* Cf. Sir Roy Harrod, who wrote: "There is wide empirical evidence for the proposition that rising prices are associated with increasing activity and falling prices with declining activity." *The Trade Cycle* (New York: Oxford, 1936), p. 39.

† Writing on the measurement of business cycles, A. C. Pigou observed: "Either (an index of production with trend removed) or an index of workpeople employed will serve as a rough measure of industrial production." On the next page, in an overlay diagram, to portray the cycle, Pigou uses a curve of an index of "general unemployment percentage inverted." See *Industrial Fluctuations* (London: Macmillan, 1929) 2d ed., pp. 8–10.

In 1957–1958 there was a mild stagflation disorder in the United States.* Prices edged up, output moved sidewise, jobs turned down. This was our gentle, fraternal initiation to the anomalous combination. But it has taken the years since 1969, years of overt, distinct, and serious distortion of old patterns, to make us cognizant of new forces that do not succumb to the old remedies, no matter how earnestly the entrenched orthodoxy tells us that nothing has changed. Only those who refuse to confront the facts can seriously maintain that "the economic structure has not altered." Echoes of "economics as usual" will do nothing to allay the virulent and perverse outbreak.

The "stagflation-slumpflation" debacle must give us pause. Now, modern economists must deal with a dual malady that never confronted their predecessors and that remains immune to conventional remedies. Learned papers, embellished by mathematics, piles of data, and the powers of the computer, recount innumerable versions of minute permutations of discredited stabilization policies. Meanwhile, stagflation persists under a remarkable cop-out of will to conjecture new blueprints to relieve the stalemate. Audiences too often are titillated instead with sallies about the incurability of the disorders or the unimportance of the instabilities. The gravity of the phenomena has not evoked comparable energy and originality in analysis or in policy response. The greater fidelity has been devoted to preserving obsolete theoretical structures.

Keynesians and Monetarists

Reference has been made to the Keynesian-Monetarist "half-a-loaf" dialogue. Generally, Keynesians espouse policies for thinning unemployment, largely by means of fiscal policy such as lower taxes or increased government spending, and an easier money policy. (Later, it will be contended that some Keynesian themes proceeded incautiously from Keynes' great work.†)

Monetarists largely fear the inflation sequence, which they believe is incubated in a lax monetary posture.‡ They blame the Federal Reserve in the United States and the central banks in other countries for sharp price outbreaks. They intimate that if the central bankers are not acting in cahoots to engineer "world inflation," they are at least in tacit collusion—or delusion. If only a handful of money managers were ousted and replaced by Monetarists who "understand" money, inflation would dissolve. Their solution: fire the central bankers.

---

*   It was the 1957–1958 phenomenon which led me to a new formulation of the price level, in the belief that something was amiss, that the economy was not conforming to old rules. See my *A General Theory of the Price Level* (Philadelphia: Chilton, 1959).

†   Cf. Chapter 10.

‡   Cf. Chapters 4 and 9.

To be sure, Monetarists are apt to concede that the immediate result of tighter money policies would be unemployment. But this is presented as the "price," the "sacrifice" *we* have to pay to abort inflation and achieve a stable price level. How long it would take, or what alternatives could be adopted if the policy faltered once again, are subjects on which they are unduly laconic. They stake all on still another frontal assault, without any protective safeguards in the event of further stagflation.

So far, there is no record of any prestigious advocate of unemployment as a salubrious public policy employed in academic, banking, or government circles, who has resigned a post to join the ranks of the militant unemployed inflation-fighters. Unemployment for the unskilled, for minorities, for individuals at the bottom of the income heap, is programmed. The direct welfare benefits of unemployment are not so enticing as to be embraced voluntarily by Monetarist propagandists.

Nonetheless, Monetarists do have a policy for inflation, with mostly a rarefied faith that "ultimately" job markets will recover. What happens thereafter? Apparently, there will be another turn of the boom-bust cycle. There are, to be sure, soothing reassurances idealizing the "long-run natural equilibrium" that will come to pass.

Keynesians, on the other hand, have been prone to derogate inflation as a false bogey. Even as inflation has accelerated under their eyes they have been apt to ignore it as a bogus scare tactic so long as unemployment exists and idle production capacity abounds. At the political level, some opportunists have convinced leaders in the Democratic party in the United States and the Labour party in England either to do nothing or, when pressed, to dust off some outmoded wage-price control diversions, with the latter (in most any form) sure of arousing strong opposition, and with slim survival prospects. The mindless-blindness inflation posture is politically comforting for it precludes taking unpalatable political stands on money-wage excesses and labor-union behavior, while opening a welcome political retreat and professionally sanctified avenue for denunciation of the Federal Reserve or Republican presidents. This contorted reasoning, for example, prompted Senator Hubert Humphrey in 1976 to sponsor a full-employment bill calling for mandatory hiring of workers for government jobs without a word about the tie between excessive wage boosts and inflation. To do so, he remarked, would offend labor.

Monetarists are fearful of inflation and tolerate unemployment, considering it a "natural" consequence of stabilizing measures aimed at prices. Keynesians consider unemployment intolerable, and regard inflation as a conservative bugaboo.

Each side in the great "ideological" debate thus grappled over a prized "half-a-loaf" economic performance. To fight inflation, Monetarists usually pontificated in favor of annual increases in the money supply of 3 to 5 percent per annum as "about right." Keynesians, equally solemn, demanded a rate of 7 to 9 percent to turn the job trick. The content of the argument degenerated into one of the shallowest and most intellectually appalling disputes ever to divide "liberal" and "conservative" camps—Democrats and Republicans in the United States, and parallel political rivals in other countries.

Thus a money-supply discrepancy of 4 percent separated the adversaries. So much noise over a paltry 4 percent ideological schism! Chairman Arthur Burns, of the Federal Reserve, with a keen sense for sifting empty pedantic palaver, usually walked the tight-rope to split the difference in his policy count-downs. To paraphrase Churchill, perhaps never before in macroeconomic policy has so much been made of so little for so long, by way of diagnosis and prescription in the worst job debacle since the 1930s and the most terrible price surge. One group was carefree about unemployment, the other about inflation.* Both somehow retained the faith that measures which had continuously failed—monetary maneuvers—must somehow succeed in the future under a new dosage of insidious ineffective medicines.

If we contend that inflation and unemployment are both evil demons, then we will have to devise a means to demolish both: it will require more than a perpetual series of bland monetary gestures. As Nobel Laureate Jan Tinbergen might say, so long as the one arrow of monetary policy is aimed at two darting targets, the bulls-eye of economic stability will elude us and capitalism will be under siege.

The "Slows": Lincoln and His Generals

President Lincoln desponded over his generals during the Civil War.† He had lavished on them manpower and matériel to the point of overwhelming the Confederate enemy stores, but it seemed to him that the generals preferred drill field and parade exercises to waging a decisive campaign: their disposition, until General Grant assumed command, was always to postpone the fight to another day. Lincoln mourned the others, more in sorrow, as being afflicted with the "slows."

There is a sad analogy in this anecdote to the performance of the economic advisers installed in the Nixon and Ford years, 1969–1976.‡ They continuously spoke of a "gradual" approach, a "game-plan," intoning the "natural" forces of recovery and price stabilization, mostly waiting like Micawber for something to turn up. The degree of inactivity made it seem as though they were

---

* As individual Keynesians and Monetarists shade off from the sharp stands assigned to them, some will protest that the descriptions are caricatures. Yet considerable evidence could be assembled, consisting of prominent names, to document the interpretations.

† See T. Harry Williams, *Lincoln and His Generals* (New York: Knopf, 1952), Ch. 7.

‡ It is the Republican party that is censured for its shortcomings in the United States; in Canada, it would be the Liberal party; in the United Kingdom and Australia, mainly Labour. Failures cut across the political spectrum for, mostly, the policies were stale and orthodox.

awaiting an act of God in lieu of exercising their brains and initiative to extricate the economy from its plight. In contrast, recall the story of Arnold Palmer, superb golfer in his prime, who was asked how he would play out from behind the trees. He responded: "I got in, didn't I?" This resolute imaginative spirit has been conspicuously absent during our economic slide, playing havoc in the world economy in view of the example that the United States sets, and the great weight it casts (through its import absorption) on the economic fortunes of other countries.

The "gradualist" game plan: the "slows"

Entering office in January 1969, the Nixon advisers were confident that tighter monetary policies would be a sufficient prophylactic to upend inflation and maintain the economy at stable, near-full employment after some temporary lapse. To use the folksy football metaphors indulged in by the impeachable President, the administration had a "game-plan." The money "strategy" was intended to rein the annual inflation rate at 3 percent by year-end, from the 6 percent mid-1968 to mid-1969 rate. On too many occasions the Nixon team strutted with confidence, declaring that they would "eat" the textbooks if the program failed. (Of course, the menu would consist of over-age Monetarist tidbits, and there is no subsequent record of a smorgasbord book feast.)

The predictions were repeated monotonously—while the number of inflation-rate fumbles accelerated. Quizzed on their intercepted price signals, they stoutly prophesied that the game-plan would win "gradually," that the money supply had been so "inflated" during the Johnson Vietnam quagmire that monetary "lags" constituted a deceptive opposition decoy back in motion. "The lags are larger than expected," became a programmed chant. (Charitably, nobody blamed President Abraham Lincoln for some delayed reactions to the Civil War greenback issue.) Railing at the Johnson Democratic administration also offered a diversionary gambit—there was much to rail about. "Everybody" knew that wars led to postwar inflation. While this contrived history satisfied a gullible press in the honeymoon phase of the new administration and a patient public anxious to believe in something after the Johnson "credibility gap," less concern was paid in the orchestrated optimism to the induction notices tendered to a new growing army of unemployed. The stagflation practices were to lap many football seasons.

By 1971, over two and a half years after the inauguration of the "gradualist game-plan," the inflation rate ballooned, compounded by growing unemployment. The consumer price index stood at 106.7 in January 1969 (1967 = 100) and the unemployment rate at 3.4 percent. In July 1971, the corresponding figures were 121.8 and 5.9 respectively. The jobless (seasonally adjusted) numbered 2.2 million more in the army of the idle.

Under the urging of Secretary of the Treasury John Connally, a political sage to whom elections overshadowed Monetarist shibboleths, President Nixon was persuaded that his renewed political lease was endangered by the stagflation debacle. Viewing the prospective wreckage of his personal fortunes, acting out his flexible principles, Nixon reversed his field, and enacted a sequence of price and wage controls, beginning with a dramatic announcement on TV on August 13, 1971. Although he had often vowed that he would *never* invoke controls, a program was drafted, albeit by advisers usually hostile to anything beyond monetary expedients plus balanced budgets.* General Marshall's maxim (in another context) that new policies required new men had not been heeded in the economic domain; it was more the fable of the fox guarding the chicken coop.

Thus began the Nixon Phases. For 90 days there was a price-wage freeze; successful, the episode proved mainly that the economy could endure practically anything for three months. In Phase 2, a wage limitation of 6.2 percent (5.5 before fringe benefits) was imposed. While this still ensured a price rise, intended to be contained at about 3 percent per annum, ad hoc rulings punctured the wage stipulations. The rationale behind the approximately 6 percent mandated wage advance was that the figure was a reasonable drop from the earlier 9 percent-plus grabs.

The Nixon Phase 2 was successful, measured by the rise of 3.4 percent in the consumer price level in 1972. To be sure, in the 1968 campaign the Republicans had lambasted the Johnson administration for its inflation rate which averaged 3.7 percent over 1966–1968, including 4.7 percent in 1968. Also, in the spring of 1972 monetary policy was eased—as it could be with the wage and price blocks in place—and the President accelerated the tempo of defense expenditures, especially in the aerospace complexes of Texas and southern California, electoral areas vital to his reelection. Too, he had delivered the oracular words that he, too, was a "Keynesian."†

With the November 1972 election safely won, President Nixon, under the prodding of his more conservative Monetarist advisers (specifically, Secretary of the Treasury George Schultz and Council of Economic Advisers Chairman Herbert Stein), effectively dismantled the Phases in January 1973. They sputtered on for a few months, lapsing first into decontrol, then into "monitoring" price and wage movements (reporting postmortems), and then, under President Ford, into widely unread "studies."

---

* The commitment to balanced budgets was mainly verbal, for political mileage; over the fiscal years 1970–1975 the cumulative deficit totalled just under $115 billion. The New Deal outlays under President Roosevelt were positively miserly in retrospect.

† Conservatives, properly faulting liberal blunders, should recall that Secretary of Defense Charles Wilson, of "what's good for General Motors is good for the U.S." fame, muttered in the Eisenhower years that if government outlay was necessary to get higher employment (and elect Republicans) the Eisenhower "team" would get the message. In this climate, the Interstate Highway Program was born: anyone who sold automobiles would appreciate fast turnpikes. Railroads were frozen out by the auto raid. Politically, when it will serve them, presidents understand fiscal facts.

The rest is history, with an 8.8 percent consumer price rise in 1973 and a double-digit 12.2 percent figure in 1974.* Some "improvement" over the Johnson *war* inflation! In spring 1974, Alan Greenspan was appointed as Council chairman. Totally devoted to "gradualism"—the "slows"—he reiterated at convenient opportunities the stale myths of the "natural" forces in the economy slowing inflation and assured jaded media reporters that the economy was "bottoming out." As a ritualistic Wall St. chartist of business cycles, he discerned that recessions were an old, not a new phenomenon: the stagflation aspect failed to dent the natural healing ideology. For about a year, Treasury Secretary William Simon (suffused with homespun doctrines of alarm fresh out of McKinley) and Greenspan kept vigil in a meticulous mid-wife study without motion over our deepest postwar "bottom." Each sign of improvement was gleefully broadcast as a miraculous sign of strength—while distress was compounded.†

Through 1974, despite the excessive unemployment, the Simon and Greenspan team kept insisting on the need for a tax *increase* to avert inflation through deficit finance. Short-term interest rates on Treasury bills, be it noted, had risen to 8.74 percent in August, with the full interest rate spectrum at about the highest levels in our modern experience. Prime commercial paper rates approached 12 percent. Tight money, *and* unarrested inflation, were in the saddle.

Unemployment, at 7.2 percent in December 1974, still did not diminish the rhetoric for a tax increase; the shambles in the housing industry, where new construction fell from 2.4 million units started in 1972 to 1.4 million in 1974, did not faze the recession-bent advisers. As late as mid-December 1974, they still called for a tax rise, amid gossip that Simon would otherwise resign. Suddenly, recognizing the political danger in the job crisis, President Ford also reversed his field, discarding his WIN buttons (for Whip Inflation Now) and his Spartan request for a 5 percent income tax surcharge to up-end inflation. Instead he urged "quick" action by Congress to *cut* taxes!‡ Petulantly,

---

*   All figures are from either the *Federal Reserve Bulletin* or *Annual Report of the Council of Economic Advisers.*

†   Some of the inflation can be assigned to the Arab oil boycott and the new muscle of the OPEC cartel. Yet the leap in oil prices alone would constitute a *relative* price surge rather than being itself the stuff of price-level inflation. See Chapter 3 below.

‡   Writing in November 1973, for publication in January 1974, I had recommended a tax *cut*, accompanied by a pledge by labor for wage restraint, as a two-pronged attack on inflation and unemployment. See "A Tax Cut to Avert Stagflation," *Challenge* (January 1974). The administration used only half the opportunity; Treasury Secretary Simon rationalized the tax reversal on the apologetic that the rise in unemployment had come faster than expected, i.e., read, *intended.* Apparently, the political cost of a job hemorrhage was heavier than slow blood-letting. Professor A. P. Lerner caustically equated the Ford fiasco to the Herbert Hoover depression era. (This was not wholly fair to President Hoover.) See *New York Times*, December 19, 1974.

when this "urgent" act was deferred into early 1975, the President denounced *congressional* vacillation! In this remarkable spin-around fashion, bedecked with high-priced talent, computer printouts, and handsome charts at the Treasury and Council, grave economic decisions were made, here now there now and a penny for ideological conviction.

September 1974 was also the time, shortly after the unlamented Nixon resignation, of the economic "summit" conferences at the White House. Those invited were mostly Keynesians and Monetarists prominent in the two political parties; too many remained mindful of their sponsors and their political allegiance. Concerning inflation, Keynesians, as usual, focussed on unemployment; Monetarists rallied around a summons "to bite the bullet." The Monetarists wanted to tighten money despite the ominously rising unemployment rate—or bite a bullet and smite the disadvantaged in another blow to jobs. Consistent, realistic on the issues, as well as having a plan to deal with the twin-heads of stagflation, to his everlasting credit for courage and independence, J. K. Galbraith recommended a restoration of price and wage controls. (More on these later; despite my doubts concerning their efficacy and survival features, they constitute a recognition of the problem and a program.)

A recent *Council of Economic Advisers* (1976 Annual Report) is a litany on "gradualism" and a capitulation to the slow-growth thesis. Thus: "If we do not commit ourselves to a gradual recovery over a period of years, we may increase economic instability . . ."* Apparently, a sick economy need not fear becoming ill. Robustness is eyed as the danger. Fortunately, this Report spared us from game-plan moralizing.† After eight years of economic blight there remained unwavering faith in gradualism and the complacent, distorted theology that while wallowing in substandard performance do-little government will aid the market economy survival.‡

What of the future? Programs, of course, take time to legislate and enact, to implement, and to take hold: this can be the only meaningful sense of

---

*   See Annual Report, *Council of Economic Advisers* (1976), p. 21.

†   Not entirely: "The challenge to current monetary and fiscal policy is to set the stage for a gradual transition from stimulation . . ." (p. 21). Or: "The thrust of fiscal policy will also have to change gradually" (p. 22). A cherished word, "gradually," and chronic worry about future *high* employment as present output slips away. Its abiding passion was for an unsatisfactory future, by lacking a serious inflation policy as unemployment either remains high or dwindles to lower and more optimal levels.

‡   The "slows" has an arcane, bemusing ancestral whimsy in Jeremy Bentham, patron of utilitarianism, who wrote that the motto, or watchword of government ". . . ought to be—Be Quiet." Bentham wrote this in protest of the restrictive strangulation of trade under mercantilism in an earlier age prior to modern industrial capitalism. Bentham, wanting to *conserve* freedom, would have opted for compatible institutional modifications, we might surmise, to permit the full functioning of the system for the "greatest good." *Manual of Political Economy* (1798). See S. Howard Patterson, *Readings In the History of Economic Thought* (New York: McGraw-Hill, 1932), p. 184.

"gradualism." But there must first be a plan to prevent the disorders rather than relying on the naive faith that by moving the economy to high unemployment the distress will somehow alleviate unemployment! The untapped query remains: what comes for inflation after fuller recovery?

One guess is that we will revert to the stagflation mess, or to the older boom-bust cycle. The scenario will only have to be updated from the file of sorry past oscillations. The crisis of capitalism is thus unlikely to abate in a happy clinch of contented actors. The inflation–unemployment pathos will stay with us in an interminable drama if present policies continue. The time is ripe, indeed overdue, for a revision of methods to banish the old sores of the market economy.

The Kennedy years of expansion

One further historic episode is worth recalling. In the Kennedy-Johnson years, from early 1961 to late 1968, the economy reported about 94 months of practically uninterrupted output rise and employment advance.* It was in this era that ecstatic Keynesian economists were prone to believe that through fiscal policy, as under the tax cuts engineered by Walter Heller, chairman of the Kennedy Economic Council, the business cycle was obsolete. The experience confirmed that an undeflected trend was possible.

If we think about it, an unremitting advance should occur: each year the population and labor force grow, and technology (and thus output per employee) generally improves: each year thus should be the *best* output year on record. Nobody is surprised that production today exceeds output in the U.S. in 1800, when population numbered about 3,000,000. The year 1800 is distinguished from the year before last only in being more remote in time. Successful economic policy should thus succumb only to infrequent departures from annual growth, attributable mainly to natural calamities such as earthquakes, floods, and droughts. Output and job slumps always attest to *some* failure in economic steering.

The Kennedy years were accompanied also by the *Guidepost* policy designed, through exhortation and public support, to maintain annual wage settlements at about 3.5 percent to avert a wage-price spiral. Guideposts, however, relied on goodwill and persuasion rather than incentives or coercive teeth to deal with firms and unions that transgressed the norms. When U.S. Steel, after what was deemed a favorable wage settlement negotiated under administration auspices, attempted to hike prices unduly, President Kennedy fumed and brandished the threat of antitrust punitive actions to compel a price rollback.

Success in wage-price balance is likely to elude us if each exasperating price-wage blowup is treated ad hoc, requiring presidential intervention, and placing the prestige of the office on the line in sporadic and acerbic encounters.

---

* By some measurements of output, rather than employment, another 11 months would be tacked on to November 1967.

A general policy must be mandated, conformable to the operations of a market economy, and with a minimum of administration harassment. Time has passed Guideposts by.* There must be a better way of preventing inflation while sponsoring full employment. Formulating details on a more rational program for quickly realizing and maintaining a fully stable economy is the unfinished agenda of the market order. Unless the quest is successful, market adherents will lose credibility to tireless foes eager to uproot its virtues as well as its vices. Retention of capitalism requires reform.

The Price and Unemployment Record

By past standards, the modern inflation and unemployment sequel is appalling, not only in the United States but in most of the more democratic market economies. Yet a certain perspective is required, especially with respect to joblessness. For example, over 1953–1965, after the 5.8 and 5.9 percent 1950 and 1951 price surge in the Korean War, the consumer price level rose by an annual 1.3 percent average increment from 1952 to 1965. In retrospect, over his tenure (1953–1960) President Eisenhower appears as an economic wizard rather than a golfing, part-time caretaker administrator meticulously shunning economic or political innovations: at least the price record for his administration shines when compared to the Nixon-Ford shambles.

In unemployment, the Eisenhower years were unsatisfactory but superior to the stagflation morass: annual jobless rates were 2.9 percent in 1953, 6.8 percent in 1958, 5.5 percent in 1960. Over 1960–1968, the consumer price index moved (1967 = 100) from 88.8 to 104.2, an eight-year rise of 17.4 percent. Since 1968, in eight years, too, the price index jumped about 72 percent. Unemployment has soared from the low of 3.6 percent in 1968 to 8.5 percent in 1975 and at 7.7 percent in 1976.

Only when judged by the Great Depression can the modern unemployment position impart modest cheer. For example, the United States figure in 1933 averaged 24.9 percent of the work force; as late as 1939 it was 17.2 percent. Keynes wrote his *General Theory* (1936) in an era when, from 1922 to 1935, unemployment in the United Kingdom ran from 9 percent to 22 percent per annum.† In the Germany of the Weimar Republic, the scourge of unemployment in the early 1930s struck about one-third of the labor force, paving the way for the fiendish Hitler and the Nazi ideology aimed to quench the human spirit and its capacity for diversity into a martial totalitarian conformity.‡

---

* I had recommended a policy similar to Guideposts in 1969, of "watchtower" control, discussed often in the summer of 1969 while visiting with Walter Heller at the University of Minnesota. See *A General Theory of the Price Level*, Chapter 10.

† See William Beveridge, *Full Employment in a Free Society* (New York: Norton, 1945), p. 27.

‡ Cf. C. W. Guillebaud, *The Economic Recovery of Germany, 1933–1938* (London: Macmillan, 1939).

By these dismal standards the free world, even in the stagflation decade, has performed much better in providing jobs for work aspirants than it did some forty years ago.* The problem, however, is that we still fall far short of an optimal achievement. Inflation has been the horsefly in the job salve; to smite it we have made a practice of engineering unemployment in order to keep the price-level lid nailed down. But the maneuvers have compounded the miseries: rather than the one instability lapse there has been the dual deviation.

Table 1.1 contains some data on price and unemployment trends in Western market economies. It is well to note that what the market economies encounter, on present policies, are persistent cumulative increases of 5, 10, maybe 15 percent inflation rates per annum. It is misleading to invoke analogies of hyperinflation, as in Europe in the aftermath of World War I where prices in Germany rose in 1923 by some trillion percent compared to 1913.† In the more recent price paroxysms, the index in Chile was 1 in 1948, 100 in 1963, and 718 in 1971.‡

Before examining the statistics, we might reflect on how various rates of inflation, compounded annually, alter the price level after 5 to 20 years on 5, 10, 15, and 20 percent inflation rates. Table 1.2 thus yields a better sense of the price tendencies; rough interpolations for index numbers can be made for intervening years and intermediate price rates.

Obviously, a price rise in any one year at any one of the rates could be absorbed, yet a persistent cumulative price trend could overturn rational calculations based on some sense of "normalcy." Fundamentally, therefore, it is a price-level policy for a "decade" rather than for a "day," or a quarter-year or a year, that we must implement, bearing in mind, however, that the long run is made up of a collection of short runs during which the policy must be effective.

---

* Over 1954–1968, for OECD countries and the United States, unemployment averaged about 3.3 percent, with the United States shading to the high side at 5 percent. For price and unemployment statistics and analysis, see Geoffrey Maynard and W. van Ryckeghem, *A World of Inflation* (London: Batsford, 1976).

† The German inflation has been chronicled by C. Bresciani-Turroni, *The Economics of Inflation* (London: Allen Unwin, 1937), Millicent Sayers, translator. The author, however, neglects the price-level impairment attributable to the wage-price spiral. For a review demolishing the overhanging Quantity Theory theme in a few pithy remarks, see Joan Robinson, *Economic Journal* (Sept. 1938). Also, for some account of the German inflation debauch, see Frank D. Graham, *Exchange, Prices, and Production in Hyper-Inflation: Germany 1920–1923* (Princeton, 1930). For an account more sympathetic to the Joan Robinson stance (and my own), see Karsten Laursen and Jørgen Pedersen, *The German Inflation, 1918–1923* (Rotterdam: North-Holland, 1964).

‡ In Argentina, the figures were: 3 in 1948, 100 in 1963, 512 in 1971. For Brazil, 4, 100, and 1269 over the same dates. See *International Financial Statistics, 1972 Supplement* (International Monetary Fund).

Table 1.1

Consumer Price Indexes (1970 = 100) and Unemployment Rates, Selected
Countries for 1968, 1970, 1975 (*P* = consumer price index, *U* = unemployment rate)

Country	1968		1970		1975		1976*	
	P	*U*†	*P*	*U*	*P*	*U*	*P*	*U*
United States	89.6	3.5	100	4.9	138.6	8.5	146.3	8.0
Canada	92.6	4.7	100	5.9	142.5	7.1	153.0	7.6
Japan	88.3	1.1	100	1.2	172.4	1.9	187.6	2.4
France	89.3	—	100	—	152.8	—	164.9	—
Germany	94.7	0.9	100	0.7	134.7	4.7	141.5	5.2
Italy	92.8	3.4	100	3.2	171.1	3.3	197.7	3.5
Netherlands	89.1	1.4	100	1.1	151.3	4.8	164.5	5.2
United Kingdom	89.2	2.5	100	2.6	184.4	4.4	212.3	5.6
Australia	93.6	1.5	100	1.4	162.8	4.2	176.7	4.7

Source: *Monthly Bulletin of Statistics* (United Nations), August 1976
*   Mid-year or latest month available
†   1969

Table 1.2

A Price Index of 100 at Inflation Rates Compounded Over Time

Inflation rate (%)	5 years	10 years	15 years	20 years
3	116	134	156	181
5	128	163	208	265
8	147	216	317	466
10	161	259	418	673
15	201	405	814	1637
20	249	619	1541	3834

Scanning Table 1.1, consumer prices rose about 11 to 13 percent in all the countries listed from 1968 to 1970, or a simple average of about 5.5 percent per annum. Between 1970 and 1975, the *low* rise was 35 percent in Germany, and the high was 85 percent in the United Kingdom. By year-end 1976, most figures should be 3 to 5 percent higher than those listed for the first-half year. Over the period since 1970, then, inflation rates averaging out toward 8 percent have not been uncommon.

This is the dimension of the inflation problem. For unemployment, with rates under 4 percent commonplace in 1969 (in all countries except Canada), only Japan and Italy reported similar figures in mid-1976 (some would be skeptical of the Italian tabulation). Percentage-wise, the unemployment swing is astounding. Together, the *U*- and *P*-data confirm the magnitude of the stagflation dilemma. Absolutely, the jobless in the listed countries totaled 5.5 million in 1969 and 14 million in mid-1976.

The Destroy-to-Revive Fantasy

Even the most simple compilation of price level (P) and unemployment (U) rates discloses an economic travesty that portends an ongoing crisis of capitalism. Too, the extracts on policy positions reveal a fantastic destroy-to-revive philosophy riding high in the saddle: in the United States and elsewhere, tight money has been mandated to shake down real output and employment in order to thwart inflation. Presumably, after the market destruction, it is intended to restore jobs and revive production, hopefully without inflation. The entire thrust has elements of madness and insensitivity: if the objective is to depress P, rationality would condone actions to dampen P directly without destroying jobs. Yet the P-failures are pronounced, while the anomalous U behavior mocks economic acumen. Desired is an objective of "slow on prices, go on jobs." Results have been "go on prices, and no on jobs." Despite the Madison Avenue sorcery of "gradualism," designed to sell an unpalatable program and beguile a battered public, the program can only be judged a fiasco, evidencing stark complacency at the misfortunes of others and a myopia to the fate of the market economy.

In the boom-bust of past cycles some might detect an (illusory) rainbow having redeeming features, for P fell in the downturn as the good-output years "compensated" the lean depression harvest. On present trends, even P-relief by price falls is denied, while the ubiquitous fears of inflation, which obsess the profound policy executioners, obstruct recovery. To still the alarms over inflation with high employment they act to maintain unemployment *with* inflation.

Policy-makers have thus instituted at least eight recent years of programmed economic chaos. All of it confirms a strategic breach in our stabilization mechanism, and a gap that must be repaired in order to check inflation in an economy operating at full employment.*

---

* As yet, after five months into 1977 of continuing inflation approaching the unsatisfactory pace of the Ford years, nothing has been done by the Carter administration that might be described as a serious new initiative. To be sure, there has been more concern, in Keynesian fashion, with unemployment—in slow restoration targets.

The Costs of Inflation and Unemployment

The whole tenor of the remarks so far conveys omens of costs and danger from chronic inflation and unemployment, operating singly or in tandem. Their perpetuation undermines the sanguine idealized "equilibrium" versions of capitalism depicting optimal performance for the market economy. The observable shortfall satirizes the harmonious models.

Yet there are some who downplay the toll of the P or U lapses from the visionary state. There is thus some point in considering the grief—and possible beneficence—in departures from low U and flat P-trends.

The unemployment indictment can be made succinctly; only those who see job layoffs as a discipline on labor, somehow conducive to work efficiency, and others who can callously regard human distress are indifferent toward the objective of higher employment.

The Costs of Unemployment

Full employment is ordinarily defined as a situation in which all who are willing to work at prevailing *real* wages—or slightly lower—are able to find jobs with employers who value their work at the same real wage (or slightly higher). Thus there would be the voluntary meeting of minds of employers' estimates of skills, and wage earners' acceptance of the proffered terms. Full employment would be compatible with some transitional unemployment, as workers quitting one job for another, or some "frictional" unemployment through temporary work stoppages, or more costly wage earner locational shuffles.

For immediate purposes this discussion need not be pursued for it raises fine and, at this time, irrelevant theoretical discourse.* For the United States it would be an enormous accomplishment to return to the officially measured unemployment rate of 1968, 3.8 percent. A target of, say, 4 percent would comprise reasonably "full" employment in this country: if achieved, we could then consider whether we might not do a bit better.

Unemployment means a loss in the Gross National Product (GNP) of output or goods and services that might be produced; on the other side of the coin, it implies a vanished Gross National Income (GNI) of wages, salaries, and profits that could be earned on the lost output. A very simple definition of excess or superfluous unempolyment, signifying some malfunctioning of the economy, would be:

$$\text{Excess } U' = \text{Actual } U' \text{ minus 4 percent.}$$

According to a frequently quoted computation (Okun's law) it is presumed that each one percent climb in unemployment above 4 percent leads to an output fall-off of about 3.2 percent, not least because employers who anticipate merely a short production downturn temporarily retain excess personnel. Employers hold on to their desired staff to meet the turn-around; meanwhile they stay underemployed for some time interval.†

Table 2.1

Excess United States Unemployment and Estimated
GNP Output Losses, 1969–1976 (in billions of dollars)

Year	Excess unemployment	Estimated output loss in 1972 prices
1970	1.0	$ 11.0
1971	1.9	21.0
1972	1.6	18.7
1973	1.0	12.3
1974	1.6	19.4
1975	4.5	53.4
1976	3.6	45.0
Totals, 1972 prices		$180.8
Totals, 1976 prices		$236.6

* Every statistic rests on a definition, consistently applied. In the United States data many questions arise, about excluding from the work force those "not seeking work"—when the only factory in town is shut down so the local job search would be pointless—or the teenagers who have never been employed, and thus escape the jobless tally.

† Cf. Arthur M. Okun, *The Political Economy of Prosperity* (New York: Norton, 1970), p. 137.

Table 2.1 calculates the cost of the excess unemployment from 1969–1976, where the excess is measured as over 4 percent. The GNP losses are computed as simple percentages of output totals; for example, 2 percent excess unemployment is counted as a 2 percent output loss. Others may prefer to about *treble* the GNP losses stipulated in the table, first in 1972 prices and then in 1976 prices.*

The output-loss total is stupendous, amounting on a *very* conservative estimate to a cumulative figure of $235 billion at 1976 prices. Employing Okun's law suggests that the total suppressed output may have been over $800 billion at 1976 prices. In other words, the cost was in hospitals, schools, day-care centers, libraries, museums, etc., worth at least $400 billion at a fairly minimal figure—approximately 400,000 useful projects of $1 million each were casualties, maimed before conception through unemployment.†

These figures impart some comprehension of the social costs of unemployment: the consumer goods, capital equipment, and communal projects that might have been, never were. The useful labor services available (and equipment depreciating through time) are, with trifling qualifications, vanished forever.

In 1978 the United States labor force will total about 100 million. Thus 1 percent excess unemployment will involve nonwork for 1 million persons.

Government budgets

At another level of social costs, excess unemployment is likely to throw government budgets into a state of shock. Assume that each unemployed individual costs, through unemployment compensation, welfare, food stamp assistance, administration, etc., $10,000 out of the public purse. Every 1 million unemployed will thus cost $10 billion, or $50 billion over 5 years. Annual output (and GNI) losses of $50 billion—just to get some idea of magnitude —might entail a $10 billion sacrifice in tax revenues. Thus the budget scales become unbalanced at all levels of government: revenues (say) $5 billion less than they might be together with outlays $10 billion more result in an unem-

---

* Any calculation must contain a good degree of guesswork, considering our inability to recapture the situation of past years. The figures, however, even on "low" grounds, cinch the point of egregious output-income losses.

† The figures understate the loss according to the Ford *Council of Economic Advisers*—hardly anxious to overstate the loss. Over 1969–1976, at 1972 prices, on a 4 percent unemployment (in 1972 prices) the GNP gap was $626 billion. At 4.9 percent unemployment the gap would be $348 billion. With 1976 prices one-third greater the figures are $835 billion and $464 billion, respectively. *Economic Report* (1977), p. 54.

Including Europe, total stagflation unemployment in 1976 amounts roughly to 15 million, or about 16 percent of the United States labor force. An output loss of upward of $250 billion, well surpassing most countries' output, is implicit.

ployment "deficit" of $15 billion.* The budget unbalance is capable of "crowding out" worthwhile government projects on the double excuse of lost revenue and the burden of welfare outlays, both emanating from the same unemployment havoc.

Business profits likewise suffer in underemployment: almost without exception, profits peak as jobs climb. Lower profit aggregates mean lower rates of return on existing investments, and offer less incentive to undertake new capital projects while at the same time drying up some internal finance to underwrite an expansion. Private sector growth thus tends to be suppressed, inhibiting the buoyancy of capitalism and blemishing its record relative to the collectivist nonmarket economies.

Individual losses

Beyond the adversity tolled in the aggregates, unemployment entails non-quantifiable individual losses and personal suffering. To the individuals out of work, any closure of job markets constitutes a "depression": there is no need for the affected to be reminded of the horrendous Great Depression. Their time of tribulation is now.

Rhetorically, it is beguiling to aver that "labor suffers through unemployment." Yet it is not labor generally, but the unemployed who are hardest hit; many of those who remained in jobs at unchanged pay in past (pre-World War II) depression eras might react casually as prices plummeted—so long as their own jobs remained secure. Labor generally would suffer only if the work-loss was shared equally, say with 5 percent excess unemployment signifying 2.5 weeks of pay losses for everybody in a 50-week work-year. With the turnover in the ranks of the unemployed, the individual penalty is mitigated in the wider sharing of the burden.†

In psychological, sociological, income, and political dimensions unemployment exacts its toll in frustration and rejection through negative responses in job search. Chipping away job opportunities hardly *wins* friends for the market economy. Income misfortunes are bound to provoke political unrest, and arouse latent antimarket sentiment. Unemployment has been second only to an unpopular war as a social and political cancer, wounding egos, personal pride and dignity, and family life. It takes a valiant sense of loyalty to retain a faith in the bounties of the market system when the individual feels abandoned by it.

---

* For 1975 and 1976, a multiple of about three would have to be given to these figures. More precise econometric calculations would probably render the facts more, rather than less, stark and shocking.

† To illustrate, in 1975, with the unemployment rate averaging 8.5 percent, or 7.8 million, the average duration of unemployment was 14.1 weeks. This suggests closer to 30 percent of the labor force affected by unemployment for shorter or longer intervals (though there can be duplication for persons subject to a short hire-fire-hire cycle).

Teenagers who want to work at a first job escape the statistical tally. Estimates of urban black teenager unemployment have run as high as 40 to 60 percent (1975–1976) in several of the larger cities. The lack of jobs is not entirely unrelated to the crime count: while violence and theft debase civilized living, an anticrime program without a drive to expand job opportunities attacks only half the problem.

There is some tendency to blame unemployment on "search costs."[*] It is alleged that jobs are available, although information on where or what kind is incomplete to job-seekers, with better knowledge being costly in time and transportation. This conception is largely predicated on the belief that if the unemployed were willing to accept lower real wages they could always find work.

An analysis of the effects of a widespread cut in *money* wages, as is ultimately posited in the search-cost literature, in the conviction that this is tantamount to a real-wage cut, is deferred to later pages.[†] Under ample demand outlays for full employment, the search-cost thesis would have more plausibility, with jobs and applicants roughly equated. Likewise, we can fathom discrepancies within regions where there may be fewer applicants than jobs in some places and particular industries and an abundance of inquiries elsewhere: mismatches of skills and posts fall under the mantle of "frictional" unemployment.

Yet a 1 percent or more annual rise in the unemployment rate almost invariably has reflected a lack of aggregate demand, especially through a decline in housing starts and the "multiplier"-dependent industries. Any attempt on the part of individuals in building construction to relocate elsewhere, or to secure other jobs, would have to be reversed under a different milieu of interest rates and mortgage-money availability. Transporting individuals about geographically, and vocationally, apart from any sentimental wrench, can involve personal and social costs that are redundant and capricious after a loosening of the monetary screws. "Search-cost" unemployment might have a more intrinsic bearing in a flat P-environment where the monetary authority was not jousting about, locked in intermittent mortal combat with inflation, and inducing unemployment in its futile quest for stability. Search-cost theories have overlooked the tenuous contribution that would follow wide-

---

[*]   The arguments are attributable mainly to Armen A. Alchian. See, e.g., "Information Costs, Pricing, and Resource Unemployment," in E. S. Phelps, et al., *Microeconomic Foundations of Employment and Inflation Theory* (New York: Norton, 1970).

    See also Edmund S. Phelps, *Inflation Policy and Unemployment Theory: The Cost-Benefit Approach to Monetary Planning* (New York: Norton, 1972), Chapter 1. While the authors concentrate on "frictional" unemployment the concept of search-costs often appears to swallow *all* unemployment.

[†]   Keynes was dubious of the ability of labor to engineer a real-wage cut, considering the intimate connection of money wages to prices. The arguments are never answered by "search costs" theorists. Cf. Chapter 5 below.

spread money-wage attrition by the unemployed, for this would signify, on average, general money-wage cuts; ultimately this would maintain the same rate of joblessness unless investment activity spurted. Lower money wages, lower prices, more bankruptcies, could make the job climate worse. Search-cost theories, in ignoring the price-level impacts of money wages, have reinstated a premise of harmonious automatic full employment "equilibrium" through lower money wages. A place for aggregate *real* demand management is precluded in their *models*—not by the facts but by their assumptions.

Finally, there is the more haughty attitude that under the prevailing unemployment and welfare handouts, unemployment is tolerable for personal disposable income is, after all, sustained. This interpretation likens layoffs to temporary retirement. Curiously, this notion is often promoted by those who proclaim most loudly their dedication to freedom, to unfettered market choice. Yet unless the unemployed are content with their lot, the "leisure" is coerced, imposed rather than freely embraced. Damage to self-esteem along with throttled output remains.

Others regard unemployment as a labor-disciplining mechanism, with widespread firing somehow fostering labor efficiency. Within a firm, the weeding out of inefficient workers, slating them for lower paid posts, might aid productivity. It can hardly apply to wholesale job losses for these would reflect widespread "inefficiency"—or *normal* productivity facts. On the proviso that the punishment should fit the crime, only the slack workers should be dropped. When punishment is meted out indiscriminately and universally, the efficiency argument has a Gilbert and Sullivan air, to be hummed lightly. It smacks of the attitude of the disciplinarian desk sergeant (wearing an academician's hat) rather than providing a coherent principle for utilizing free labor with all their productivity frailties: rates of pay might better be adjusted to their failings rather than having the system mete out a sentence of exile to the reserve army of unemployed—as Karl Marx might phrase it. Ultimately, the faith (for such it is) in disciplining labor is irrevocably tied to Phillips curve heroics, wherein unemployment is deemed to be a potent factor in restraining money wages. This identification will be discussed later.

Democracy, and its market economy adjunct, will be best served when jobs are abundant and individuals hold an economic stake in the system: workers are unlikely to drive freshly purchased automobiles in a fiery revolutionary protest parade. Jobs and rising real income can best thin the agitators' ranks. High unemployment becomes almost inevitably a political time bomb. On this premise, democratic economies cannot temporize with full-employment goals.

Whether the route to full employment should be tagged with more private, or more public, sector jobs is a matter that, for our purposes, can be set aside. There is much useful work to be performed in both sectors—in urban renewal, in transportation, health, and environment generally. Even under full employment (as under unemployment) the issue will provoke contention, depending on the evaluation of needs and the estimate of benefits from each sector. There is ample room for accommodation of both schools, considering the unemployment facts of recent years.

The Inflation Impacts

On the subject of the pains of inflation, there are few inherent gains that cannot be achieved more rationally in a sidewise P-path. Recent analyses confirm that it is only *unanticipated* inflation that is economically corrosive (anticipated inflation will be considered later).

Living with inflation

Any appraisal of an inflationary impact is contingent on whether the price spurts per annum are small or steep, sporadic or cumulative. We have often been advised, in tones of either airy disdain or solemn surrender, that: "We can live with inflation, but we cannot afford a stagnant economy."* At the time these views garnered support inflation was cantering in the 5 to 6 percent range per annum. Shortly after these sanguine assurances, the Nixon Phases were inaugurated as an overdue response to an imminent price gallop.

To be sure, we will continue to "live" regardless of the price rate: a price upheaval is not exactly a physical calamity in the sense of a fire, flood, earthquake, or the human carnage of war. Physical injury is not inflicted, at least not immediately and overtly. But there can be immense harm, and some chaos. Individual suffering could be relieved, lives could be better organized, and resources more wisely used if the erratic price blips were subdued by acceptable means.

The advice to live with inflation, and to ignore it, reflects a defeatist attitude. Inflation impairs social welfare; medicine would hardly countenance bodily illness without exploring ameliorative remedies. By inadvertence, erosive nibbling inflation can develop into the more pernicious and irrational Latin-American-style hyperinflation which would compel the erection of sturdy roadblocks. Those who urge us to tolerate inflation will often put forth a mixed bag of "correctives," such as indexing money incomes by cost-of-living formulas, or concocting a variety of complex expedients to denominate contractual obligations so as to preserve their initial purchasing power.†

---

* James Tobin and Leonard Ross, "Living With Inflation," *New York Review of Books*, May 6, 1971, pp. 24, 26. Also, Peter Passell, "Learning To Live With Inflation," Editorial Notebook, *New York Times* (June 2, 1977).

† "Corrections" for pensioners and others were recommended in the article cited. Apparently, it was thought that if inflation was treated lightly while running at 6 percent or so, it would disappear. See also the American Economic Association presidential address, James Tobin, "Inflation and Unemployment," *American Economic Review* (March 1972). Here, Tobin remarked (p. 15): "The prediction that at low unemployment rates inflation will accelerate toward ultimate disaster is a

Beyond a nod of skepticism, we need not, at the moment, evaluate the potential success—or bankruptcy—of the "corrections" policy.* Indexing could underwrite worse inflation, and with a devastating effect on the foreign-exchange value of the dollar. Sooner or later, after a "corrections" fling, the inflation problem would have to be confronted. If later, best now, before compounding the price iniquities.

Accompanying the "living with inflation" theme are frequent assertions that inflation is not a "real" problem (aside from some avoidable unemployment) for it does not impair output but "merely" plays some redistributive tricks on relative incomes. Manifestly, the esoteric art of solving riddles by posing enigmas retains a quaint theoretical charm.

By the same "real" output test, nonviolent crime also partakes of a "merely" redistributional shuffle: theft, burglary, embezzlement, corruption, and bribery involve a robbing of Peter to enrich Paul. Filching, however, is usually frowned upon in our society. Condoning inflation as "merely" redistributing income in a blind and unpremeditated way hardly complies with democratic ideals of fairness. Further, the addendum urging "corrections" for the distributive upsets of inflation is casuistic; if a market economy could readily iron out income discrepancies, the ugly imbalances would long ago have been repaired. "Corrections" promise a proliferation in the array of redistributive measures, with predictable old imperfections and unpredictable new inequities.

Entirely overlooked in this unreasoned acceptance of inflation in the interest of creating jobs is the size of the price binge. One may perhaps scoff at a price rise of 5 percent, but will 10, 20, 50 . . . percent per annum, or higher, be welcome? When does haphazard income redistribution have "real" effects?

One must also note the uneasy premise that inflation does not portend inefficient resource use, or invite conduct irrational in a stable price climate. Long-range planning by individuals, business firms, and government is highly unlikely to be as balanced under erratic price upswings as under a flat price trend.

The trouble with inflation

Inflation has some analogy with "The Trouble With Harry," the character who, often given up for dead, keeps popping up at inopportune times. Inflation can have diverse characteristics in different historical circumstances, with

---

theoretical deduction with little empirical weight. In fact the weight of econometric evidence has been against acceleration, let alone disaster." Alas, Tobin's econometrics were performed prematurely: the following years brought double-digit inflation and *growing* unemployment in several of the free-world economies. A greater sense of urgency to deal with the "double-digit" 1974 outbreak reflected some disenchantment with the ignore-inflation prescription. See *Op. Ed., New York Times*, Sept. 6, 1974.

* See below, Chapter 8.

manageable impacts under mild outbreaks accepted as the random "rub of the green" in golf.

1 Inflation is said to redistribute income blindly, and thus is bound to create some social and political disaffection damaging to the free society. Indiscriminate income shuffles are less likely to be the handiwork of a virtuous Robin Hood adhering to an egalitarian tenet than of a villainous Blind Jack pillaging the underprivileged.

But the imagery must be interpreted carefully for in the market economy, where demand and cost conditions vary, relative incomes are always subject to flux, carrying redistributive omens. Sometimes, it is said that *if* all money incomes moved proportionately to prices, inflation would be deprived of distributive havoc: this is to say that if inflation created no problems it would exert no damage. Modern inflation, however, must be appraised against a backdrop of growing productivity, and compared to general distributive trends in a stable price-level regime.

Under a stable price level, with average money wages moving up under normal productivity gains, even those whose money income stayed fairly *constant* would avert real-income discomfort, even though their niche on the income scale would be relocated adversely compared to money-wage gainers. Largely, however, there would be general real-wage benefits and few real-income casualties.

Under an inflationary binge, *average* money wages will usually outstrip the price move by the productivity advance: everyone whose income move lags the price flare will suffer income deterioration. Considering that the most powerful labor blocs are likely to grab the spectacular wage prizes, the inflationary sequence is likely to reveal ragged edges within the total wage share. A substantial labor segment can be disaffected: the aggressive unions will be overcompensated at the expense of docile labor groupings. The real income transfer, even under a constant wage share, may not be from capitalists to labor but from one labor group to another labor sector, with a premium placed on union belligerence. The meek are likely to be exploited in the inflationary income race.* The unevenness in the money-wage blowup can leave many workers disenchanted when "a dollar no longer buys a dollar's worth." This untidy incidence would be precluded under a stable price level.

Focus here is on the employed members of the labor force. The unemployed, without income and having meager financial reserves, have to endure even greater hardship: welfare recipients, likewise, continuously find their handouts becoming less valuable even as taxpayers vociferously protest mounting public costs as payments are belatedly enlarged. Teenagers on paltry allowances find these depleted: the rewards of crime pay more.

---

* Contrary to the sanguine remarks of Tobin and Ross that labor's relative share does not deteriorate, the important point concerns inequities within the cut of the pie going to labor. On movements in the total wage share, see below, Chapter 3.

Retired pensioners will also be victimized with each price rise, with their real fortunes partially repaired by Social Security correctives: they are consigned to be even more craven wards of government, hostages of budget priorities subject to the vicissitudes of government largesse and visible prey for ideological political cross fire. So far as private pensions go, the real impairment is seldom counterbalanced.* Implicit is a real-income switch from the elderly, with modest Social Security correction, to the young who earn in their first job a real (and a money) income that might have taken the retired parents 20 years or so to achieve. The intergenerational income transfer can, given a sufficient cumulative price rise, be cruel, and condoned only in a callow view of human relations; the aged are put in the position of supplicants while the real-income fortunes of the young, enjoying living standards beyond earlier parental imagination and promised even more in the future, are further enriched. Compared to the hesitant and degrading "corrections," a steady price climate would be welcomed by the older, least adaptable members of society. Residual life planning would be far better appeased than through the hoax of imperfect corrections.

Indubitably, redistribution can be accomplished more sanely and surely under a stable P. Inflation distorts our perception of income inequities by disturbing the *individual* income shares. The indiscriminate income dealings are exasperating to those who suffer and, perversely, to many who benefit. Counting on the exorbitant money-wage accretions to be a real enhancement, there is some sense of being jilted and cheated at the erosion of prospects when prices spiral. An accelerated chain reaction can set in for the next round of wage negotiations, with labor demanding even bigger pay hikes to touch off a weird case of the frenzied dog chasing its meandering tail.

2 Inflation clouds rational long-range economic planning. At the personal, business, and governmental levels, plans would be more clearly ordered in a stable price environment. Costs and benefits, especially the timing of home purchases, durable goods acquisitions, factory construction, equipment installation, and long-range government projects, could be more unequivocally assessed without fitful price-level gyrations. Imperfectly perceived inflation induces economically costly advance buying by the venturesome, a behavior pattern which is superfluous in a stable P-environment.

An enterprise economy is a *contract* economy—despite the sedulous neglect of contractual relations in models of perfect certainty. Wage contracts run for a year or two, rental contracts often cover 10 years or more, bonds carry fixed interest charges for 20 years or longer, etc. Uncertain and diverse estimates of inflation inject another vague and costly parameter into agreements and, depending on which side is more nearly right or wrong, affect income distribution. Serious inflation is likely to lead to short-, rather than

---

* For a pension of $800 a month, half Social Security-half private, an imperfect inflation corrective will ordinarily apply to only half the income.

long-run agreements, which can be unreasonably costly to one side or the other.* Uncertainty about the P-path thus deters some otherwise longer-run financing ventures, usually for a worse growth score when tested against a more rigid price trend.

Economists assign high marks to the price mechanism as a beacon, an economizer of information facilitating purchase and sale decisions and influencing careers requiring expensive educational preparation or vocational training. Inflation can befuddle decision making and induce protective patterns of resource use, inhibiting longer-range strategies while inflicting wild redistributive blows, skinning some and elating others through institutionally conferred price-level forays unrelated to underlying taste, factor ownership, or resource-productivity phenomena inscribed in stable Walrasian equilibrium models.

3 Traditionally, it is argued that debtors revel in their luck and creditors mourn their losses in a zero-sum inflation game: that is, on contracts written in the past, any unforeseen change in the price spiral will filch from one to console the other. Those owning bond indentures stipulated in fixed money sums, or savings deposits, will face some erosion of wealth. Populists are accustomed to suppose that the debtor is usually the decent fellow. However well this generalization fits the older, rural, farm-mortgaged economy, the assumption requires at least some review by age-group categories.

Banks, for example, are usually classed as "creditors." Yet as their deposit liabilities are also denominated in dollars there is partial cancelling out of what they owe against what they own. Most importantly for them, however, is that their income depends on interest earnings which have hit historic highs: net interest in the national income has risen from 3.3 percent in 1965 to 6.7 percent in 1975. Farmers are unlikely to cheer the borrowing terms. The little (and politely) studied, and gently whispered, economic power of banks in our market economy has surely not been devastated in the stagflation era of limited loan availability and tight money. Their power-broker position has been enhanced—and ignored in inflation discourse.

Insurance policies, dispersed widely in small packets, have suffered a cruel depletion. Consider one example: World War II GI life insurance of $10,000 was initially intended as covering about three years' average income (of $3,500 per annum, in the dim sights of the 1940s). Currently, the face value provides less coverage than an average one-year income.

The tight money policy to fight inflation, and the inflation premium in long-term interest rates, have depressed (1971–1975) stock market prices. For most people, this is a matter of casual concern. Yet low equity prices signalize higher capital financing costs. This has its distributive ramifications as well as damping the growth process.

---

* Short-term borrowing is one response, creating refinancing consternation for firms and possible domino effects in capital markets under credit-crunch episodes during bouts of tight money. Cf. H. Minsky, *John Maynard Keynes* (New York: Columbia, 1975).

4 Linking to the above is the erosion in the real value of depreciation accumulations amassed by corporations over time and intended to finance new investment through internal sources. Either more of the investment outlays will have to be defrayed through external borrowing reliance on creditor-finance, or replacement and modernization projects will be deferred till accumulations warrant.

5 Just as urban crime alters living styles and fosters costly security measures, including preventive flights to suburbs, expectation of continued inflation challenges ingenuity to indulge in various speculative practices to outwit the crowd and excel in an ill-defined game. Some otherwise frivolous activity is undertaken, e.g., excessive real estate acquisition, a flight from the stock market, speculation in foreign currencies, gold, silver, and *objets d'art*.* The covey of activities, redundant in a more balanced P-setting, can occasion real costs: some of the best brains are preoccupied in a game for survival in protective luxury while the economy writhes under stagflation.

6 Concern with inflation, because of its significance to personal income, distracts public focus from other complex subjects. Preoccupation with prices as a compelling human story competes for the limited public attention-span; ventilation of other serious and controversial issues becomes crowded out. Budget-wise, governments shelve overdue programs as "inflationary." The price of this preoccupation can run high.

7 Governments, as debtors, hack away the real value of the national debt—at the expense of individual bondholders, directly or indirectly, as in insurance companies, banks, or corporate bondholdings. Likewise, in a progressive income tax structure the higher money incomes encounter higher tax rates, pouring in revenues to sustain bloated government costs. An analysis of the "ultimate" benefit or burden via tax mechanics would be extremely complex for it would have to be contrasted with results along a flat P-course, and maybe in a full-employment economy. Nonetheless, as a debtor on capital account, the government fleeces its bondholders in some internal income transfers.

8 Internationally, foreign-exchange reverberations and balance-of-payments upsets, with real-income implications, will occur so long as the P-trends vary significantly among trading countries. The terms of trade will alter, with the country reporting the best price-level record finding its exchange rate generally appreciating, making claims on world resources easier. The final onus

---

* Historically, the stock market was believed to be an inflation hedge. However valid this might be in the hyperinflation economy, equity prices are about the only sector that has been depressed: the New York Stock Exchange industrial index (Dec. 31, 1965 = 50) was at 48 in 1970, 66 in 1972, and 52 in 1975. Bombed by inflation and tight money, the stock market has been ailing—even as Wall Streeters place their faith in miraculous monetary remedies on the premise that what has continually failed must "ultimately" succeed.

of domestic price inflation, therefore, is likely to be in the world economy: a country oblivious to its price gymnastics will end in shearing the foreign exchange value of its currency. As its currency depreciation outruns the speed of world price adaptations there will be a deleterious interim twist in the terms of trade: foreign goods will command premium amounts of domestic items in exchange.* Travel for its citizens will become more prohibitive. On capital accounts, contractual foreign debtors will reap a harvest in acquiring the currency for debt servicing at depreciated rates, or for amassing landed property, business firms, or *objets d'art*. Domestic debtors owing sums denominated in foreign currencies will be sorely tried through burdensome foreign exchange bites for debt servicing or principal repayment.

It is no accident that the rise in value of the German mark and the Japanese yen have made world travel amenities and luxury good imports easy for their people, and harder for United States and United Kingdom citizens over the last decade.

9 Under hyperinflation people will be eager to avoid money, disgorging it about as fast as it is received: money velocity climbs precipitously. Under the recent nibbling cumulative inflation, the same phenomena must tend to occur, mitigated only in degree as individuals try to economize their cash balances. One way or another, the money mechanism is made a less efficacious instrument for consummating optimal dating of purchase decisions.

10 As inflation progresses and irritation abounds, there will be protests to "do something." Price controls become an obvious recourse, opening up a bag of economic irrationalities. Resort to the conventional monetary and fiscal tools will rear renewed unemployment. New tensions, new frustrations, new disorders, will exert an extra toll in the mindless historical saga.

Mischievous Potency of Inflation

The income marauding is enough to condemn inflation; pocketbook grievances are bound to fester. Most of us feel strongly that we deserve the relative income portion we have—and more. Karl Marx saw income inequities as the nemesis of capitalism, ushering in revolutionary violence and abrupt, harsh change. Inflation, depending on its degree and disaffection, can mean a perilous joyride for free societies. Resolution would relieve social tensions and mitigate personal anguish while, in the modern context, the unpremeditated income shifts carry a concomitant multiplicative distress in unemployment.

---

* Under floating exchange rates and massive capital flows, as in recent years, currency speculation is usually triggered by expectations of inflation trends. In mid-1976, for example, newspaper accounts reported residents, and transient tourists to the United Kingdom, flocking to the shops for bargains in London as the British pound plunged precipitously to historic lows.

Income-distribution upsets, depending on the particular details of each inflation experience, must also affect consumer demand and resource use: only in theoretical resignation can it be contended that the bouncy price trend will be free of real costs.* Running all through the points above are resource-use implications. Long-range investment decisions and consumer durable-goods purchase patterns, such as house buying, are inevitably affected by the uncertain price parameters. Young people hasten to acquire "properties" with more space than they require immediately: why wait if prices will climb later? Public sector decisions are muddied in cost-benefit calculations. International import-export patterns are also not immune from the disparate price events. Multinational investment decisions come to lay weight on the imponderable foreign currency perturbations. One way and another, inflation is capable of inducing physical output, real income, resource use, and income-distribution configurations hardly captured in models hypothesizing the "perfect foresight" mirage.

If we postulate that the race goes to the swiftest, and in the haphazard inflationary world to the combination of luck and perception, it will largely be upper-income groups with know-how and access to funds who are best able to win the scramble, in real estate or other hedges, to acquire an edge in the distributive chase. Lower-income groups are also likely to cling longer to the money illusion of "a dollar being a dollar." It is a reasonable surmise, therefore, that greater egalitarianism and a stronger democracy would be promoted under a stable price level, although the proposition remains impenetrable to proof: we cannot restore the past and insert a flat price level to prevail while the previous preference, government budget, monetary attitudes, and productivity circumstances are resurrected for comparative outcomes. Nonetheless, rational distributive objectives are more likely to be realized if the value of money is held more nearly constant.

A flat price trend

Condemnation of inflation implies the optimality of a sidewise price trend. But the lateral path need not be interpreted rigidly; it could be reconciled with oscillations of a few percent up one year, and slightly down at other times, without abrupt departures from a flat norm. Alternately, a persistent edging up of one to two percent per annum, or a long-range moderate annual dive of one-half percent or so might be bearable. Reasonable stability over time would be the aim. Older arguments would have opted for a slight annual tilt upward to alleviate the debt burden, and tempt entrepreneurs to activate investment plans secure in the knowledge that "small" miscalculations would be compensated through higher revenues without undue scraping of creditor

---

* Implicit is a compartmentalized theory of the independence of output and resource-use phenomena despite price jumps and distributive perturbations. It is as if full-employment output is always an identical package.

equities. At the moment, until macroeconomic policy is able to demonstrate mastery over the price level, more extended evaluation of the merits of alternative paths is premature. Reasonable stability in particular historical contexts would clarify the issues on deviations up and down.*

Anticipated Inflation

A diversionary smoke screen is released in the contention that the ordeal can be dispelled if inflation is *correctly* anticipated. The assertion that "anticipated inflation is harmless inflation" is an oblique evasion of a piece with the preposterous myths in economic models of "perfect certainty" and "perfect foresight," which have long obstructed pertinent analysis.† With perfect foresight, economic, social, and political organization and activity would alter unrecognizably: there even arises the question of interest in living under perfect foresight. Why submit to "this vale of tears" when life is an open book already experienced in anticipation? Banks, money, stock exchanges, insurance companies, brokers, armies, weapons systems, education, police, fire, religious orders, lawyers, courts, etc., would be dispensable—as we know them—if we seriously inhale the gossamer "perfect foresight" pipe dream.

Must "correct" inflation anticipations be held universally? How far ahead, till the end of time or for a year or two? How *confidently* are the expectations to be held? Are there institutional blocks that preclude realization? Must behavioral attitudes be consistent, or otherwise obstruct individual adaptations?

For example, suppose wage earners expect an inflation rate of X percent over the next year and businessmen agree on the same guess. Also, suppose that wage earners demand a wage increase of $5X$ percent while firms feel free to grant only $2X$ percent at the expected prices. What then? If wage earners succeed in obtaining $5X$ percent, will firms acquiesce in the X percent rise, or will prices be drawn higher, falsifying the predictions? Participants would have to agree not only on the expected price rise but also to act consistently with the expectation, otherwise the outcome will confound the conjecture.

Consider what "correct" anticipations entail in a pervasive market-contract economy. Wage bargains commonly run for one to three years. Business rental arrangements can go for one, or five, or twenty years: the permutations are

---

* For a brief but illuminating discussion of the comparative advantages of the alternatives of *gently* rising or falling price levels, see the ever-fresh volume of D. H. Robertson, *Money* (New York: Pitman, 1948 revision). I see no warrant for E. S. Phelps' interpretation of Robertson being counted among those who "took prominent inflation positions." Cf. E. S. Phelps, p. XII.

† The quote is from Tobin and Ross, p. 24. Much of the volume of E. S. Phelps is executed on this premise. Incredibly, there are recent volumes on *money*, almost entirely a product of uncertainty, that proceed glibly on perfect foresight assumptions. As an antidote, Paul Davidson, *Money and the Real World* (London: Macmillan, 1973) makes *uncertainty* the prominent feature of his analysis.

legion. Moneys are borrowed for one month to twenty years, sometimes longer. On the "correct" anticipations thesis, the price level must be "correctly" predicted in advance by all market participants. Looked at in these terms, the assumption fits some dream-land without contact with real events. It would be interesting to have some evidence on pre-1920 predictions of the twenties or thirties, or 1930 views on subsequent events, or 1970 forecasts of post-1971 price experiences!*

It would be nice indeed to have "correct"—and *certain*—anticipations, not for all time, but for a day or two on Wall Street in a bouncy stock market—or at the race track on a day for long shots. It would be best of all to have a banker with the prevision to discern your prevision—and finance it. This would guarantee a sure—and safe—road to quick riches. The models go even further and invoke clairvoyance for *everybody*, and apparently for infinite time! If correct anticipations were universally held that stock market prices would bound sharply higher in the near future, prices would leap up to (approximately) these levels today, and without any transactions, and to the consternation of financial journalists stretched to explain the price convulsion on "no volume"! It is not a matter of record, however, that any economist building "perfect foresight" models has ever retired prematurely, aided by revealed prescience in riskless Wall Street speculation.

Gamblers at the race track are rarely comfortable with merely confident "anticipations": reputedly, they bolster their anticipatory lights—the dope sheet "models"—by drugging horses and bribing jockeys. A deeper faith resides in their astrologers after they lend a hand to fix up crucial relations.

Universal anticipation of inflation—or stock market prices—can be a self-fulfilling prophecy *if*, and only if, certain other relations are satisfied in money wages, productivity, and income shares *regardless* of the conjectures of market participants: given the evolving relations the prior expectations would hardly matter. A pervasive "belief" that the stock market will soar will not advance prices unless there are individuals with purchasing power or owning stocks, and willing to act in support of their surmises.

The bland assurance that inflation is "only" a problem under imperfect foresight encourages a digressive ramble into metaphysical space, and fleeing reality. The past inflation record, and future omens, inject some extra uncertainties to befuddle decision making. Slipped in, too, is the illicit premise that the genesis of inflation is universally known, and that the omniscient economic actors are so gulled as to tolerate the known causes responsible for the penetration of the price stratosphere. Governments would be pressured to assert mastery of the price level if a vast consensus prevailed, for their operations are supposed to facilitate life by eliminating dispensable uncertainties; infla-

---

* The date of some of the "perfectly-anticipated" inflation analyses referred to may be noted; there was absolutely no inkling of the double-digit United States, United Kingdom, or Australian experience in any of the cited works that underplayed inflation and demoted it to sham-issue status.

tion ranks high on the mischievous list of economic griefs that deserve to be expunged. Largely, the only "inflation"—or price level—capable of being "correctly anticipated" is a flat price path of $P(t_0) = P(t_1) = P(t_2) = \ldots$. Minor aberrations would inflict only minor harm and, on balance, major benefits through systemic stability and rational intertemporal planning of private and public decisions would adhere.

Finally, ranking high in analytical and practical irrelevances is the proposition that with anticipated inflation the one "ultimate social cost" is that the price march involves "extra trips between savings banks and commercial banks" to get the necessary money for payments.* Apparently, even hyperinflation, based on this anticipatory perspective, does scant damage; it merely presupposes computer minds busy at work (all day?) in rational calculation of behavioral responses to random astronomical arithmetical posers.

Inflation as a Brain-Drain

One of the harshest indictments of inflation is that it entails an enormous intellectual distraction that dims our focus on other grave problems. This may be the most monumental long-run bill when all the costs are toted up. Spectator sports may be a healthy safety valve for pent-up energies to fill in leisure time; they are socially frivolous when they divert an array of professional talent from preoccupation with necessary specialties.

Inflation is hardly a new problem. The typewriter clack can fill libraries. Yet we permit it to endure. Too many pontificate that "even economists are confused," or that "nobody has a solution." So it rolls on, victimizing people in tolling up income inequities, arousing income fears, hatching escape routes, impairing employment, aborting potential output, and twisting the terms of trade.

Could we control the price binge, our intellectual and political energies could be devoted to the long laundry list of new societal puzzles. Instead, we pile up still another generation of economists to parade lock-step, singing stale theoretical tunes while their commanding academic mentors assure them that archaic inflation premises, invigorated by updated statistical massages, are prime candidates for dissertation prizes awarded for originality and perception. Recital of sterile remedies follows, by rote, the fresh data.

The age of inflation shoves the formidable problems of cities, energy, nuclear alarms, ecology, etc., into a subordinate place; the inflation bug infects talents and provides respectable escape models for *a priori* apologists to defer innovations in troublesome areas. The price precipice beclouds the budgetary process; it warps rational evaluation of priorities; it subdues a dialogue on the human evolution by evoking fears of more inflation. In the casualties inflicted on other programs, the prospective social loss is incalculable—to others be-

---

* Cf. Tobin, p. 15.

sides those whose ideological temperaments favor *laissez-faire*, come what may. Yet they too should welcome the clearer delineation of deeper issues without the perfunctory diversions of inflation aspects under a flat price path.

Skirmishes over inflation theory and policy should be able to vault ideology, renewing the philosophical zest for meaningful controversy never revealed by quarrels over the preservation of fox hunts (about which differences of opinion hardly matter) but on human life-styles and institutional response. Persistent inflation, and the replication of economic policy atrocities, with only the date of repetition being new, dwarf all other "brain-drains" to which the economics profession is exposed.

Experimental sciences abandon approaches that have spelled failure, and demonstrate an eagerness to undertake trials with new concepts. Economics is stigmatized by a tyrannous obsession: there is a vested commitment to the principle that what has conspicuously failed has really not been vigorously pursued. New theoretical directions and innovative policy techniques are decades overdue.

PART 2

The Theoretical Structure

Introduction: The Money Wage and Money Price Level Connection

The theoretical structure for understanding the inflation-unemployment ordeal occupies the next set of chapters. As averred, the current wave of unemployment has largely been generated by the application of more or less conventional monetary maneuvers intended to control inflation. The results of this tinkering with formulas mainly obsessed with money supply targets have operated to aggravate the problems instead of solving them: besides the ascent in the price level, the economy has suffered from instability in job markets. In spite of this, the Monetarist contention that monetary discipline will save the day still pervades in policy and academic quarters. Others see the source of monetary laxness and the lapse from monetary rectitude in bloated government deficits: they castigate fiscal profligacy as the root of all disorder. Others regard big business and big labor, with or without big government, as the monopolist rascals behind the crisis of market capitalism.

In a fuller study all of these origins could be evaluated for their validity and influence. Yet all of the ideas can be absorbed as secondary and partial explanations, as theoretical supplements within a more general formulation. In the modern industrial economy theoretical eminence and emphasis must be assigned to the imbalance of money incomes to physical output volume as the price-level destabilizer. The key in generating the price-level sparks is the ratio of average money incomes—comprised substantially of average money wages and salaries—to average labor productivity.

This is the essence of the money-income theory of inflation. In other times, and in other societies, it would be possible to opt for other explanations which presently are less pertinent to a money-wage market economy where employee payments comprise far and away the bulk of business costs and the source of consumer demand in the circular economic process. Subsequent analysis will flesh out this imagery.

After developing the money-incomes theory (or the WCM, as it will later be called) it will be necessary to dress the theme to show how money enters the circle. The associated WCM theory of money naturally evokes implications for monetary policy that collide with conventional Monetarist doctrines: the altered perception will be treated in some detail. Attention will also be devoted to a serious gap, even an embarrassing chasm, in the Monetarist conception of the inflationary process in an evolutionary economy.

Because of its vital significance in the ensuing WCM theory below, and in a stabilization policy to avert the stagflation crisis, the theory of money wages will be surveyed at some length. Curiously, economists too often have simply presumed that this was a tidy, decorative, and completed corner of economics; only intermittently have students been informed of the large void on the subject. Theory has had, to be sure, much of importance to say about *real* wages, largely decked in a marginal productivity costume. Our concern, however, is with money wages—a phenomenon of a different color. Even in its real-wage uniform, the marginal productivity theory is a lot less robust than its proponents admit.*

Keynesianism and Monetarism

It is fashionable nowadays to speak of paradigms.† In this sense the money-income theory is the newest entrant claiming attention for illuminating and ameliorating the problems that menace the market economy. The theory deserves more careful scrutiny than it has so far received in professional circles, where the consensus stays pinned to older models despite their failure to abate the stagflation-slumpflation crisis.‡

Keynesian and Monetarist models of inflation suffuse the textbook and professional literature. Keynesianism, often loosely identified with Keynes, initially came to be systematized in the Hansen-Samuelson "45-degree-cross" or the *IS-LM* curves emanating from J. R. Hicks. Keynes, if alive, might view

---

*   See my "Marginal Productivity and Macrodistribution Theory," *Keynes and the Monetarists, and Other Essays* (New Brunswick: Rutgers University Press, 1973). (Hereafter cited as *KaM*.)

†   Cf. T. S. Kuhn, *The Structure of Scientific Revolutions* (University of Chicago, 1963).

‡   For fresh evidence, see D. E. L. Laidler and J. M. Parkin, "Inflation: A Survey," *Economic Journal* (Dec. 1975). This is committed to standard Monetarist fare even as it glosses over shortcomings which, in a two hundred plus year doctrinal history, should have long ago been corrected—if the breaches could be repaired.

with some consternation the acclaim for the doctrines that bore his name, for they were synthesized into a set of fiscal precepts for augmenting government expenditures and cutting taxes in order to dispel unemployment, and instructions to reverse the tap to block inflation. Manifestly, the instructions are a recipe for confusion in a stagflation-slumpflation setting. The impasse has led to the disruption and dismemberment of a once-confident school of thought.

An account of Keynes versus Keynesianism is relegated to Chapter 10 in order to permit an easier and more direct communication of the WCM theme, without embarking upon a theoretical digression. While the WCM theory of money is discussed in Chapter 4, along with some of the major aspects of Monetarist doctrine, a host of uncompleted issues are also reserved for later comment, in Chapter 9: the items involved are dispensable for establishing the major propositions for our immediate study. Also, for some effort at inclusiveness, the matters of monopoly pricing in inflation, and government largesse in causing the inflation troubles, are also reserved for later exposition.

All theories profess generality. Peering behind the theoretical scaffolding at the policy precepts usually proves most instructive in apprehending the structure of ideas. For in each theoretical redoubt, about whose particulars disciples may differ, it is possible to allege that "all" variables are included, that nothing has been forgotten or omitted. This is particularly demonstrable when appeal is made to a general equilibrium listing.

Affirmations of inclusiveness must, however, be ingested cautiously for it is necessary, somehow, to break into all reasoning chains to spot a strategic entry point for optimal control of the behavioral mechanics of the economic process. It is thus the instrumental variables selected for guiding the system onto a balanced path that best exude the content and spirit of a theory. There is an uncanny methodological wisdom in the biblical injunction that "by their fruits ye shall know them" (Matt. 7:20).

CHAPTER THREE

The WCM Theory: The Double-Edged Demand and Cost Blades

Archimedes, delegated to nudge the price level onto a sidewise path in the modern "money income industrial economy," would have to set his considerable talents to the construction of a lever long enough to tilt the *money* income advance into balance with output growth. The income-output counterweights comprise the gist of the wage-cost markup (WCM) theory of inflation.

Any temptation to label the thesis a "cost-push" doctrine must be rejected as a casual half-truth. To be sure, in consumer market macrotheory, no less than in microtheory, "cost-push" and "demand-pull" comprise the two blades of the Marshallian price-scissors. In the macroeconomy both sides are forged simultaneously from identical income materials, released to cut and click in unison. Also, it can be deceptive to describe the economy as a price system; instead, it is best viewed as an industrial order in which labor is hired by firms to produce output, and paid in advance of expected profitable market sales. In paying out money wages, firms weld the cost side of the price-making equation; the same money wages (and salaries) constitute the household purchasing power establishing the demand magnitudes. Demand and cost blades snap to the same fingers in settling consumer prices and purchase quantities. If labor were paid in shoes, bread, TV's, and cars, a barter system, instead of a money price mechanism, would prevail.

Money supplies remain offstage in the immediate exposition of the WCM theory. This is not to deny the importance of money. Quite the contrary; money supplies and monetary policy are potent elements in shaping the output and employment volume; but they touch the price level only peripherally. As this proposition confutes orthodox doctrine, it will be explored at length in Chapter 4.

The General Price Level in the Closed Economy

The market sector general price level can be identified with the price deflator extracted from the Gross Business Product (GBP). This concept omits the nonprofit activities of government, households, and eleemosynary institutions, included in Gross National Product (GNP).* Initially, a closed economy is envisaged.

Money incomes and the price level

Definitionally,

$$PQ = Y, \tag{3.1}$$

where Y = GBP (or gross money income), Q = real output, P = the price level. It follows that:

$$P = Y/Q. \tag{3.2}$$

By dividing Y and Q by the number of persons employed (N), then:

$$P = y/A, \tag{3.3}$$

where $y = Y/N$, $A = Q/N$ = average labor product.

Thus y = money income per person employed, including money wages and salaries, profit, depreciation, business taxes, rents, and interest payments. Alternatively, y translates as the average *gross* income per employee or average gross labor earnings.

A steady price level thus requires: (1) that aggregate money incomes rise at the same pace as total output, or (2) that gross income per employee correspond to average labor productivity. "Simple and obvious" as these relations are, it is mystifying that it has taken so long for the implications to be discerned. They still remain underrated in learned discussion of inflation policy.

Over time, where magnitudes change, the elements determining the $P(t)$ course become:†

$$(\Delta P/P) = (\Delta Y/Y) - (\Delta Q/Q) = (\Delta y/y) - (\Delta A/A). \tag{3.4}$$

P will thus change whenever the relative Y move surpasses the relative Q list, or whenever relative money-income trends per employee outrun the employee output pace. Regardless of money supply, money velocity, government

---

* GBP series are published by the United States Department of Commerce along with GNP statistics. Less inclusive, they ordinarily attract less attention although they comprise the nearly pure data of the market sector ordinarily in mind in the inflation context. The P-term in Eq. (3.2) reflects the general price index implicit in the GBP statistics.

† The derivation is conveyed more precisely by differentiating $\log P = \log Y - \log Q$ with respect to time as:

$$(1/P)(dP/dt) = (1/Y)(dY/dt) - (1/Q)(dQ/dt). \tag{3.4a}$$

Where the time trend of a variable is involved the notation of $P(t)$ or $P(t+1)$, or $P(t+2)$, etc., will often be used.

expenditure, monopoly practices, import prices, or the volatility of inflationary expectations, P cannot be subjugated unless Y matches the Q tempo.

Sharpening the theory is a derived formulation which emphasizes the crucial bearing of the ratio of average money wages (and salaries) to average labor productivity.*

$$Y = PQ = kwN, \tag{3.5a}$$

where w = average wage and N = employment.

$$P = kw/A, \tag{3.5b}$$

where k = the average markup of prices over unit labor costs (w/A) or the reciprocal of the wage share (ω), where $k = 1/\omega$.

$$(\Delta P/P) = (\Delta w/w) + (\Delta k/k) - (\Delta A/A) \tag{3.5c}$$

Equation (3.5b) is the WCM (= wage-cost markup) equation. With Eq. (3.2) it comprises the theoretical foundations of Incomes Policy. By positing: (1) $k = \overline{k}$, or $\Delta k = 0$, primarily year-to-year as reenforced by factual evidence, and (2) imputing causal significance from right to left, from unit labor costs (w/A) to P, the truism is transformed into a theoretical conjecture.

Reiterating, for clarity, (w/A) = unit labor costs. If merely $\Delta(w/A)$ is underscored as the ΔP pacesetter, the argument is of a piece with the "cost-push" thesis. Shortly, however, the implicit demand-aspects inherent in Eq. (3.5) will be elaborated.

Truisms, theory, and institutions

Equations such as those presented are sometimes disparaged as "truisms." Inescapably, theory—and all logic—must proceed from truisms which disclose relations not casually apparent: in mathematics and in physics, chains of cogent reasoning are frequently the culmination of manipulations founded on truisms. Pathological aversions to truisms presumably intimate that logical thought should originate in "falsisms"—and thus derive spurious results. Ejecting k from temporal short-term influence in altering P unquestionably converts Eq. (3.5b and c) into a hypothesis in the accepted conditional sense.

Sometimes theories which stress the critical leverage of the money wage on the price level are pejoratively referred to as "institutionally" oriented; monetary theories are praised as immune from institutional taint.

Surely it is a virtue to admit prevailing institutional circumstances. Likewise, monetary theories are hardly pure, natural, or noninstitutional; certainly

---

* For an early statement see my *A General Theory of the Price Level*. Money wages, henceforth, will always be interpreted to include salaries. It is not easy to separate the two in either published statistics, or in concept, unless we arbitrarily call all employee income below, say, $15,000 wages, and above the threshold, salaries. But this is to deal in income size rather than in a common attribute.

As $k = PQ/wN$, it is clear that k is the reciprocal of the wage share, wN/PQ or ω.

modern money is an institutional creation, a phenomenon of central bank operation under its legal mandate. Money has *always* been an institutional phenomenon arising out of custom in distant ages singling out gold and silver as conventional *institutional* media of exchange.*

The near-constancy of k

The WCM theory builds on the hypothesis of $k = \bar{k}$, or nearly so. Practically, k changes very little year-to-year or over the long run, so we may ordinarily ignore any fluctuations as inaudible P-noise.

It is not vital that k hold rigid; what matters is that its annual variations are generally too miniscule to explain the P-surges that have occurred.† Variations in k cannot account for the trebling of the United States (GNP) price level since 1946, or the 75 percent climb since 1967. Indeed, over the long term k has been falling and there is evidence over the last decade that k has slumped in the United States and in the United Kingdom, especially in recent years. This should have fostered *falling* prices rather than an intense surge in prices in that beleaguered country.‡

Explanation of why k holds so remarkably steady over the short term and so relatively steady over an indefinite term is still inconclusive; economists have devoted little attention to the subject.§ Nonetheless, for P-theory and policy we can proceed as if k will hold firm, or vary only slightly over the near future. In the United States GBP data in recent years k has been at approximately 1.8; even if k were somehow to drop miraculously to 1,

---

* Nicole Oresme (1320?–1382) described the gold and silver coming into common use as being the work of "clever men." See A. E. Monroe, *Early Economic Thought* (Cambridge: Harvard University Press, 1924).

† Cobb-Douglas production functions, it might be recalled, are predicated on share constancy, or $k = \bar{k}$, and then applied to explain output growth as dependent on the growth of capital and labor inputs.

‡ Cf. Peter Wiles, "Cost Inflation and the State of Economic Theory," *Economic Journal* (June 1973), p. 381.

§ The constancy of the wage share was noted many years ago by A. L. Bowley, and hence it is sometimes referred to as "Bowley's law." Bowley used national income data (as then defined) for the United Kingdom. See *Wages and Income in the United Kingdom Since 1860* (Cambridge University Press, 1937).

Michal Kalecki, however, drew attention to the analytic significance of these facts in his demonstration of the constancy of the wage share of *manual* employees. See his *Essays in the Theory of Economic Fluctuations* (New York: Farrar & Rinehart, 1939), pp. 16–19.

Joan Robinson wrote that "the divorce between theory and realistic investigation . . . is a standing reproach to academic economics," especially on "the mystery of the constant relative shares." This was 35 years ago. See *An Essay on Marxian Economics* (London: Macmillan, 1942), pp. 92–93.

For my own attempts at some explanation, see *Some Aspects of Wage Theory and Wage Policy* (New York: Greenwood Press, 1963 reprint), Chapter 3.

so that *all* gross income went to wages (making other income and depreciation allowances nil), the WCM facets would signify even more strongly the need to align $(\Delta w/w)$ to $(\Delta A/A)$. In the market economy k can hardly plummet to 1; even in "ideal," and certainly in the actual collectivist economies, $k > 1$.

International differences in k would be attributable, in a complex way, to variations in economic structure, including the size of the farm sector, nature of industrialization, foreign trade, tax laws, oligopoly price practices, and the bargaining strength of labor. How these matters intersect to affect k remains a sedulously unexplored subject.* It may be surmised, however, that the k-values are unlikely to erupt so violently as to distort an inflation strategy based on the w/A alignment: signals of an unrecognizable systemic transformation in the distribution of income and operating mechanics of market economies would have to be emitted; even political and economic upheavals may shake k by less than one might imagine. Although the names of the "haves" may change, quick, drastic societal income reshuffles are rare.

Figure 3.1 traces the absolute size of k for the United States. Its index movements over time appear in Fig. 3.4.

Compared to the other "great ratios" of economics, k (or its reciprocal) has been most nearly constant: its sidewise trend is pronounced when measured against ratios of capital-output, capital-labor, the average propensity to consume, or money velocity.† Past facts warrant the surmise that k is unlikely to explode dramatically in the near future.‡

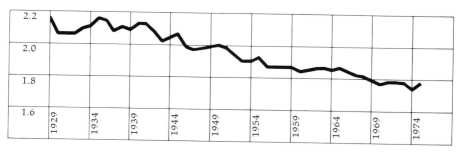

Fig. 3.1   Value of markup k in gross business product, 1929–1975

---

*   For some comparative data, see John Hotson, *International Comparisons of Money Velocity and Wage Mark-Ups* (New York: Augustus Kelley, 1968).

†   Cf. L. R. Klein and R. F. Kosobud, "Some Econometrics of Growth: Great Ratios of Economics," *Quarterly Journal of Economics* (May 1961). Note, however, that to use a long series the authors employed Simon Kuznets' income definition which includes only the portion of government output covered by taxes as intermediate goods in C and I. This creates anomalies for the war years.

‡   In a major article Franklin M. Fisher argued that Cobb-Douglas production functions succeed in "explaining" production growth with some accuracy only because they build in the hypothesis of constant shares, and that any mathematical function making the same assumption might serve equally well. Fisher also notes the

Egalitarian prospects

The k facts neither support nor oppose egalitarian goals. It is humane to favor measures intended to correct inequities in income (and wealth) distribution: the facts, however, reveal some obdurate rocks and realities. In the United States, for instance, the 1970–1975 corporate profits before the income tax ran to between 5.6 and 7.4 percent of GNP, and after the income tax to between 2.8 and 4.3 percent. Thus the possible margin for maneuver in diverting profits to wage and salary income is narrow.* If the scaling was performed the bleak questions would be: (1) What would egalitarian proponents do for an encore after the profit sums were obliterated? P-stability would thereafter compel a rigid link between w and A once $\Delta k = 0$ with $k = 1$ by some legerdemain incompatible with a market economy. (2) As the corporate tax levy would yield zero income to the Treasury, would the onus of the personal income tax rate be heavier? (3) How would the economy be run? Without the profit prizes, how would production be organized?

Advocates of guillotining k are more concerned with egalitarianism than with inflation, and often heedless of production implications. But the perplexities of inflation will endure even with zero profit margins unless money incomes behave rationally. In collectivist societies, inevitably $k > 1$ so long as the state amasses tax proceeds from producing firms and allows some retention of depreciation allowances for replacing (or expanding) capital equipment.

The Consumer Price Level

The theory of the consumer price level (P_c) is of special significance for *real* wages, or the relative buying power of money wages, and is reflected by the w/P_c ratio.† Largely, the C-sector price level devolves from the same w/A ratio *even when we start entirely from demand aspects*, endowing a low profile to cost attributes. "Cost-push" and "demand-pull" in consumer markets are thus nourished on a common wage-salary root.

The C-Sector in the closed economy

For the *supply* side of the consumer price level, write:

$$P_{cs} = k_{cs}w/A_c, \tag{3.6}$$

where c denotes the C-sector and s the supply aspect.

---

sparse theoretical concern with the constancy issue. Ultimately, the problems are less with constancy but with why the share ratio became stuck, and why it refuses to get "unglued." See his "Aggregate Production Functions and the Explanation of Wages: A Simulation Experiment," *Review of Economics and Statistics* (Nov. 1971) and "The Existence of Aggregate Production Functions," *Econometrica* (1969).

*   For nonprofit k-components, see Chapter 11.

†   In practice, P_c would be given by the consumer price index, the CPI of economic and financial reporting.

In Eq. (3.6) k_{cs} can be interpreted as the *target* markup aimed at by producers, while P_{cs} is the targeted macromarket supply side consumer price level. The average money wage (w) is assumed to be uniform for all market sectors.

The *demand* side of total consumer outlays is given by:*

$$P_c Q_c = c_w wN + c_r \lambda R + \theta, \tag{3.7}$$

where: c_w = average propensity of wage earners to spend out of pretax income; c_r = average propensity of nonwage earners to spend out of pretax income; N = total employment in GNP output; R = gross *nonwage* income, excluding only wN from GNP totals; θ = transfer incomes; λ = payout ratio from firms of nonwage income.

Equation (3.7) simply defines "consumer market sales equal to purchases," grouping buyers by income source. The wage bill includes *all* GNP wage earners—not only GBP sectors. Likewise, $R = (GNP - wN)$, where R includes all of GNP outside of the wage bill. Inasmuch as depreciation allowances, corporate taxes, and undistributed profits are not disbursed as individual incomes, the λ-payout ratio is inserted to restrict the purchasing power influence of R. Too, the c_w and c_r coefficients are reduced not only by personal savings but also by personal tax payments. The θ-term is a catchall for transfer incomes by way of Social Security pensions, unemployment, and welfare benefits.

To extract a demand-oriented price level from Eq. (3.7), divide through by the wage bill (wN) and multiply by N_c/N_c, denoting C-sector employment. Clearing:

$$P_{cd} = (w/A_c)(c_w + c_r \lambda R' + \theta')N/N_c, \tag{3.8}$$

where $R' = R/wN$, $\theta' = \theta/wN$.

In Eq. (3.6) the C-sector price level was based wholly on *supply* aspects; in Eq. (3.8) wholly on *demand* elements. Joining the two in equilibrium *and* disequilibrium, it follows:

$$k_c = [(c_w + c_r \lambda R' + \theta') N/N_c]. \tag{3.9}$$

The markup that emerges from market phenomena is *always* equal to the right side of Eq. (3.9). Equilibrium would require $k_{cs} = k_c$, with the *targeted* markup expected by producers coinciding with the market outcome; entrepreneurs would apprehend (on a macrobasis) a coalescence of their expected and realized gross profit margins.†

---

*   Cf. my "Comment on Cost Inflation," *Economic Journal* (June 1974).

†   In Walrasian equations it is usual to write the demand equation for any good i as a function of all product, and all factor, prices in terms of a common *numeraire*, as $p_1 = 1$. Thus:

   a) $Q_i^d = f(p_2, p_3, \ldots, w_1, w_2, w_3, \ldots)$,

where w_i = factor prices. In a money income economy this would probably have to be written as:

If the realized k_c remains constant over time, any P_c upheaval would be wholly attributable to the w/A_c ratio. Wriggles in k_c, whether of a cyclical or secular origin, would impose some P_c perturbations.* Nonetheless, an intuitive grasp of the 75 percent 1967–1976 leap in P_c, with available k-data trending almost flat, suggests that k_c variations are more likely to provoke ragged price blips rather than spur a price bulge: the inflation fires are stoked by a sharp flux in w/A_c ratio.

Sample values can illuminate Eq. (3.9); the numbers are rough indicative guesses: the econometric art should yield more precise values. Note that the c_w- and c_r-terms are calculated on personal income *before* income tax.

$$k_c = [0.8 + 0.5 \, (0.6) \, (0.6) + 0.3] \, (1.55) \approx 2 \qquad (3.10)$$

These tentative estimates place the C-sector markup factor at close to the economy average.

The "wage earners spend capitalists save" simplification

An elegant simplification (of Kalecki-Kaldor-Joan Robinson) can illuminate the analysis by stripping the theory to its bare essentials.† In a simplified model, "wage earners" are presumed to *spend* all their income while "capitalists"—nonwage earners in our classification—*save* all their income. Thus:

$$P_c Q_c = wN, \qquad (3.11)$$

and

$$P_c = (w/A_c) \, (N/N_c). \qquad (3.12)$$

In Eq. (3.12) the C-sector price level depends entirely on the wage-productivity ratio and the relative size of the C-sector.‡ The K-K-R hypothesis can be modified slightly to make it more general:

$$P_c Q_c = \alpha wN, \qquad (3.13)$$

---

b) $Q_i^d = f(P_1, P_2, \ldots, Y)$ or $f(P_1, P_2, P_3, \ldots, kwN)$,

where the P's are money prices and $Y = $ money income. For Walras, unit cost $=$ price, with neither "profits nor losses" in firms or industries, so that:

c) $P_i = k_i w / A_i$.

Stipulating $N = N_f$ (as Walras assumes full employment), it follows that money wages comprise a demand *and* cost parameter in consumer markets.

* Using the ratio (GNP/C) as a proxy for (N/N_c), and thereby assuming constant capital-labor ratios in all sectors, the structural N/N_c variation has moved from 1.49 in 1950 to 1.56 in 1975, conveying a price step-up of 5 percent against the 140 percent jump in the C-sector price index.

† For references, see "A Macro-Theory of Pricing, Income Distribution and Employment," in *KaM*, Essay 8.

‡ N/N_c, or its proxy GNP/C, is obviously linked to Keynes' multiplier. Taking $Y \equiv $ GNP, for the multiplier we have $Y = \chi I$ as against $Y = \chi' C$ for N/N_c, so that $(\chi/\chi') = (C/I)$.

with α = a multiple of the wage bill,

$$P_c = \alpha(w/A_c) \ (N/N_c). \tag{3.14}$$

If $\alpha = 1$, the K-K-R perspective survives with an extended twist: either their proviso applies or wage-salary savings and tax obligations are exactly offset by nonwage earner "capitalist" consumption. As Table 3.1 indicates, for both the United States and Canada, the K-K-R simplification would have missed the mark by under 5 percent in recent years, and from 1 to 4 percent in the United States between 1967 and 1975. In these cases the approximation "thinks through" reasonable results at a glance. For an impressionistic, quick brush portrait of C-sector outlay trends, the pristine K-K-R surmise constitutes a fertile working premise.

In both the United States and Canada the recent close convergence of wN to C-outlays after the mid-1950s undoubtedly reflects the legislated welfare state income redistribution trends.

The simplification in a time context

In a time context the K-K-R simplification (with the α twist) displays the *major* forces operating on consumption outlays more prominently than the more elegant disquisitions on the consumption function; also, as the latter run in *real* terms the relations usually have to be restored to current money sums by some price-level projections.

For relative changes in C-outlays over time:

$$(\Delta C/C) = (\Delta\alpha/\alpha) + (\Delta w/w) + (\Delta N/N), \tag{3.15}$$

where $C = P_c Q_c$. With employment increasing by 2 to 3 percent per annum, depending on a natural increase in the labor force, immigration, the business cycle, and growth forces in the economy, a big C-outlay burst is not apt to come from the N-term. Likewise, if trends in α are steady, then Eq. (3.15) discloses that the important impact on retail sales figures emanates from changes in w. An explosive Δw will stimulate sales growth and inflation flutters.

Table 3.1
Ratio of Consumption Outlay to Employee Compensation,
United States and Canada, 1947–1974

Years	United States	Canada
1947–1949	1.25	1.35
1950–1954	1.14	1.28
1955–1959	1.11	1.26
1960–1964	1.10	1.23
1965–1969	1.05	1.12
1970–1974	1.02	1.04

Source: U.S. Department of Commerce, *Survey of Current Business; Economic Council of Canada*

This almost self-evident result would not deserve amplification except for the astonishment expressed, whenever money wages rise in the Detroit automobile region or the Pittsburgh steel mills, that local retail trade figures also mount. Equation (3.15) conveys the reasons more simply than the recondite consumption-function printouts.

Sectoral price levels

Formulas similar to Eq. (3.8) and Eq. (3.14) can be confined to a narrower price sector, say for foodstuffs.* While the elements would be the same, each c-term would also embed implicit substitution effects, and thus implicit demand elasticities, depending on food prices relative to other items in the consumer budget. Insofar as the c-terms remained fairly taut in household budgeting, the sectoral P would likewise dance to w/A tunes: thus foodstuff prices also react to money-income gains. As Δw grows, demand pressures lift food prices. Even with bumper farm crops food prices can soar, according to WCM precepts.

Oil prices

On the critical energy and oil problem, a sketchy C-sector model would assume not only that oil is purchased solely by final consumers, but that even the ability of firms to sell products whose price encompasses a sharp increase in oil prices would be contingent on Δw trends. Specifying the domestic consumption of oil as derived from domestic and foreign supplies, Q_d and Q_f, and that a common price prevails at the filling station, then:

$$P(Q_d + Q_f - E) = bwN, \qquad (3.16)$$

where E = industrial purchases. The coefficient b is a measure of the link between the wage bill and outlay on oil products: a slow-up in Δw should restrict energy outlays, retard the rise in oil prices, and check the value of oil imports. Although the analysis can be extended, there is the salient point that oil prices and import outlays also come to reflect the money-income growth.

The investment sector price level

It might seem natural to develop the I-sector price level in an analogous way, especially by invoking Keynes' truism of $S = I$, savings equal investment. Yet this would imply that savings are immediately channeled into I-purchases in any market period, as if those who save directly buy the new capital goods.†

---

* Cf. a related approach by Nicholas Kaldor, "What Is Wrong With Economic Theory," *Quarterly Journal of Economics* (August 1975). Kaldor argues (p. 354) that the income of the agricultural sector is truistically equal to the expenditure of the industrial sector on farm products, with the former determining (in multiplier fashion) "the level and rate of growth of industrial production."

† In a circular-flow economy, such as envisaged by Joseph Schumpeter, *The Theory of Economic Development* (Cambridge: Harvard University Press, 1934),

In the C-sector we can accept as valid (for most consumers) the income restraint on purchases; in the I-sector the plant and equipment purchases are financed either by: (1) commercial bank loans (directly or indirectly) and thus by demand-deposit creation, or (2) internal financing by firms out of past profits and depreciation flows, and (3) capital market borrowing. Back of it all lies the central bank and its assessment of the economic scene, with the ability to affect investment through its money maneuvers. Hence for the I-sector a markup formula is likely to prove most useful, with k_i subject to the forces of competition and monopoly, and sensitive to the order backlog and the amount of idle productive capacity.

Money Wages in a Time Setting

Money wages have been thrust on center stage in the price-level script.

From t_0 to t_1

Suppose money wages are universally raised at time t_0 to rule until t_1 with the $t_1 - t_0$ interval being a "year." Immediately, from the cost side at t_0 there are pressures on each firm to raise prices fairly proportionately, or for leftward shifts in supply curves under pure competition. Possibly, if markups were unduly high firms may temper the price increase. Likewise from the demand side, the wage rise must tend to lift consumer-demand curves, and hence prices.

Schematically, if we assume that all wage and salary income changes occur on January 1 (t_0), then again on t_1 a year later, there will be some tendency for a ratchet price leap every January 1 if k is inflexible. As the year grinds on, prices will drift down at the pace of productivity progress. Thus in Fig. 3.2 $t_0't_1$, $t_1't_2$, etc., slide down along a gentle grade.

Actually, some wage bargains are consummated in January, others in February, others in March, etc. In the continuous wage progression, with each adjudication boosting the average wage fractionally, there is finer continuity to the price advance, as suggested by Curve 2 in Fig. 3.2.

As output drops in a recession firms may be reluctant to fire valued employees, clinging to the chance that the slump will be short-lived. Temporarily, the work force may be redundant as employment holds steadier than output: with $Q_2 < Q_1$, and $N_2 \approx N_1$, then $\Delta A < 0$.* Thus Fig. 3.2 might be amended for "hoarded" labor hire in a stagflation context.

Redvers Opie, translator (1911 edition), where savings flow back to investment goods purchases, we would have: $P_i = (w/A_i)(s_r R' + s_w)(N/N_i)$, where s_w, s_r denote the respective savings ratios, and $R' = R/wN$. See my *Classical Keynesianism, Monetary Theory and the Price Level* (Philadelphia: Chilton, 1961), p. 127.

Keynes, likewise, noted that a closed-circuit price-level formula for the I-sector would be contrived and overly mechanical. See *A Treatise on Money* (New York: Harcourt, Brace, 1930) Vol. 1, pp. 140–146; also, *Collected Writings* (London: Macmillan, 1973), Vol. XIII, letter from Richard F. Kahn, pp. 203–207.

* The elasticity of labor productivity would take a value below unity, as $E_{QN} =$

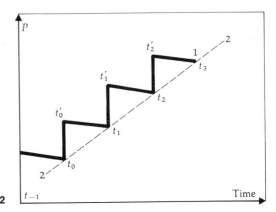

Figure 3.2

In Fig. 3.3, if we take maximum productivity improvements per annum at about 4 percent, and minus 2 percent as an extreme descent, the productivity path might follow the cyclical (ac) productivity curve; under slumpflation any deceleration in $\Delta w/w$ is in part neutralized by a decline in $\Delta A/A$. In a rapid upswing the P-consequences of wage excesses are tapered by productivity flashes.

Profit Inflation and Income Inflation

So long as k is constant, or falling, only a rising w/A ratio carries a price clout.

If money wages were geared to A, and prices mounted, k would have to rise: the outcome would constitute a "Profit Inflation."* Through taxing profits away it could end as a "tax inflation," involving a Treasury bonanza. Available data on k, however, reject the hypothesis of profit-inflation in the

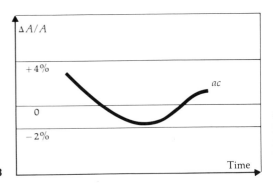

Figure 3.3

$(N\Delta Q/Q\Delta N) < 1$. In the recovery phase, then, $E_{QN} > 1$. The latter, plus new technological improvements, would explain marked labor productivity gains in a cyclical stagflation system.

* Cf. Keynes, *Treatise*, Vol. I, p. 155.

United States, Canadian, United Kingdom, or Australian experience over the past inflationary decade. It is doubtful that the facts were different elsewhere. So long as the w/A barrier held firm, a profit inflation could be dispelled through the corporate income tax or abated by keener antitrust surveillance.

It should be mandatory for those who elicit causes beyond the w/A ratio to submit evidence of a notable change in k to account for the extraordinary price leap over the last decade, and explain how money wages (or money incomes generally) can grossly surpass productivity without ushering in an inflationary sequel.

Historical Trends in WCM Components

To lend concreteness, Fig. 3.4 displays the movements in w, A, and k since 1929, based on Department of Commerce series; for comparative purposes, the 1929 values are assigned an index of 100 with the semi-log scale designed to exhibit rates of change. The flatness (and downtrend) of k, the rather steady ascent in A, and the explosive skyward thrust in w are graphic.

Five-year averages of the same variables since 1950 are tabulated in Table 3.2; they amply confirm the chart tracings. For some comparison, the Canadian data are also included. In Canada, A and P ran nearly along the same track until the 1970 period, with the implication that

$$(\Delta P/P) = [(\Delta w/w) \pm (\Delta k/k)]/2.$$

That is, the relative P-movement reflects half the relative wage and k changes. Over the quarter century, in the Canadian GNP, the k descent exerted about a 10 percent *deterrent* to the 76 percent price escalation fueled by the 212 percent wage rocket.

Table 3.2

Five-Year Averages of Indexes of WCM Components,
United States and Canada, 1950–1974

Period	United States, 1958 = 100				Canada, 1961 = 100			
	k	w	A	P	k	w	A	P
1950–1954	104	77	89	87	106	65	81	85
1955–1959	101	97	99	97	104	86	95	94
1960–1964	101	118	113	105	101	105	104	102
1965–1969	98	148	126	115	99	141	118	118
1970–1974	96	206	137	144	95	203	130	150

Note: Figures for Canada are from GNP data; an exclusion of Public Administration and defense salaries led to no significant differences in the series. The P-term denotes the GNP deflator. For the United States the data refer to GBP components, including the GBP deflator.

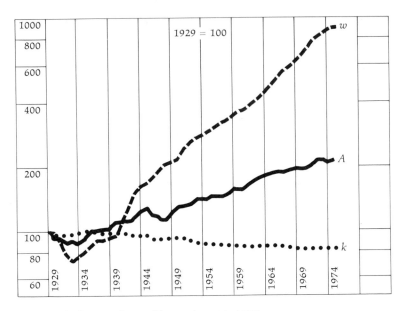

Fig. 3.4 Index numbers of k, w, A, 1929–1975

The Price Level in the Open Economy

For the United States the closed economy provides a good approximation to price-level events; other countries must keep a more watchful eye on external influences. Still, in a regime of floating exchange rates only a fairly simple revision in the basic WCM theory is entailed.*

In practically every country there is a tendency to blame price woes on "imported" inflation: inflation appears as a unique phenomenon which everybody imports and nobody exports.† Even United States officials, with less warrant than elsewhere, conjure visions of global inflation to exonerate their own price-level ineptness.

The doctrine of imported inflation furnishes a comforting rationalization; if the problem is "global" then the ball is tapped into the courts of other countries; the corollary is that rescue must await an international conference rich in vague communiques and short in concrete steps to bank the price fires. To be sure, economic analysis stemming from the classical economics of Hume and Ricardo, and an older gold-standard world, or even the postwar Bretton Woods commitment to (relatively) fixed exchange rates, lends some plausibility

---

*   Cf. my article of the same title in *Kyklos* (1977) for some extension of these remarks.

†   In lecture visits to about 27 countries, including the major trading nations, the complaint of imported inflation is as prevalent as the common cold: everyone catches the infection, nobody admits to spreading it.

to the theme of imported inflation. Nonetheless, ideas on sheltered industries, and the sporadic exchange-rate variations over the last quarter century, plus the contemporary exchange-rate floating, impel revision in the older fixed-exchange-rate inflation-transmission mechanism.*

In defining the degree of "openness," our telescope is on trade interdependence. In other contexts migration, interest-rate interdependence, capital flows, the international transmission of knowledge, technological absorption, literary communication, or external political stimuli might command attention as a test of the open society.

To anticipate the conclusion, the world inflation is unlikely to abate until the major trading nations act, mainly independently, to control their own (w/A) fate; a more resolute policy stance will be imperative when other countries are remiss in their performance. A concerted international program could be mutually reenforcing, permitting less stringent domestic initiatives.

The price equations in the open economy

In view of the prevalence of GNP data, and the snares in disentangling imports destined for government use, the analysis leans on the GNP rather than GBP concept.

In the open economy the new complication is that both exports and imports affect the quantities of goods available for sale domestically and, thus, the domestic price level. We can visualize the economy as selling domestically the entire range of final goods and services bought by consumers (C), investment by firms (I), and absorptions by government (G). Further, there are exports (X), which sell domestically—as C, I, or G items—for the same price as the unit proceeds rendered after conversion from foreign currencies. Embodied in all these goods is the import content (F), as raw, and semifinished materials or final goods in the C, I, G, X categories.

From Gross National Product (GNP) accounting it follows that:

$$C + I + G + X - F = \text{GNP} \equiv P_d Q_d \qquad (3.17a)$$
$$C + I + G + X = \text{GNP} + F = PQ = P_d Q_d + P_f Q_f \qquad (3.17b)$$
$$\frac{(C + I + G + X - F)}{(C + I + G + X)}(C + I + G + X) \equiv \text{GNP} = nPQ \qquad (3.17c)$$

where: $P_f Q_f$ = import prices and quantities; $P_d Q_d$ = prices and quantities of domestic output content; P, Q = prices and quantities in the open economy, embodying import content; $n \leqq 1$ = domestic content of each money unit of $C + I + G + X$.

---

* As a recent survey article (by economists predisposed to the doctrine of global inflation) observed: "Nevertheless, major discrepancies between the inflation rates experienced by different countries persisted . . . and these divergences need explaining." D. E. W. Laidler and J. M. Parkin, "Inflation: A Survey," *Economic Journal* (Dec. 1975), p. 783.

Running down the equations, the first is merely the conventional GNP aggregate.* Equation (3.17b) severs the relation to display the domestic and import price-quantity set: P denotes the price level inclusive of imports. In Eq. (3.17c) the value of output (PQ), *gross of import content*, is reduced by the n-term to elicit domestic GNP content.

The n-term provides a wedge for classifying economies by the degree of "open" or "closed"-ness. As n varies the home market P becomes more, or less, buffeted by external price winds. The alternative WCM open-economy relations thus become:†

$$nPQ \equiv n(P_dQ_d + P_fQ_f) = Y, \text{ or } P_d + P_f(Q_f/Q_d) = Y/nQ_d \quad (3.18a)$$
$$nPQ \equiv n(P_dQ_d + P_fQ_f) = kwN, \text{ or } P_d + P_f(Q_f/Q_d) = kw/nA \quad (3.18b)$$
$$P = (P_dQ_d/Q) + (P_fQ_f/Q) = (kwN/nQ) = kw/nA' \quad (3.18c)$$

In Eq. (3.18) n denotes the domestic component of the gross internal output containing import content.‡ Thus if $n = 0.9$, then 90 cents of every dollar of $(C + I + G + X)$ consists of domestic output (and income), with 10 cents or $(1 - n = n')$ being the import-content in each sales dollar. The price level, gross of imports, is weighted by the price level of home output, and of import prices weighted by their quantitative importance as indicated in Eq. (3.18c).§

Some comparative calculations of domestic content

In the *fully* closed economy, $F = 0 = X$. Conceivably, $F = 0$, with $X > 0$, where the exports amass international reserves unless cancelled through foreign aid grants. In any event, with $F = 0$, $n = 1$, so that the pertinent P-theory is that of the closed economy; "imported inflation" is precluded.

At the other extreme, $Y = F$, and $n = 0$, so that *all* goods (and services) are "imported." This is a far-fetched instance of nil domestic production: in descending from $1 \geq n \geq 0$ the economic door becomes progressively ajar to "openness." Changes in the inclusive home price level, as in Eq. (3.18c), can reflect either internal or external price-quantity changes, or varying n-content. Often the price-quantity influences will exert counteracting pulls. A falling n, attributable to rising import prices or quantities, tends to elevate P or negate some of the price deterrence of A.

Some illustrative n-values can be computed from data published by the *International Monetary Fund*. In all cases Gross National Product statistics were used (in domestic currencies), together with the accompanying infor-

---

* GNP thus nets out imports.

† Using a Fisher-type equation of exchange the formula would be $MV = nPQ$. (See Chapter 4.)

‡ It is worth reiterating that n is a ratio, of $1/(1 + P_fQ_f/P_dQ_d)$. Thus n can vary with changes in either or both import prices and quantities even with a fixed P_dQ_d sum.

§ The term $A' = Q/N$, where $Q = (P_d/P)Q_d + (P_f/P)Q_f$.

mation on imports. Results appear in Table 3.3 where economies are classified as "Almost Closed," "Amply Closed," "Moderately Closed," "More Open," etc.

It is astonishing to find India heading the list as the most closed economy of all! Undoubtedly, this is part statistical illusion, in view of the substantial amount of nonmarket—maybe about half—GNP output in Indian statistics.* As imports belong to the market price system, on market GNP data India would drop to a more open setting, maybe with $n = 0.85$ or so. A parallel distortion probably taints the n-values for all countries as the GNP data embed disparate amounts of nonmarket output.

The United States is obviously a very closed economy; Japan and Australia also rank high on the list. While refinement of the GNP totals may revise the ordering, based on the raw GNP data both countries appear less open than the United Kingdom, or Canada, over the period covered. Germany and France have more openness, and the Scandinavian and Low countries even more. Israel and Luxembourg are prime examples of open, "Westernized" market economies.

Price level independence and interaction in the open economy

Suppose an open economy tried to pursue an independent price-level policy, whether the objective be a flat P-trend or a controlled path. Using subscripts for dates t_1 and t_2:†

$$(P_2/P_1) = (n_1 Y_2 Q_1)/(n_2 Y_1 Q_2) = (n_1 k_2 w_2 A'_1)/(n_2 k_1 w_1 A'_2). \qquad (3.19)$$

On the heroic assumption of "other things unchanged," meaning $\overline{\text{GNP}}$ $(= Y)$ and $\overline{Q}$, the composite price rise will turn on:

$$(P_2/P_1) = (n_1/n_2). \qquad (3.20)$$

Thus the price move will equal the reciprocal of the fall in domestic content: if n drops from 0.9 to 0.8, or a doubling of the *value* of foreign content from 0.1 to 0.2, the upward price thrust will be 12½ percent so that even a shocking 100 percent import price upheaval (with Q_f/Q_d held rigid) will evoke a limited P response. If $n = 0.8$ and sinks to 0.06, the price jump will be 33⅓ percent: openness spells higher inflation vulnerability.

Normally, world price eruptions of such magnitude come as part of a cumulative process over some years, rather than as an instant rash. Annual bites on importing countries are thus scaled down. "Other things," of course, will also change. If the Q's are inviolate, as the monetary authorities strive to maintain employment, then:

$$(P_2/P_1) = n_1 Y_2/n_2 Y_1. \qquad (3.21)$$

---

* For an attempt to place the Indian statistics on a market basis, see my *Growth Without Inflation in India* (Delhi: National Council of Applied Economic Research, 1965).

† Note: The interpretation of $A' = Q/N$, meaning output *gross* of import content.

Table 3.3

Domestic Content of One Currency Unit of Gross Domestic Product, 1970–1974

	High	Average	Low
"Almost" closed economies: 1 > n > 0.9			
India (1968–1971)	0.978	0.958	0.945
United States	0.948	0.938	0.919
Argentina (1970–1973)	0.942	0.928	0.919
Brazil (1970–1973)	0.934	0.924	0.915
Turkey (1970–1972)	0.922	0.909	0.902
Mexico	0.917	0.909	0.895
"Amply" closed economies: 0.9 > n > 0.85			
Japan	0.916	0.899	0.864
Uruguay (1970–1973)	0.901	0.888	0.876
Chile (1970–1972)	0.893	0.886	0.873
Australia	0.885	0.870	0.861
Spain (1970–1973)	0.866	0.857	0.843
"Moderately" closed economies: 0.85 > n > 0.80			
France	0.863	0.848	0.807
Greece	0.847	0.827	0.801
Germany	0.835	0.827	0.804
Venezuela	0.836	0.825	0.815
Italy	0.842	0.823	0.770
Canada	0.827	0.815	0.792
United Kingdom	0.828	0.806	0.755
New Zealand (1970–1973)	0.812	0.803	0.795
"More open" economies: 0.80 > n > 0.75			
South Africa	0.813	0.795	0.764
Sweden	0.811	0.794	0.748
Finland	0.783	0.771	0.742
Denmark	0.788	0.768	0.741
"Substantially" open economies: 0.75 > n > 0.70			
Austria	0.763	0.748	0.729
Switzerland	0.758	0.748	0.739
Costa Rica	0.730	0.715	0.677
"Extremely" open economies: 0.70 > n > 0.65			
Belgium	0.713	0.693	0.650
Iceland	0.713	0.692	0.677
Norway	0.712	0.691	0.663
Ireland	0.715	0.690	0.628
Netherlands	0.695	0.673	0.646
"Practically" open economies: 0.65 > n > 0.55			
Israel (1970–1973)	0.654	0.638	0.601
Luxembourg (1970–1973)	0.563	0.559	0.556

Source: *International Monetary Statistics,* International Monetary Fund (Dec. 1975)

If $n_1 \approx n_2$, the composite price bulge hinges on the domestic money income (GNP) development, of (Y_2/Y_1). Under limited GNP advances an inflation debacle through external price events becomes less ominous. Implicitly, however, domestic money-wage restraint is entailed in establishing this conclusion—along with productivity gains.

So long as P_f spurts faster than P_d, substitutionary demand forces should work to replace some import wares; countries with high domestic supply elasticities should not be battered by external inflation.* By containing the w/A ratio, and defending the home price level, exchange-rate appreciation over time should also operate to nullify the domestic impact of world inflation; comparative domestic purchasing power ratios should overwhelm capital flow influences, over the long haul, in settling foreign exchange rates.† The recent strength of the German mark and the Swiss franc is not unconnected to the capital flows on the widespread expectation that their economies will best abate the price upheavals; the inflow of funds helps make this premise a self-fulfilling prophecy by raising the exchange value of their currencies. For economies grappling with more dubious P-prospects there is a feedback from inflation, to exchange-rate depreciation, and to more inflation.

The consumer price level in the open economy

The consumer price level equation can also be amended to cover the open economy. Equation (3.8) must thereby: (1) add a term on the right-hand side to cover exports of consumer goods (X_c); and (2) subtract imports entering consumer purchases (F_c). Also, to adopt a more comprehensive view, add a term to cover (3) increases (or decreases) in consumer output entering business inventories (V_c). Furthermore: (4) government buys consumer goods (G_c) to store, or for foreign aid, or to dispense to flood victims, or for school lunches, or through food stamps, etc. For V_c and G_c it is as if these goods are "exported," though the G_c disposition is capable of influencing the c_w, c_r, and θ magnitudes insofar as the government programs affect consumer outlays.

Equation (3.8) would thus be supplemented by:

$$B' = (X_c + G_c \pm V_c - F_c)/wN). \tag{3.22}$$

Largely, relative to wN and through the negative F_c, B' will ordinarily be "small." However, with massive grain exports (say to Russia and else-

---

*   Thus $(Q_f/Q_d) = f(P_f/P_d)$, with a negative sign on the first derivative. Fairly constant domestic prices of import competing wares will tend to neutralize rising world prices as a home market inflation-maker.

For some elasticity derivations, see my *Kyklos* article.

†   So long as purchasing-power parity doctrines hold even partially, the *tendency* of exchange rates to appreciate will impart substance to the argument that most affluent countries can control their own price-level fortunes even in the face of global inflation. A full assessment of the theory of the open economy would transcend the scope of this chapter. In essentials, substitutionary forces and capital flows should buttress the argument.

where), or inventory buildups, or direct G_c purchases, the B' term may compel occasional P_c lurches.

Imported inflation?

Control of the domestic w/A ratio, a high elasticity of import substitution, and accompanying exchange-rate appreciation as a matter of policy or ensuing from market forces, could permit the major affluent economies to mark their own price destiny with minor deflections.* Price levels are generally "made at home"; imported inflation appears to be a comforting apologetic to support inaction, evading the w/A leverage.

One-crop, one-mineral, or one-commodity underdeveloped lands are likely to have a more difficult time in exerting P-discipline because of the lack of stabilization instruments, ineptness in their use, political instability, or apathy. Imported (and nonimported) inflation is one more price of economic and political backwardness; some relief could follow from a better record in affluent countries.

Not Why, But How

The WCM theory constitutes a *general* theory of the price level: any ΔP force must, one way or the other, operate through w, k, n, or A. With k practically subdued, it is through w and A that we must look for ΔP guidance. Later, in examining the staple diet of competing theories, each in turn will be tested against the WCM categories.

The proliferation in the same textbook of several theories resembles a menu listing the house specialties for the reader to make a selection. It is as if Einstein catalogued several theories of the physical world and invited his audience to pick one out. A general theory, however, must encompass all phenomena, otherwise the model is suspect for its inadequacy in embracing relevant factors. The WCM formulation is able to absorb all other explanations in a consistent way, including the pernicious stagflation and slumpflation phenomena. Older theories cannot make the same claim, either in the diagnostic, prescriptive, or prognostic phases.

Rear-guard defenses of outmoded doctrines tediously invoke the query "Why did the wage level 'suddenly' break out of its past norms?" For it is the flight of money incomes into economic outer space that has demolished the past ambivalence to the WCM theory, refusing it a respectable airing among economists rendering lip-service to innovative ideas.

---

* On a conscious application of exchange-rate appreciation, along with domestic steps to subdue the price level, see Lars Calmfors, "Swedish Inflation and International Price Influences," Seminar Paper (Stockholm: Institute of International Studies, 1975) and "Swedish Inflation and International Price Influences," *Skandinaviska Enskilda Banken* (Stockholm, Quarterly Review 4/1975).

The WCM theory has always been pertinent to the industrial economy. That money wages behaved better in the longer past, and that they could be aligned to labor-productivity advances through monetary policy—at a price in unemployment in the boom and bust cycles—tended to obscure their significance. Too, in a more rural agricultural order with modest and nonbellicose unions the cutting edge of the WCM thrust could be blunted. Surely, more than a glimmer of the WCM theory was discerned by Keynes over forty years ago.* Likewise, even for the German hyperinflation of the twenties, Joan Robinson saw the mischief inherent in the hourly "indexing" revision of money wages in the Ruhr Valley.†

As for the "why" in the recent unruly income binge: part of the explanation is undoubtedly attributable to the more permissive life-styles and the more hedonistic drives for instant gratification in material goods, sex, drugs, easy education, and rewarding careers. This is not to be construed as a blanket indictment—it is merely a recognition. The visual TV and movie media, the auto and its quick mobility, the airplane, and speedy communication have aroused a craving for the goods and gadgets of industrial society and the urge to possess them *now*, quickly. Inflation itself intensifies the drive to buy now; for instance, to acquire excessive house space to beat the higher prices that are likely to occur later.‡ To the ordinary citizen the obvious means to material riches consists in fingering "more" in the pay envelope; while the quest for "more" has never been absent in the economic person or the labor movement, it has been magnified to "more and more"—and more quickly.

Between the spirit of the age and coaxing by TV glamor—wholly sustained by advertising—pay demands have burst their previous bounds. Often overlooked is the fact that our energy-using durable goods culture is a very late arrival. Universal auto ownership, even in the United States, is largely a post–World War II phenomenon. The "big ticket" refrigerator, air conditioner, home-movie camera, hi-fi, cassette, and, above all, TV, date from the mid-1950s. That these items are commonplace adornments of normal living standards bears testimony to the common availability of products that are short-lived in terms of human existence. By the late 1960s in the United States the possession of these goods became a normal expectation.

It is a remarkable accomplishment to have been able to mass-produce these goods within so short a period, say 1950–1965. In other countries, the lag

---

* In the *General Theory of Employment, Interest and Money* (New York: Harcourt, Brace, 1936). Nearly a half century back, in the *Treatise*, there is explicit recognition of "efficiency-earnings," in his effort to dislodge the Quantity Theory. Ibid., Vol. 1, pp. 135–137.

† Cf. her sparkling review of Brescioni-Turroni, *Economic Journal* (Sept. 1938), p. 150.

‡ Wiles writes: "It is, surely, the communications revolution which, making everyone instantly aware of everything, has sharply increased the amount of envy and imitation in the world, and reduced the number of things that are sacrosanct." *Economic Journal* (June 1973), p. 378.

behind the United States' abundance was about 10–12 years. Worldwide, the same types of goods pour out of multinational factories and are dispersed in a widening arc. Familiarity has fed desire, with escalating pay demands.

Impatient aspirations thus convey one possible explanation.* Even if it is not wholly persuasive, the serious concern is not with "why" but with "how," on means to arrest inflation while restoring jobs and output.

Once money incomes lunge forward the only imperatives are to deter the ascent or to accept the inflation. Each annual pay sequence can sport a different coloration. Group A insists on 15 percent more this year because one year, two years, or just three months back, Group B garnered 8, 12, or 20 percent more. Then C, D, and E groups vie, followed by A and B again— or B and A. There is pressure on the part of each group to get "the mostest fastest," to extract its due; the pellmell process carries each group along to roughly the same relative position as each acts to protect its place on the income scale.

So the vigorous struggle to get ahead in the *money*-income race impels inflation. Entrepreneurs, likewise, act to protect their own profits from being eroded, and counter by raising administered prices directly after tabulating the wage pressures. At the same time, in competitive markets prices are carried up by the tandem agents of costs *and* demand. One way and the other, the wage share holds constant while inflation is recorded; real incomes, to be sure, still follow the productivity course.

Without inflation some glaring income inequities could more readily be dispelled and more rational purchase patterns implanted under normal real-income improvement. With full employment, per capita real income could be larger, and the income distribution deflected into some match with the consensus on ethical criteria. A disciplined money-wage evolution can alone spell the larger benefits in a less rancorous society.

---

* Without collective bargaining it might seem that with unemployment an employer could replace employees with unemployed workers at lower money wages, thus making the money wage flexible downward. Whether it would be conducive to full employment is another matter. (See Chapter 5 below). But even this hypothetical "assuming away" of unions neglects the historical force of custom in money-wage settings. Mill emphasized this a long time ago. Cf. "The Full Employment Model," *KaM*.

CHAPTER FOUR

Money in a Money-Wage Economy

A revision of monetary theory and policy, away from M to P-causation and over to P-accommodation and Q-causation, is inherent in the WCM model so that conventional ideas on monetary theory and policy invite amendment.* Accenting the Monetarist refrain that "money matters—indeed," the strike-arm of money emissions in the WCM rendition is poised over Q and N terrain rather than on the P-front. The theoretical divergences thus carry practical overtones.

Not so long ago it was inadvertently alleged that only "empirical" issues confronted monetary theory, that the theoretical perceptions commanded maximum assent.† Shortly thereafter, Professor Friedman was besieged in a 140-

---

* Further aspects of the theory of money, beyond the needs of the main theme, appear in Chapter 9. Several passages in this chapter have been drawn from my joint article in collaboration with Professor Paul Davidson, "Money as Cause and Effect," *Economic Journal* (Dec. 1973), and from my lecture on *A Theory of Monetary Policy Under Wage Inflation* (University of Queensland, July 1974), sponsored by the ANZ Bank, Brisbane, Australia.

† Thus Friedman remarked: "One purpose of setting forth this framework as I have is to document my belief that the basic differences among economists are empirical, not theoretical . . ." See "A Theoretical Framework of Monetary Analysis," *Journal of Political Economy* (1970), closing passages.

In an article devoted to theoretical evaluation, decorated with a Phillips curve wage equation and adorned with "expected" price changes, "excess" labor demand, and never pausing over the concept of a homogeneous stock of capital—despite the devastating criticism of Mrs. Robinson on the concept—Jerome L. Stein concluded: "I have shown what empirical specifications imply monetarist or fiscal conclusions; and the controversy can be reduced to a set of testable propositions." There is nary

page journal symposium devoted to conceptual structure.* Apparently, more remains to be said on the theory of money. The episode is reminiscent of John Stuart Mill, writing in 1848 just before the dawn of the marginal utility revolution, that: "Happily, there is nothing in the laws of value which remains for the present or any future writer to clear up: the theory of the subject is complete."† Mill's mishap should have instilled some Monetarist reserve in heralding the New Quantity Theory of Money (NQT).

The Macrodemand for Money

It will be useful first to consider how money fits into the economy as a medium of exchange employed to settle transactions. Obviously, money is used daily by firms to pay out incomes and then used by income recipients to make their usual household purchases. Firms also demand money to make their purchases of materials alongside of the payments to productive factors, notably as wage sums to labor. The initial remarks thus deal with the *transactions-motive*, as Keynes termed the main source of demand for money; thereafter we shall look mainly at money supplies before returning (in Chapter 9) to the demand thesis.

A fundamental synoptic proposition

The conception of how money enters into the economic process can be capsuled in a few words. Beyond its description as a price system, our economy is primarily a money-wage system. In the *expectation* of sales receipts, employees are hired. Businesses pay out money wages and salaries—by drawing on their business bank accounts and by borrowing from banks—which sets up the cost side of market phenomena. The same money-wage and salary payments constitute the major component of demand, or purchasing power, in consumer markets. Through the dual forces of money demand and money cost, prices evolve.

In the fully "circular-flow" stationary economy ably described by Schumpeter, the pace of income payments to factors, and outlays by income recipients, and the outlays and receipts by firms, even when they were not perfectly

---

a word on even the possibility of a WCM theory, as faith springs eternal that the dispute can be settled by churning out correlations for "proving" that both Monetarists and Keynesians are sometimes right and sometimes wrong. See his "Unemployment, Inflation, and Monetarism," *American Economic Review* (Dec. 1974), p. 887.

* "Symposium on Friedman's 'Theoretical Framework,'" *Journal of Political Economy* (Sept./Oct. 1972).

† John Stuart Mill, *Principles of Political Economy* (Ashley ed., 1909 reprint), p. 436. Friedman, to be sure, has quoted Mill approvingly on "the veil of money" under a steady rule of money-supply augmentation. See below.

synchronized, would form an undeviating pattern.* If time "stood still," as in a world where all activities were consummated in a flash, the receipts and payments would balance out, with receipts equal to the payments made; the money stacks would pile up in the "hoards" of those who disgorged them. Money holdings after transactions would match the sums held prior to the exchanges. (To be sure, to press the point, in the instantaneous circular-flow a unit of money could have an infinite velocity of circulation so that the money supply would tend to be nil. Further, if the economy were stationary, and *known* to be so, there is the deeper question of whether there would be any need for money. But these profundities can be set aside as extraneous to our experience: transactions take time and decisions are made under uncertainty).

Breaking into the circular-flow, it is, as Schumpeter has emphasized, the decisions of the entrepreneur on output levels, the hiring of productive factors, and the paying out of money incomes for their services that typify the motions of the capitalist economy. It is this linkage that shapes our conception of the market process.

By and large, the ensuing theory of monetary policy is an exploration and elaboration of the implications of the synoptic propositional chain. Anterior to money prices are money incomes. Theories which commence with the hypothesis of consumers coming to market, and already enriched with money to make purchases, start one stage too late in the circle by failing to identify the *source* of the household purchasing power as emanating from the hire process where definite money-wage and salary incomes are disbursed.† Analogously, those theories which invite us to "imagine" an increase in the money supply as exogenously realized—for example, from a helicopter "bombardment," where the streets are littered with new money—obscure the origins of household money balances.‡ Underplayed in this simplistic version is the *demand* for money by firms to make income payments at prevailing wage-salary levels and, thereupon, the ultimate supply pressures on central banks to consummate their designated function of "creating" money to support Q and N at any given or enhanced w figure.

---

* Cf. the vivid description of the circular-flow economy in Joseph A. Schumpeter, *The Theory of Economic Development.*

† Cf. Don Patinkin, *Money, Interest, and Prices* (New York: Harper & Row, 1965), 2d ed., Part I for a prestigious illustration.

‡ While Friedman employs this image to simplify his analysis, there is a mental residue which affects his theoretical account. The concept impedes recognition of the *endogenous* pressures on the monetary authority to contend with unemployment in the modern context of wage, and thus price level, inflation inasmuch as the central bank is powerless, by and large, to arrest ΔP without acquiescing in intolerable unemployment. See his title essay in *The Optimum Quantity of Money and Other Essays* (Chicago: Aldine, 1969).

The monetary authority, whether the central bank or the Treasury, will be referred to as the MA. Colloquially, less in affection than in disillusion, the "Fed" is short-hand for the United States Board of Governors of the Federal Reserve System and the Federal Reserve Banks.

The Monetarist and WCM version of money demand

Manifestly, the WCM model rejects the Monetarist's updated version of the Quantity Theory of Money (QTM) proposition that M is the strategic key to lock P. As the Q-potential has a technological and behavioral base fairly immune to quick swelling, M has been seized upon by Monetarists as the instrument for an inflation strategy eminently amenable to institutional MA control. Central banks have acted on this premise to puncture the inflation balloon—with a conspicuous record of missions foiled. Monetarists have unremittingly reproached the MA for laxity in command.

In developing the transmission mechanism whereby M affects Y, after a helicopter drop or ad hoc-MA emissions of ΔM, as households and firms sort their (M/P) real-balances under the new money surfeit, after some time lag, prices are presumed to drift upward. The exposition is simple in some renditions, complex in others which treat money as one asset among many held in a portfolio spectrum suddenly disturbed by the ΔM variation. The full portfolio thereupon undergoes compulsive review, and the assorted financial claims thereafter become methodically rearranged.* As the behavioral perturbations unwind there is likely (in the Keynesian views) to be some fall in interest rates (r) and a rise in investment (I) and consumption (C).

On the demand side, there is an exaggerated fascination in the Monetarist NQT with *household* reactions to enlarged money balances. In the WCM it is the business firms, confronted with $\Delta P > 0$, and with Δw playing the kingly role, who run to the banks to borrow more money to finance their higher payrolls at any $Q = \overline{Q}$. Thus a partial demand function for money can be written as:

$$M^d = M(w, Q, \ldots), \tag{4.1}$$

with $(\partial M^d/\partial w) > 0 < (\partial M^d/\partial Q)$.† If added funds are not forthcoming, as when the MA strives to hold ΔM under wraps despite $w(t) > 0$, the burden of adjustment falls not on P but on Q and N. In the NQT, rather than Q or N it is ΔP that is assumed to absorb the backlash of retardation in ΔM. In the WCM the pace of ΔM has little to do with P (by and large) and much to do with Q and N.

The business firm thus occupies the driver's seat in the WCM theory of money demand. The current money wage-salary bill in the United States surpasses $1.1 trillion. A 10 percent annual wage climb will compel firms to

---

*   For a portfolio-theory statement, see James Tobin, "A General Equilibrium Approach to Monetary Theory," *Journal of Money, Credit and Banking* (Feb. 1969).

†   Note that against Friedman's real-demand function (M^d/P) for money, the stress is on the demand for *nominal* money, contingent on P as a determining variable. For a similar view favoring the retention of a demand function for nominal money, see W. L. Smith, "On Some Current Issues In Monetary Economics," *Journal of Economic Literature* (Sept. 1970), p. 774.

borrow, on a crude velocity of about 4, about \$28 billion more from banks.*
If $\Delta M = \$28$ billion is not forthcoming, then the ramifications will spread
rather quickly to jobs and output. When steel mills, auto companies, and arms
makers—or universities—are faced with a higher wage bill because of wage
hikes, more money will be required by them to finance their previous volume
of operations.

Thus it is not a random—or manna from heaven—augmentation *forced*
on firms by the MA that accomplishes the inflation. Instead, the situation is
that *after* the price inflation has ensued through unit cost and demand pressures, extra money is imperative for maintaining Q and N. Without a ΔM
flow the inflation and unemployment script of stagflation and slumpflation
woes will materialize. The initiating impulse for demanding more cash balances comes from the desire to sustain (or enlarge) Q at the *fait accompli* of
$(P + \Delta P)$. "Real-money" balances of firms eroded by a price upheaval energize firms to act to restore them; when they fail to acquire the funds they are
compelled to cut their work force. In the NQT, the extra ΔM has nowhere to
go except to raise P (until recent—and reluctant—ΔQ concessions).

The Potency of the Money Supply

It is a misconstruction of the WCM analysis to interpret it as denying the
potency of monetary policy or of MA operations. On the contrary, discretionary monetary policy is crucial, vital, indispensable. Its decisive thrust, however, is on Q and N. P-impacts are far less than assigned by Monetarists,
sometimes even contrary to the conventional indictment; far from being culpable, central bankers are very unlikely accomplices in the inflation trial.

The WCM price level transmission effects of monetary policy

To shape our thoughts, consider an attempt to impose a monetary choke on
inflation, according to the WCM price-level theory. Clearly, a tight-money
vise can create unemployment—or, euphemistically, "slow up" the economy
—to take the "steam" out. According to all the variants of this theme, unemployment will subdue the inflation monster.

Producing enough unemployment would, in the longer past, curb wage
settlements and inhibit the price upsweep: this is good Phillips curve doctrine.
The cost: lost jobs and vanished output. Note, however, that according to the
WCM formulation, the price-level improvement must be won *indirectly:*
following the direct clout of reined money supplies on jobs, thereafter money
wage-salary terms are hit.

---

* On changes in money wages and the demand for money, see Keynes, *General
Theory*, pp. 249, 263.

Given a submissive response by labor to an unemployment bath, leading unions to moderate their bargaining stance, monetary policy can thus act as a subtle and artful form of Incomes Policy; its sting entails lost jobs and its precondition is a supine labor response. In recent years, despite growing unemployment, labor has refused to play the game by the old rules and has exacted disproportionately higher money-wage increments. This is at the bottom of the "shifting Phillips curve" anomalies that have confounded the mechanical conclusions drawn by economists persuaded of the regularity of labor behavior in the early enchantment with Phillips curve regressions.*

Pricewise, even unemployment may be counterproductive in checking the improvement in labor productivity. A taut monetary policy tends to curb the installation of new equipment and plant modernization, so that the price path will lose some of its productivity deterrent. Indirectly, tight money may finally have an inflationary impact.

Symbolically, the orthodox monetary doctrine of combatting inflation through unemployment entails, in WCM terms (where $U =$ the unemployment rate, and the subscripts refer to successive time frames), the *supposition* that:

If $U_1 = U_0$, then

$$w_1 = w_0 \left(1 + \Delta\, w/w_0\right), \tag{4.2}$$

where $(\Delta w/w_0) =$ the "normal" wage change when $U_1 = U_0$.

If $U_1 > U_0$, then

$$w_1 = w_0 \left(1 + \epsilon \Delta w/w_0\right), \tag{4.3}$$

with $\epsilon < 1$.†

While the wage drift may have been lessened by the unemployment bouts in recent years, we shall never really know; we cannot recreate the past for an experiment. The doctrine, however, may be more guilty of neglecting productivity impacts on ΔP resulting from $U_1 > U_0$ under the money maneuvers. Using static reasoning, following the venerable "laws of return," then:

If $N_0 > N_1$, then

$$A_0 < A_1. \tag{4.4}$$

Less employment would mean higher labor productivity, and thus act as a leash on prices. In a dynamic context, however, tight money will deter investment on usual "marginal efficiency" grounds. Likewise, labor availability through unemployment will make labor-saving capital techniques less urgent. Thus in a dynamic vision it is possible that Eq. (4.4) is reversed, to read:

If $N_1 > N_0$, then

$$A_1 > A_0. \tag{4.5}$$

---

*   Phillips curves, as taught in economics textbooks, trace out the negative relation between rates of money-wage change and rates of unemployment. See Chapter 5.

†   Presumably, under Friedman's "steady-rule" for money augmentation for price-level stability, a "normal" $(\Delta w/w_0) = 3\%$.

Conceivably, greater price steadiness through wage restraint may only be hypothetical, while productivity retardation may be real. Thus tight money, *if* it is effective in price stabilization, succeeds mainly by compressing the time path of w more than the time course of A. The delay in technological improvement implies some deferment in real-income growth, and in real wages over time; the unemployment inflicts an absolute loss of income and jobs.

Monetary policy has thus served imperfectly and erratically as an Incomes Policy in disguise, operating under a cloak and having baneful side-effects that negate its effectiveness as a money-wage stabilizer.

Monetary policy and the WCM

Some perspective on the connection between monetary policy, the QTM, and the WCM theory can be derived by recalling some familiar formulas.

$$MV = Y, \tag{4.6}$$

where: M = money supply, V = average money velocity. Equation (4.6) is, of course, the truistic underpinning of the "New" Quantity Theory, linking money supplies to money income Y. For immediate purposes, whether M is to be interpreted as M_1, M_2, M_3 . . . in the ascending series of measurements, can be set aside for engaging controversy by monetary specialists.*

Equation (4.6) is more tautologous than the robust Fisher "Equation of Exchange" (EOE), of Old Quantity Theory distinction:

$$MV = PQ, \tag{4.7}$$

where $PQ = Y$.†

In Eq. (4.6) M is at most tied to the two terms V and Y, while in Eq. (4.7) there are three possible links, V, P, and Q. For a monetary theory of inflation,

---

* Thus M_1 = currency and demand deposits; M_2 = currency, demand, and time deposits at commercial banks; M_3 includes all time deposits, etc. Higher M's could include a variety of money "substitutes."

† Irving Fisher, *The Purchasing Power of Money* (New York: Macmillan, 1911). Fisher, to be sure, acknowledges his debt to that versatile genius in the Ben Franklin mold, Simon Newcomb, *Principles of Political Economy* (New York: Harper, 1885). See also Knut Wicksell, *Interest and Prices* (London: Macmillan, 1936), R. F. Kahn translation of the 1898 German edition.

Fisher would have used T instead of Q, as $MV = PT$ where T encompassed *all* transactions. But the use of Q here will tie P closer to the GBP price level. Using M_2, M_3 . . . or other definitions of money compels variations in the size of V to retain the truistic content.

There is always a tendency to pretend that the Monetarist theory is more profound than an elaboration of the content of Eq. (4.7). For example, George Horwich, after a protracted verbal, geometrical, and mathematical exposition, concludes (after 447 pages) that: "Any policy calculus needs an organizing framework, and there is none better for this purpose than the equation of exchange." Would that we were told this sooner. See *Money, Capital, and Prices* (Chicago: Irwin, 1964). Cf. the pedantic repetition of the same point in the otherwise excellent historical

the EOE—or a near cousin—retains its traditional price-level status. As at long last, and after many false trails, this has again been recognized, we can avoid a defense of the restoration of Eq. (4.7); Monetarists for too long confused an equation for the *demand* for money, intended for explaining V, with a price-level equation.* Hastily ejected at the front door by the NQT, a welcome mat has had to be laid at the kitchen entrance. Less momentous controversies center on whether the Fisher-type or a Cambridge "cash-balance" equation should command loyalty.

From Eq. (4.7), and neglecting terms such as $\Delta M \Delta V$ and $\Delta P \Delta Q$:

$$(\Delta M/M) + (\Delta V/V) = (\Delta P/P) + (\Delta Q/Q). \tag{4.8}$$

Changes over time in the money supply are linked in Eq. (4.8) to changes in *both* prices and output. The interactions in Eq. (4.8) contain the necessary clues on the chain locking monetary policy to price level and output events: despite its pristine trimness, Eq. (4.8) has erected a veritable Monetarist maze. Truistically, if the right-hand side grows by 10 percent, the left-hand side must report the same lift. Money and money-velocity rates must match price and output rates of change.

Despite its primordial importance for policy-makers, detailed examination of the $\Delta V/V$ can be bypassed here; in the strict mechanistic Quantity Theory the attitude was that $(\Delta V/V) = 0$, or that velocity was constant so that for predictive purposes it could be ignored. At the present stage of the art, and after so much inner debate by Monetarists, the revealed secret is that $(\Delta V/V)$ = a constant—but greater than zero.† If the conclusion is warranted, we can largely drop conjectural concern with $(\Delta V/V)$ in Eq. (4.8).

The central bank will have to estimate $\Delta V/V$ for the forthcoming time interval to which money policy is to apply. Much of the success of central banking will hinge upon the correctness of the guess; judgment, intuition, happenstance, as well as inferences from studious evaluation of past data, will assist the accuracy of the policy projections: price-level calm would contribute mightily.

---

exegesis of Arthur Marget, *Theory of Prices* (New York: Prentice-Hall, 1938, 1942), 2 Vols.

Because of nonincome payments for debt repayments and refinance, if driven to choose an EOE, Hyman Minsky sees merit in the "model-T." See his *John Maynard Keynes.*

* Cf. the restoration of Eq. (4.7) in a Cambridge cash-balance form in Friedman, "A Theoretical Framework."

† Thus Friedman places the United States estimate at about 0.84. See *The Optimum Quantity*, p. 227. Estimates for Canada suggest that $(\Delta V/V) = 0$, from calculations of an elasticity of demand for money of about unity. Cf. George Macesich, "Supply and Demand for Money in Canada," in *Varieties of Monetary Experience* (Chicago: University of Chicago Press, 1970), David Meiselman, ed., pp. 286, 288.

Price and output components

To focus on money supplies, Eq. (4.8) can be rewritten as:

$$m(\Delta M/M) = (\Delta P/P) + (\Delta Q/Q), \tag{4.9}$$

where $m = 1 + (M\Delta V/V/\Delta M)$. It appears that usually $2 > m > 0$.*
    Substituting for $(\Delta P/P)$, and recalling $Q = A \cdot N$:

$$m(\Delta M/M) = [(\Delta w/w) + (\Delta k/k) - (\Delta A/A) + (\Delta A/A) + (\Delta N/N)], \tag{4.10}$$

where

$$(\Delta Q/Q) = (\Delta A/A) + (\Delta N/N), \tag{4.11}$$

with N = measured employment, ΔN = annual employment increase. Elements of economic growth are contained in Eq. (4.11), with ΔQ reflecting productivity improvements and employment growth. Clearing terms:

$$m(\Delta M/M) = (\Delta w/w) + (\Delta k/k) + (\Delta N/N). \tag{4.12}$$

On the proviso that $\Delta k = 0$, this simplifies to:

$$m(\Delta M/M) = (\Delta w/w) + (\Delta N/N). \tag{4.13}$$

Thus the money supply is inextricably linked to money wages and jobs. If the money wage jumps precipitously and money supplies hold firm, then ΔN will suffer—so long as m holds practically constant. On sample values, merely for illustration:

$$2(\Delta M/M) = 10\% + 4\%, \text{ so that } (\Delta M/M) = 7\%. \tag{4.14}$$

That is, if velocity rates hold steady so that $m = 2$, once money wages climb by 10 percent, in order to advance employment by 4 percent through a natural expansion of the labor force and an absorption of the unemployed, the money supply would have to rise by 7 percent. If the unemployment rate held constant so that only the natural increase in the labor force in the range of 1.5 percent had to be provided for, then the necessary money augmentation would approximate 5.7 percent under a 10 percent money-wage increase.

Money supplies in a time context

Clearly, in the irreversibility of history, the economy is always moving forward in time, with the MA only able to effectuate future variations in ΔM. It is well to develop the implicit economic process embodied in Eqs. (4.8) through (4.13) in a time context before considering the theory of monetary policy in an era of wage inflation. The results depart substantially from the Monetarist recipes which have poured into MA thought recesses and inspired search for new ΔM operating formulas in recent years.

---

*   The Macesich Canada calculation implies $m \simeq 1$.

Starting at t_0, say January 2 of the calendar year, suppose the central bank authorities instruct their technicians on the extent to which member banks' reserve balances are to be enlarged through open-market operations, and the amount by which the money supply is to be augmented over the quarterly interval, up to date t_1 on March 1.* Further, suppose that the ordered increment ΔM will be executed at a smooth pace, with fresh instructions intended to be issued beyond t_1 as policy is continuously reviewed and revised under evolving events. Of course, before March 1, like any strategic commander, the MA always retains its options to countermand the earlier directives as new facts warrant.

In the interval t_0 to t_1, therefore, $\Delta M/M > 0$. As money wages will also be escalating during that time frame, some of the monetary increase will thus serve to support the prevailing t_0 employment at the higher price level engendered by $(\Delta w/w) > 0$. Whether or not employment grows will depend on $m(\Delta M/M) \gtreqless (\Delta w/w)$. Likewise, over the interval there will be productivity changes, $\Delta A/A$. With $\Delta A > 0$, there will be some neutralization of the price-level rise. Largely, the facts entitle us to ignore Δk which, at worst, may edge slightly either way.

On this evaluation it is only the residual, or that part of ΔM which is not drained off to finance the prevailing $Q(t_0)$ at the new $P(t_1) > P(t_0)$, that can exert a positive effect in influencing output, as a rule through the rate of interest. Functionally, where we take the dependence of Q on M directly, rather than through investment and the rate of interest, we would have:

$$\Delta Q = f(\Delta M_s - \Delta M_p; m), \tag{4.15}$$

where $\Delta M_s = $ the full increment in the money supply; $\Delta M_p = $ the extra money required to sustain $Q = \overline{Q}$, when $P(t_1) > P(t_0)$, given the Δw and ΔA variations; and $m = (1 + \Delta V/V)$. Not all of the increase in the money supply, therefore, will influence ΔQ; part of ΔM will be siphoned off to support $Q = \overline{Q}$ at the higher price level. Too, the MA will have to predict m, to guess whether velocity will vary and in what direction.

Over the $t_0 t_1$ time span, the MA w~ .ld thus have to anticipate all of the price-level variables that are in motion, and make allowance for them merely to *sustain* production. The money increment could then be enlarged, depending on the central bank's aim for sponsoring output growth after estimating unused resources, especially labor unemployment, and the likely production speed under possible bottlenecks and balance-of-payments restraints. Foreign payment considerations can hamper the advance because of imbalances coming from complementary imports.

---

* The knot tying open-market operations and M_1 (or $M_2 \ldots$) is seldom foolproof. However, *The Monthly Review of the Federal Reserve Bank of St. Louis* has often cited a high linear correlation of the two.

As the MA is compelled to peer into the future in exercising its mandate, while possessing only imperfect past data, there can thus be a good deal of both "endogeneity" and "exogeneity" in its ΔM actions.

Money in a WCM Model

The WCM theory thus also waves the flag that "money matters," in the same way that liberals and conservatives agree that government matters, but are at loggerheads over how, and how much.

Yet an entirely different assessment attaches to monetary policy. According to WCM theorizing, once a money-wage inflation erupts about all that the MA can do beyond adopting a valiant posture as the defender at the gates is to create unemployment. In the noxious euphemism, it can "slow up" the economy and, in good Phillips curve fashion—with nicely cooperating workers —it can flatten the wage ascent. After victimizing workers and provoking enough misery, it can then announce—someday—"slower" rates of inflation, declaring it has held the inflation dragon at bay. Unfortunately, as "slow" recovery ambles on and encounters outsized wage boosts, the hibernating price dragon can emit new fire.

Monetary policy thus intrudes, on the best interpretation, as a vague and miscast form of Incomes Policy. When labor refuses to abide by the Phillips curve wage game rules and insists on higher pay because prices have risen, or are expected to rise, the MA muster of money pawns becomes an ineffectual ritual, bracing itself ostentatiously for another go at the price foe, undaunted despite the monotonous regularity of unstrategic retreats and defeats.

The classification of monetary policy

The analysis permits a classification of monetary policy under wage inflation that is more precise than the nondescript "easy" or "tight" categorization, with shades in between which refer only to money-supply aggregates. The latter can obscure the P and Q dimensions of the ΔM variation. In considering production, there are three main categories:

a) *Stimulating (or Expansive)*: $\qquad m(\Delta M/M) > (\Delta P/P)$
b) *Neutral (or Sustaining)*: $\qquad m(\Delta M/M) = (\Delta P/P)$
c) *Recessionary (or*
$\quad$ *Constrictive)*: $\qquad\qquad m(\Delta M/M) < (\Delta P/P)$

In each case ΔP rests on the Δw and ΔA variations: the spillover to Q will depend (in given money-demand circumstances reflected in m) on the magnitude of $(\Delta M/M)$ compared to the $(\Delta P/P)$ absorption inherent in the prevailing WCM relations. With the ΔP perturbations ascribed to *nonmonetary* elements, the ΔM repercussions extend solely into the Q and N sphere, qualified over time for any feedback on Δw and ΔA through unemployment.

The *P:Q* matrix

An illuminating two-way classification of economic conditions attributed mainly to monetary policy, given the $\Delta w/\Delta A$ environment, also shakes out of the analysis.

Table 4.1 contains a matrix of ΔP and ΔQ combinations.* The table carries major implications for monetary policy inasmuch as the Q and N result is wholly contingent on monetary action, given a general exogenous development in w and A, where technology often governs the ΔA result. Inasmuch as money-wage and salary decisions lie beyond the reach of the central bank maneuvers, as largely exogenous and fortuitous historical variables, the Q and N results will ultimately be decided by central bank (and fiscal policy) decisions.

With $\Delta P \gtreqless 0$ viewed as a culmination of WCM relations, whether we land in row 1, 2, or 3 of Table 4.1 rests on Δw, Δk, and ΔA magnitudes. On the other hand, whether column 1, 2, or 3 prevails depends on monetary policy. Output relations may be lagged; to explore these would involve a study in itself and special circumstances would dominate the outcome at particular times. Directionally, accepting the Monetarist's $(\Delta V/V)$ estimates, the qualitative dimensions of $(\Delta M/M)$ seem less vulnerable to criticism.

Table 4.1

The ΔP and ΔQ Matrix Pursuant to ΔM Action

ΔP \ ΔQ	+	0	−
+	Growthflation	Stagflation	Slumpflation
0	Growth at constant prices	Stationary state	Recession
−	Deflationary growth	Stationary state deflation	Depression

Measured in jobs and output, our economic position, whether plight or pleasant, hinges substantially on monetary policy. The WCM theory thus acknowledges the pervasive contribution of money to the job and output climate. But P responds mainly to the w "pulls" and the A "tugs."

If P lies outside the MA probing orbit, the best it can do is to adopt a monetary policy that lands us in column 1—unless it is intent on imposing Incomes Policy through the use of indirect money levers in creating unemployment on a conviction of ultimate triumph through perseverance in job disasters. Misguided monetary ventures that disregard the $(\Delta w/w)$ upheaval

---

* Cf. my "Money Policy Under Wage Inflation."

will lodge the economy in column 2 at best, or column 3 at worst. Column 2 depicts the stagnant sidewise Q-trend. Column 3 depicts regressive Q features. Column 1 typifies the growth economy.

Row 2, in the middle, is the favorite textbook case in which growth, and cyclical recovery and recession, are discussed in "real terms," with P subdued in the heroic conjectures. The classification also demarcates stagflation and slumpflation, with each conveying extra unemployment as labor productivity advances; under stagflation, however, Q may hold fairly steady, while slump-flation involves a cutback in Q.

Including unemployment in a three-way table would swamp us with 27 macrophases. Accelerated population leaps (or dives), and technological forays into the robot age, might one day test the economist's ingenuity in concocting felicitous names to describe the variety of conceivable economic states.

In leaving Table 4.1, the lesson to be drawn should be underscored:

*Monetary policy to control inflation is not the solution: it is part of the problem, for in its inability to exercise a direct restraint on the price level it is a major force making for stagflation and slumpflation.**

The Monetarist "Hole-in-the-Middle"

The analysis surrounding Table 4.1 depicts the ΔM emissions by the MA serving both a *causal* and an *accommodating* function. This interpretation of the money mechanism affirms a tolerable coexistence of two ancient principles in the history of monetary thought: the doctrinal lineage merits some mention. Thereafter, it will be of more than casual interest to examine a self-inflicted Monetarist wound suffered by not heeding Jan Tinbergen's warning against aiming one arrow at two targets, namely, firing ΔM at both ΔP and ΔQ.

Failure in observing this injunction has exposed an awkward *indeter-minateness* in the Monetarist theory of inflation: there is a gaping hole-in-the-middle despite the automated response that money is the root of all inflation. As yet, however, the void too often tends to be hastily bypassed.

Money as accommodating and causal

Conceptually, once $(\Delta P/P) > 0$, any increase in the money supply by the central bank can be described as an *accommodating* gesture: so far as the extra money sums do not affect P, they serve merely to meet the needs of trade, as in the older Banking Principle doctrine. To this extent, ΔM lacks causal

---

* This lesson on the inability of monetary policy to deal with unemployment seems to have been lost on the leaders of the Western world at the Downing St. summit of May 8, 1977. The communiqué issued declared inflation as "one of its [unemployment] major causes." The reference should have been to monetary policy to control inflation.

thrust; as a good medium of exchange the ΔM emissions act as a facilitating agent, not the wheels of trade, but the lubricating oil, as David Hume would describe it. Money would be more the "effect" of trade at established prices.

Extra money, seeping beyond the accommodating or sustaining function, should press on the interest-rate pedal and, ordinarily, enhance I and, through the multiplier, Q. Money supplies in excess of the sustaining "needs of trade" for accomplishing the $Q = \bar{Q}$ function under $\Delta P > 0$, exert a causal prong, serving to enlarge Q and N. This would harmonize with Currency School doctrine, without the (ΔP) overtones.* It would also be compatible with the NQT of $MV = Y$, limited though to Q effects as in $MV = \bar{P}Q$. Only if inevitably, irresistibly, $Q = Q(M)$ and $P = P(Q)$, so that prices mounted significantly in some causal fashion, would the Currency Principle retain sure-fire causal P-attributes.

Contrary to the myth that the Currency Principle conveys the true religion, and that the Banking Principle represents confused thinking, it is possible to indulge both strands of thought, to discern both causal and accommodating features in ΔM variations. Currency School adamancy could be maintained only under the hypothesis of money-wage *endogeneity*, where w adapted to P without any feedback from Δw to ΔP.† This defies the modern facts though it would have somewhat more vitality in a gold-standard era under supporting conditions of labor docility fostered by unemployment.

The Friedman "puzzle": the embarrassing indeterminacy

The eclectic position embodies a critique of the Monetarist perception which, Adam Smith might say, "once made so much noise in the world."

Initially, Monetarists rallied about the NQT, asserting $MV = Y$. Years later there was the belated discovery that the NQT and the surrounding money-demand equation held a P-term in a system that was bereft of a P-equation: more recently, Fisherine and Marshallian origins have been revived, where an $MV = PQ$ or $M = cPQ$ equation (with $c = 1/V$) has again come to the rescue.‡ The restoration has involved some embarrassment because of the long interregnum.

---

*   On some history of this ancient debate with lingering echoes, see Lloyd Mints, *A History of Banking Theory* (University of Chicago, 1945) and Marget. Both come down in the Currency School camp. A bit more conciliatory to the Banking Principle is Keynes' earlier ally, D. H. Robertson. Keynes would embrace the eclectic position, as in his *General Theory* "generalized Quantity Theory" comments.

†   On money-wage endogeneity, see Chapter 5.

‡   In the "Cambridge cash-balance" equation of $M = cPQ$, the c-term facilitates the recognition of motivational factors underlying the demand for money, and thus affecting velocity. It thus tends to less mechanical statements of the content of V. Keynes embraced this Marshallian formula—which traces an ancestry to Sir William Petty—in *A Tract On Monetary Reform* (New York: Macmillan, 1923). He disengaged himself from it and from "Fisherine" versions in *The Treatise*, Vol. 1.

Recall Equations (4.8) and (4.9). Both refer to exogenous and endogenous changes in variables in an implicit time profile:

$$(\Delta M/M) + (\Delta V/V) = (\Delta P/P) + (\Delta Q/Q) \tag{4.8}$$

$$m(\Delta M/M) = (\Delta P/P) + (\Delta Q/Q) \tag{4.9}$$

Obviously, on routine conjectures the ΔM variations can knock at ΔP or ΔQ, or both—with $(\Delta V/V)$ assumed (for the while) constant. All this is ancient elementary wisdom, back to square 1 in economics.

Nonetheless, this trim EOE archeological excavation has opened the Pandora's box that is an enigma to Monetarism and perplexes policy-makers. To what extent will new money increments affect ΔP? ΔQ? It makes a world of difference whether ΔM enlarges ΔQ mainly, or ΔP only and ΔQ not at all. Or ΔP up, and ΔQ down, or vice versa. Likewise, estimates of m, for its part in the systemic drama, can only be churned from *past* data even as the MA aims to glimpse the secrets of the future. The quandaries on the m-values, and on the M, P, Q interactions, are first conceptual, then statistical, involving initial images of how the economy works; thereafter come ideas on magnitudes and the usefulness of the past data as a guide—even when good *past* statistics are available. Some policy questions remain resistant to data collection and econometric processing. Intuition, judgment, and conceptualization must dominate purported "facts."

The "simple" (Eqs. 4.8 and 4.9) crossroads are littered with treacherous hard rocks that stymie the smooth ride of Monetarism; perplexity abounds concerning how to navigate about the seemingly small, innocent, and passable blockbuster. Posed at the policy gate is a vexing test for the MA. Credibility depends (*assuming* for simplicity that $m = 1$) on whether a 5 percent increase in M fuels a 15 percent increase in P and a 10 percent *decrease* in Q (and comparable unemployment), or whether P stands firm and Q surges by 5 percent. Deprived of this insight (and precise short-term or intermediate period values of m), we know preciously little about the efficacy of monetary policy.

Surveying the gaping hole undermining Monetarism, Friedman has in several places blandly asserted that: "The general subject of the division of changes in money income between prices and quantities badly needs investigation," and that "none of our leading theories has much to say about it."*

The crack in the Monetarist armor has thus been conceded even though Monetarists are understandably reluctant to quit the stakes. Friedman is nonetheless mistaken in the gratuitous addendum that "none of our leading theories has much to say about it."

Keynes organized his money analysis about the ΔP and the ΔQ division; the partition has also been a focal concern of the WCM theory.† The solution

---

* *Optimum Quantity*, p. 279; "Theoretical Framework," pp. 222–223, 234.

† On Keynes' preoccupation, see "Keynes and the Quantity Theory Elasticities," and "Money Supplies and Price-Output Variations," in *KaM*, Essays 2 and 5 (with

readily shakes out on WCM theorizing, as in the discussion surrounding Table 4.1, where $(\Delta P/P)$ is at most tenuously connected to $(\Delta M/M)$, with different handles cranking the separate ΔP and ΔQ magnitudes.

Here then is the muddle in Monetarism which renders the theory indeterminate on the idealized subject of study, namely, inflation. Despite the fanfare, the packaged doctrines are unable to reveal definitely whether more money moves P, Q, or N—except in the "long run" where, we are assured anyway, Q and N stride serenely to "natural" levels, unaffected by P. Still, on a less fatalistic sweep of history, life might be more viable and rewarding for many if through the collection of short periods of time that constitutes the human existence economic life was made more equitable, with jobs abundant and life planning more rational as under a fairly steady price level.*

Facing the theoretical rout, a diversionary flap has been sounded to salvage *something* from the ominous NQT wreckage. Thus Friedman declares:

One theory asserts *that the change in national income will be absorbed by price change; the other that it will be absorbed by quantity change. In my opinion, this is the central common defect of the two approaches as theories of short-run change.*†

The first view—a handy but not an incontrovertible attribution—is lodged with Marshall, for invoking P-adjustments rather than altered Q's: that is, $\Delta Q = 0$ and $\Delta P > 0$. But Marshall is ordinarily regarded as the master of the short-run, of continuous Q-adaptability against the classical predilection for the long-run "natural price."

Marshall would have been engrossed in movements *along a supply schedule*, with both ΔP and ΔQ interacting, as even in his stability analysis

---

H. Habibagahi). My own work on the Keynesian defects has been concerned with this issue for some 20 years. Hicks, in a short article, has recently focused on this Monetarist indeterminacy as critical; perhaps it will finally command wider attention. See his "The Little That Is Right with Monetarism," *Lloyds Bank Review* (July, 1976).

* In "A Monetary Framework," p. 27, Friedman writes: "We have accepted the quantity-theory presumption, and have thought it supported by the evidence we examined, that changes in the quantity of money as such *in the long run* have a negligible effect on real income, so that nonmonetary forces are 'all that matter' for changes in real income over the decades and money 'does not matter.' On the other hand, we have regarded the quantity of money (plus other variables that affect velocity) as essentially 'all that matter' for the long-run determination of nominal income. The price level is then a joint outcome of the monetary forces determining nominal income and the real forces determining real income."

This is a predestined "long run" unaffected by happenings in the interim. Why then any concern with inflation? The converse is that the "long run" is an inclusive film of short-runs, with long-run disaster (and sweet memories) shaped in the collection of short-period happenings.

† "A Theoretical Framework."

generated by ΔQ variations. Further, he would have written the supply function as $Q = Q(P)$, with the Q schedule *explicitly* resting on: (1) money wages, and (2) labor productivity.* Keynes, according to Friedman, abided only Q-adjustments, or $\Delta Q > 0$ and $\Delta P = 0$.† The latter is an attenuated interpretation inevitable in Friedman's neglect of the implications of Keynes' use of the wage-unit: with (1) a constant wage unit, (2) price competition, and premising (3) the static law of diminishing returns, Keynes always retained *some* price flexibility, so that with $\Delta Q > 0$, then $\Delta P > 0$.‡ Differences with Marshall are only artificially fashioned.

Aside from the dubious historical exegesis, Friedman spotlights the Q-variability as the salient open-ended question, holding the key to the "division" of ΔP and ΔQ stemming from ΔM emissions over time.§

The rupture in the facile story of money growth beyond the Monetarist norm culminating in inflation, and the back-slide into yesterday's OQT, with ΔQ (at this post-Marshallian date!) interpreted as a "physical" quantity floating off apart from prices, places the entire Monetarist thesis in a state of analytical jeopardy and policy limbo: at best it languishes as a "full employment" theory, even as the economy endures unemployment slack, combined with Q and N growth in time.‖ Its irrelevance is patent in its preoccupation with nonexistent situations when there are 15 million unemployed in the Western world. Its chalkboard strategy of monetary caution and withdrawal under inflation is prematurely pitched to the glory of the optimal N_f realm: this has not been the environment in which recent inflation has flourished.

Further, a straw-man has been reared; nobody has advised stepped-up rates of money emissions under N_f circumstances *and* with steady w/A ratios.

---

* Cf. my "The Equation of Exchange and the Theory of the Price Level," in *Classical Keynesianism*.

† Ibid., pp. 16–20 especially. Cf. the transcription of Keynes' thinking in Paul Davidson, "Disequilibrium Market Adjustment: Marshall Revisited," *Economic Inquiry* (June 1974). This is carried on under the assumption of *given* money wages. An extension for money-wage changes appears in Davidson and Jan Kregel, "Keynes's Paradigm: Theoretical Framework for Monetary Analysis," in *Growth, Profits, and Property*, E. J. Nell, ed. Cf. my *Approach to the Theory of Income Distribution* (Philadelphia: Chilton, 1958), pp. 102–104.

‡ Cf. "The Equation of Exchange," in *Classical Keynesianism*.

§ Reflecting on this turn in Monetarism—apparently from "money matters" to "output matters"—Professor Ritter was led—in sorrow or anger?—to remark: "It takes no small amount of *chutzpa*—after twenty years of arguing about the left-hand side of the (EOE) equation, we are told that the only questions worth discussing are on the right-hand side!" Lawrence S. Ritter, review article of "A Theoretical Framework," *Journal of Economic Literature* (Sept. 1975), p. 927.

‖ On the speed of ΔP and ΔQ responses, see the earlier work of Robert W. Clower, "The Keynesian Counter-Revolution: A Theoretical Appraisal," in *The Theory of Interest Rates* (New York: Macmillan, 1965), F. H. Hahn and F. P. Brechling, eds.

Some ancient reservations

Longevity is characteristic of monetary folklore. Recently a spate of Monetarist textbooks have been assembled dedicated to preserving error in classroom tutelage, characteristically *after* the inflation applicability of the ideas has been exploded. Despite the gravity of the theoretical muddle, a new crop of students will be nursed on doctrines as thin as the *IS-LM* diversions of Keynesian textbooks.*

This belated discovery of ΔQ can only be judged bewildering for it was commonplace, in the less "sophisticated" 1930s, to qualify the EOE—which

---

* Representative samples of Monetarist opinions on inflation are the following: "The price level is then a joint outcome of the monetary forces determining nominal income (i.e., money income) and the real forces determining real income." Also: "I regard the description of our position as 'money is all that matters for changes in *nominal* income and for *short-run* changes in real income' as an exaggeration but one that gives the right flavor to our conclusions." See Friedman, "A Theoretical Framework," p. 27. Also: "Inflation is always and everywhere a monetary phenomenon . . . ." M. Friedman, "What Price Guideposts," in George Shultz and Robert Aliber, eds. *Guidelines, Informal Controls, and the Market Place* (University of Chicago, 1966), p. 18. An analogous statement appears in his *Monetary Correction* (Institute of London: Economic Affairs, 1974), p. 10. Karl Brunner: "An assemblage of all the inflationary experiences, new and old, demonstrates that the Monetarist thesis explains the whole range of experience with respect to both occurrences and orders of magnitude." See "The Drift Into Persistent Inflation," *The Wharton Quarterly* (Fall 1969), p. 26. Darryl R. Francis, President of the Federal Reserve Bank of St. Louis: "The growth of money is thus the key to inflation. . . . ," in "Controlling Inflation," Federal Reserve Bank of St. Louis, *Monthly Review* (Sept. 1969), p. 11. Also: "Monetarists have a monetary theory of the price level. . . . ," concluding section in *Monetary Economics: Readings on Current Issues* (New York: McGraw-Hill, 1971), William E. Gibson and George G. Kaufman, eds. Harry G. Johnson: "one does not need . . . to bore the court with a recapitulation of the vast mass of empirical evidence on the connection between monetary growth rates and inflation rates," in "What is Right with Monetarism," *Lloyds Bank Review* (April 1976), p. 16. J. Huston McCulloch, *Money and Inflation: A Monetarist Approach* (New York: Academic Press, 1975) writes: if "the real-demand for money is constant, the equilibrium price level will be proportionate to the nominal money supply. Doubling the money supply will double the equilibrium price level" (p. 18). Likewise: "The price level and nominal income are proportionate to the nominal quantity of money supplied," in Michael R. Darby, *Macroeconomics* (New York: McGraw-Hill, 1976), p. 109. Also: "It is remarkably easy to control the rate of inflation as long as the Federal Reserve System carries out its duties to maintain the required trend growth rate of the nominal money supply" (p. 368). Amid analytic elegance (concerning banalities) the same electrifying opinion is tucked away in David E. W. Laidler, *The Demand for Money: Theories and Evidence* (Scranton, Pa.: International Textbook Co., 1969), with a bit more attention to varying output levels. In the ponderous article "Inflation—A Survey," *Economic Journal* (Dec. 1975), exemplifying the art of elevating trivia, Laidler and J. M. Parkin write: "Inflation is, then, fundamentally a monetary phenomenon" and that "if excessive monetary expansion is a necessary and sufficient condition for sustained inflation, this immediately raises important problems in the analysis of the control of inflation" (pp. 741, 796).

was in widespread use—for variations in Q (and in V).* Apparently a matter so trite has had to be discovered after an erudite and recondite expedition.

Rummaging back to Jean Bodin (1576), perhaps the earliest recorded QTM expositor, the doctrine was more reserved even in that simpler era: he saw "the high prices we see today [16th century!] are due to some four or five causes. The principal and almost the only one . . . is the abundance of gold and silver . . ."† After Sir William Petty in 1682, John Locke in 1691, and John Law in 1705, Richard Cantillon (1730–1734?) could narrate: "Everybody agrees that the abundance of money . . . raises the price of all things" but "the great difficulty . . . consists in knowing in what way and in what proportion the increase in money raises prices."‡

David Hume (1752), like Cantillon, is universally admired for his QTM acuity in distinguishing the process in which money supplies jolt prices to the final equilibrium state. After echoing Locke and Cantillon that "it seems a maxim almost self-evident, that the prices of every thing depend on the proportion between commodities and money," Hume's dynamics qualified this mechanistic QTM view on the effects of more money trickling into the economy:

At first, no alteration is perceived; by degrees the price rises, first of one commodity, then of another; till the whole at last reaches a just proportion with the new quantity of specie which is in the kingdom. In my opinion, it is only in this interval . . . between the acquisition of money and rise in prices, that the encreasing quantity of gold and silver is favourable to industry. (p. 38)

. . . we find, that, in every kingdom, into which money begins to flow in greater abundance than formerly, every thing takes a new face; labour and industry gain life; the merchant becomes more enterprising, the manufacturer more diligent and skilful, and even the farmer follows his plough with greater alacrity and attention. (p. 37)

From the whole of this reasoning we may conclude, that it is of no manner of consequence, with regard to the domestic happiness of a state, whether money

---

* Friedman, to be sure, has estimated ($\Delta V/V$) to hold firm under his definitions of "permanent" income. Recently there is some rupture in the Monetarist camp over the prospect of greater variability in the velocity ratio. See Chapter 9.

† Jean Bodin, *Reply to the Paradoxes of Molestroit Concerning the Dearness of All Things and the Remedy Therefor*, translated in A. E. Monroe, ed., *Early Economic Thought*. On early monetary theory, see the detail in Douglas Vickers' *Studies in the Theory of Money, 1690–1776* (Philadelphia: Chilton, 1959). For adventures—and misadventures—in monetary thought and experience, see the very readable J. K. Galbraith, *Money: Whence It Came, Where It Went* (Boston: Houghton-Mifflin, 1976).

‡ Richard Cantillon, *Essai Sur La Nature du Commerce En General* (New York: Macmillan, 1931), p. 161, Henry Higgs translation. Of course Cantillon's query concerns the "transmission mechanism" in which modern rivals ritually invite more (*sponsored*) research. Cantillon himself deals with the opening of a new gold mine.

be in a greater or less quantity. The good policy . . . consists only in keeping it, if possible, still increasing; because [it] keeps alive a spirit of industry in the nation, and encreases the stock of labour, in which consists all real power and riches. (pp. 39–40)*

Astonishingly, after so many detours, modern Monetarism has become alerted to the not-so-fresh $\Delta Q(t)$ recognition.

What still remains for rediscovery is the Marshallian perception of the supply function of output, of $Q = Q(P)$, where the function is subject to the money wage (w) and productivity constraints (A).

The Steady-Money-Growth Rule

Economics, like medicine, physics, and all logical disciplines, can in the theoretical phase be assessed only by its inner consistency and, where the contacts arise, by the conformity with facts. The ultimate test, however, is more pragmatic, capsuled in the older query, "will it work?" or, in the modern idiom, "Will it fly?" The measure of diagnosis, however, is not entirely in prognosis—for this can be a product of lucky guesses—but in its strategic policy design where preventive control is feasible and ideologically acceptable. It is thus the prescriptions that reveal the spirit and practical viability of a theoretical system. A scan of the Monetarist proposals is thus vital, especially as articulated by Professor Friedman and approved by many disciples.†

After the recital of the futility of the MA striving to "peg" real quantities as real interest rates, unemployment, or output, Friedman counsels the MA to "guide itself by magnitudes that it can control," and that "a monetary total is the best currently available immediate guide or criterion for monetary policy." Too, the MA should "avoid sharp swings in policy," for ΔM injections today will erupt only after a time lag of six, nine, twelve, fifteen months —or longer.‡

On lags, Keynes once conveyed the "castor-oil bismuth" cycle, of the patient being cajoled with doses of one medicine just as he was about to suffer

---

*   David Hume, *Writings on Economics* (1752), Eugene Rotwein, ed. (Madison: University of Wisconsin Press, 1970).

†   His views have been promulgated in many writings, including those already cited. For a longer list, see Richard Selden, "Monetarism," in *Modern Economic Thought* (University of Pennsylvania Press, 1977), S. Weintraub, editor. See especially, *A Program for Monetary Stability* (Fordham, 1959). Origins go back to Friedman's 1930s graduate-student days, and the writings of Henry Simons, Friedrich Hayek, Dennis Robertson, and others.

Influential Monetarists such as Professors Brunner and Meltzer are partial dissenters, subscribing to more monetary ease in recessions and according more weight, too, to fiscal policy.

‡   When the predicted consequences of money-supply changes fail to materialize, there has been the defensive parry that "the lags are longer than expected."

the opposite disorder.* To avert mischievous timing, Friedman's protective screen entails a steady dosage of money:

My own prescription is still that the monetary authority go all the way in avoiding such swings by adopting publicly the policy of achieving a steady rate of growth in a specified monetary total. The precise rate . . . is less important than the adoption of some stated and known rate. I myself have argued for a rate that would on the average achieve rough stability in the level of prices of final products, which I have estimated would call for something like a 3 to 5 percent per year rate of growth in currency plus all commercial bank deposits or a slightly lower rate of growth in currency plus demand deposits only.†

For brevity, this will be denoted as the 3-percent rule.

The steady-money-supply rule

Much Monetarist theorizing can be described as a formidable facade designed to rationalize an automatic rule for monetary policy. Judgment and discretion at the central bank are to be suspended, with the prestigious central bank assignment being superseded by a statistical clerk, of utter integrity to be sure, abiding the rigid instruction.‡

Sometimes, as intimated in the quoted remarks, "steadiness" appears as the higher virtue, that the money gauge be set and locked. Qualms come readily: probably nobody would advocate "steady" money emissions of 3 percent per minute. Steadiness at a norm of 3, 4, or 5 percent per annum is intended; it is a *two*-part rule: steadiness at a "reasonable" rate is prescribed for the affluent Western economies.

The 3-percent rule ultimately originates in Eq. (4.8) or (4.9): $m(\Delta M/M) = (\Delta P/P) + (\Delta Q/Q)$. Separating out time series on $P(t)$ and $Q(t)$ has led to the empirical observation that "real output"—$(\Delta Q/Q)$—has grown by about 3 percent over the long haul, which allows for productivity improvements and labor-force growth. Hence, by matching the Q-trend with an annual M-increment of 3 percent the conclusion has been drawn that observing the "rule" would preclude any spillover of money into price inflation: the 3 percent annual M-augmentation would wend its way, nicely and inexorably, into Q-channels, serving only to finance extra output. The $P(t)$ path would be flat, and $Q(t)$ would burgeon at its "natural" rate.

---

* *Treatise*, Vol. II, pp. 223–224.

† "The Role of Monetary Policy," *American Economic Review* (March 1968), p. 16.

‡ For some criticism, see Franco Modigliani, "Some Empirical Tests of Monetary Management and of Rules versus Discretion," *Journal of Political Economy* (1964). A well-reasoned brief supporting the regime of an automatic rule is prepared by Martin Bronfenbrenner, "Monetary Rules: A New Look," *Journal of Law and Economics* (Oct. 1965). References to the earlier discussion are also provided.

The recipe thus invokes a fair amount of wishful thinking. It *assumes* that unions will be well-behaved, that labor generally will, without protest, accept annual $w(t)$ increases of about 3 percent. It *must* also assume that k also holds firm, with the future A-path an extrapolation of the past, for otherwise P-stability would be threatened. Pondering recent income excesses, it requires undiluted faith to presume that the "rule" would ensure price-level calm.

A rapprochement with the WCM theory?

It would be easy to subscribe to the (approximately) 3-percent $\Delta M/M$ rule *if the w/A ratio held solid*. That is, if a successful Incomes Policy was implemented to maintain the w/A ratio, and if k did not change, then the necessary annual M-increases could approximate 3 percent. For with $2 > m > 1$, 3 percent more money could sustain an annual, approximately full-employment money income and real output advance; with $m = 1.5$, the 3-percent rule could underwrite a Q-advance of 4.5 percent, consisting of productivity gains of about 3 percent and labor-force growth of 1.5 percent.

Contention over the 3-percent rule would thus be dispelled, converging mainly on the demand for money and thereby on the stability of m, if—a big conditional if—a successful Incomes Policy prevailed. Without the w/A alignment, a relentless 3-percent rule in the face of extraordinary pay boosts would be a mandated design for slumpflation. To cling to a rule despite Q and P distortions would be to prescribe medicine without monitoring the patient's initial condition or reaction, and without revision despite damaging side-effects.

Monetarists thus beg the very point at issue in *assuming* that an automated monetary policy would prevent inflationary wage and salary bargains: the rule presupposes that a successful indirect—or direct—Incomes Policy is already established.*

A steady rule and unsteady economy?

Events of the last decade bear weighty evidence that money constraints accompanying huge wage settlements have had unsavory stagflation and slumpflation outcomes: once wages are compromised beyond productivity trends, prices move skyward; all the MA can do is to affect N and Q. The "steady" rule could lead onto a more rocky road, of a disastrously "unsteady" economy piloted by the MA into a depression trough.

---

* In testing a Friedman money rule in an econometric model "considerably more monetarist than is the St. Louis model," Thomas J. Sargent concludes that "the evidence that seems most damaging in the model comes from the role that the money wage plays in apparently 'causing' unemployment and the long-term interest rate." See his "A Classical Macroeconometric Model for the United States," *Journal of Political Economy* (April 1976), pp. 207, 236. See also D. C. C. Ho and Maxwell Noton, "A Study of the Alternative Policies in the Control of a National Economy via Dynamic Programming," *Economica* (May 1972).

Money "tightness," despite money-wage-salary "ease," has also exacted a heavy toll of instability in financial markets. The higher interest rates knock down bond prices, creating liquidity havoc and bankruptcy in a credit crunch.* The historic high long-term interest rates have also deflated the stock market (1973–1976), toppling it from its position as a hedge against inflation as "bulls" turned into "bears," deranging the financial underpinning necessary for recovery.

Although central bankers have not adhered slavishly to the "steady" rule, they have been sufficiently intimidated to flirt with Monetarist doctrines to sustain their QTM predilections on the theoretical inviolateness of monetary resoluteness in quelling any P-insurgency.†

Does money really matter?

The steady-rule script must come as a letdown. After the seductive refrain that "money matters," the lesson degenerates into its own negation as the real phenomena of *relative* prices, output, and the "natural" rate of employment (and unemployment) are finely—and finally—ground out by the irrevocable Walrasian equations, so that money hardly matters, except for ephemeral interludes.‡ Adopting the "rule" would consign the theory of money to oblivion, with fascination only for anthropologists.

The Monetarist dichotomization of economic theory into a study of real forces affecting Q, N, and real r, real C, and real I, as against the nominal money overhang of P, Y, and r, fosters a two-world psyche, and a schizophrenic revival of "neutral" money innocent of real impingement on the Walrasian sector.

The position is utterly alien to Keynes' thinking and to the WCM model: our economy *is* a money-using production economy; there is no way of ejecting money *out* of the system; the economy would disintegrate as an efficient

---

* On the financial market instabilities engendered by (incomplete) Monetarist attitudes at central banks, see Ervin Miller, "The Pains of Monetary Restraint," *Lloyds Bank Review* (July 1973). On "credit-crunch" aspects, see H. Minsky, *Keynes*, pp. 86, 129.

† Cf. Selden, on the influence of Monetarist doctrines; I think he actually understates the Monetarist influence. Though central bankers may explicitly reject the 3-percent rule, they always explain that they are fighting the good battle against inflation—despite extravagant pay settlements and unemployment. Only sporadically have central bankers endorsed the quest for a workable Incomes Policy. Chairman Arthur Burns of the Fed and Governor Henry Wallich are manifestly absolved for they have been most conspicuous in recognizing the need for measures of wage-salary restraints.

‡ Friedman quotes approvingly John Stuart Mill's remark that "there cannot . . . be intrinsically a more insignificant thing in the economy . . . than money; except in the character of a contrivance for sparing time and labour." Keynes would have regarded money as a most significant social invention, so that at all times "money mattered, indeed"—so long as the tomorrows are vague and unknown.

production and distribution vehicle without money or a computerized substitute. Likewise, money *is* potent on Q, N, r, C, and I in the short *and* long run. *Money matters*, in the short season and beyond, for the ramble into the "long-run" consists of a collection of shorter intervals.

Money Wages: From Silence to Expectations

As a prelude to an examination of the money-wage issue we note here merely the reticence of Monetarists on the subject.

The QTM—new and old—has been most laconic, over most of its assertive period, on the subject of money wages: the words elude the index of Friedman's larger works.* In the symposium on Friedman's "framework," Brunner and Meltzer develop a theory of prices of real assets, financial assets, and output, positing that "we reduce the scope of our model by omitting the labor market."† This is indeed a spectacular abstraction.

In a late textbook, in conjecturing about the mere *possibility* of a wage-price spiral, Darby regales us with an illuminating riposte: "The idea is ideal for the politician, since it shifts blame from government policy, where it belongs, to greedy business executives and economists."‡ Ostensibly, the Fed can always save the day.

Apparently, all of us can secure a money-income enhancement of a thousand percent per day, and the Fed will protect us—with near total unemployment, no doubt, and ascending prices! Similarly, McCulloch writes that "if the rise in prices were not validated by a comparable increase in the money supply," then, "the wage-price spiral (would be) halted or even

---

* See also Chapter 9 for further evaluation. Cf. *Optimum Quantity of Money, A Monetary History,* or *Studies in the Quantity Theory of Money.* Friedman, in the former, prefers to speak of "factor prices"; the infrequent references to wages are generally to real wages "ground out" as relative prices in a Walrasian general equilibrium system. Long ago, with respect to the wage share, he considered it astonishing that anyone would even be interested in this ratio. See his article in *The Impact of the Union* (New York: Harcourt, Brace, 1951), David McCord Wright, ed., pp. 306, 352–353.

† Cf. Karl Brunner and Allan H. Meltzer, "Money, Debt, and Economic Activity," *Journal of Political Economy* (Sept./Oct. 1972). Their other article in the same issue is titled "Friedman's Monetary Theory." This, too, lacks any entry on money wages and inflation. With the exception of Paul Davidson, who tried to call attention to the issue, there were thus 160 tight journal pages without a significant word on money wages and the price level. For a comparable earlier performance, see the multiauthor "Symposium on Monetary Policy," *Review of Economic Studies* (Oct. 1960). To this day (mid-1977), and after nearly a decade of stagflation, there has not been *one* article accepted by the professional editors of the *American Economic Review* on money-wage inflation, or Incomes Policy remedies. The pages are "scientifically" policed for Monetarist dogma.

‡ Darby, *Macroeconomics,* p. 348.

reversed."* In an "analysis" that goes to arduous pains to misread the WCM thesis—a commissioned article, of all things—Laidler and Parkin conclude:

Wage leadership models . . . may well be interpreted as complementary to excess demand and inflation expectations models, telling us about the details of the transmission . . . of wage inflation through the economy . . .†

Do we ever find "excess demand" in conditions of stagflation or slump-flation? The post-1970 episodes are marked by *deficient* demands in any rational sense of these words.

In these "theories" of Monetarism, the $P = Y/Q$ relation never appears: however stormy the money-income tide, the MA can put its finger in the dike and resolutely block the choppy P-flow.

Reversing the Monetarist dictum, it is Monetarism that provides balm to console politicians, permitting them to cave in to outlandish wage-salary claims while denouncing the Fed for inflation; no need to alienate any political bloc, merely rail at the MA.

In the next chapter attention will be devoted to the *purported* theories of the money wage, leading a student to marvel at the extraordinary propensity for fiction writing. The theory that the MA can preclude a P-bulge regardless of (w/A) events is an idea whose time has gone.

Central Bankers: A Maligned Lot?

Central bankers are a maligned lot, living in prestigious comfort while enduring the slings and arrows aimed by outraged critics. They are castigated for creating too much liquidity and entertaining inflation, chided for supplying too little money and rearing unemployment, assailed for devotion to fixed exchange rates, and flayed for acquiescence in floating exchange rates. Judging from the attacks, they do everything wrong: battered on all sides, they are in a no-win contest. Their prescience is held in such low esteem that Professor Friedman would supplant them with an unimaginative statistical clerk who would obey a strict steady-rate instruction. Discretion would be superseded by an inexorable $\Delta M(t)$ directive.

---

* McCulloch, pp. 36–37. The word "validated" by money supplies is a favorite rationalization to deny the obvious wage-price market events, permitting refuge in $MV = PQ$. It was this word which led me to formulate the WCM truism as an answer to the EOE: the rise in unit costs must "validate" the increase in P! For an early dismissal of even the thought of a wage-price spiral, see Friedman, "The Case for Flexible Exchange Rates," reprinted in his *Essays In Positive Economics* (University of Chicago Press, 1953). There are several spicy remarks, such as "the crucial fallacy is the so-called 'wage-price spiral' " and "the emptiness of the argument" (pp. 180, 181).

† Laidler and Parkin, p. 765.

The WCM vote transcends the Scotch verdict, and is for full MA acquittal on the inflation indictment; they are not absolved, however, from the unemployment distress nor for their dereliction in alerting their governments of the need for an income apparatus to buttress their economic stabilization mission.

The proper moment for dismantling the MA, or at least observing the atrophy in its scope of operations, would be on the occasion of the launching of an effective Incomes Policy. Once P is (largely) stabilized the tortuous ΔM perplexities would abate. Fortified by an Incomes Policy the MA directives could more nearly pursue the steady rule, with the automated mission deflected by the vicissitudes of Q and N lags, A projections, m (or ΔV) oscillations, and open-economy ramifications. In remaining alert to the disconcerting perturbations of change, a stable P would permit a serene and rewarding MA career, earning kudos for inuring humanity from injurious job misfortunes. Too, the MA would be condoned for intermittent lapses from the steady rule. It would be admired for its deftness in parrying a string of small blows emanating from unexpected quarters.

More will be said on the theory of money in Chapter 9. It is more important now to examine the fictitious theories of *money*-wage determination.

CHAPTER FIVE

Money Wages: Phenomena in Search of a Theory

Flutters are predictable that the WCM analysis presumes the money wage to be an exogenous variable with a career of its own, rather than an endogenous response to supply-demand forces analogous to other prices. The clash comes to a head in how we perceive w: as a determinant of P or as an immanent determinate, along with P, of the Walrasian tastes, income, and productivity data, together with the structural and behavioral forces shaping the V- and M-magnitudes.

Singularly, the exogeneity reproach collapses on the perception that a determinate *money*-wage theory escapes economics under prevailing collective-bargaining institutions, with or without government intervention, outside a particular historical context with determining facets known mostly *ex post*. Bilateral monopoly realities of the negotiating table preclude deterministic theories that are characteristically aloof to historical complexities of power, strife, and ideological rationalization; the phenomena are resistant, if not immune, to the angular supply-and-demand etchings delineated in deterministic profit-maximization models.

It has been observed that by some standards the ΔM emissions could also be stipulated as functionally responsive to endogenous forces. Yet on recognizing MA discretion, and its erratic responses (in amplitude and sign) to latent economic phenomena, the exogenous interpretation was judged to be not unreasonable: an endogenous M^s function would be fuzzy and ambiguous on profit-maximizing principles.

The WCM theory is driven to a comparable analytic posture in admitting unpredictable union and management attitudes on the prospective settlement, beyond a fatuous demarcation of a fairly elastic zone of high and low limits prior to the final announcements of concession and agreement. Nebulous ideological human factors are ultimately muted in some conciliation to end the struggle; recessed psychological quirks come into play with respect to $\Delta w(t)$ just as they do with $\Delta M(t)$. Obviously, zonal limits for MA money emissions could also be set to bound most historical contingencies, yet few would posit an *a priori* determinate M-function to border the field of caprice on which the MA gambles, and gambols.

"We are where we are." The human lot is a mixture concocted in history and sped relentlessly into tomorrow without the power to stop the calendar. Whatever the antecedent P-events, so long as $\Delta w(t_1) > \Delta A(t_1)$, then $P(t_1) > P(t_0)$, with the degree of ascent dependent on the disproportionate (w/A) move. A 10, 20, 30 . . . percent upkick in money wages, whatever the fervor of "catch-up" arguments, and whether emanating from the Monetarist right or the "worker-friend" left, will do nothing to capsize the price tapes: cost pressures and fatter pay envelopes in consumer hands will tend to catapult prices skyward.

The WCM conception thus sustains the exogenous image of w as a P-maker, as a gravitational sun around which P rotates (given the magnetic pull of A and k).

An Exogenous-Endogenous Dialogue

Metaphysical perplexities and prolixities, capable of filling a good-sized tome—maybe without changing initial preconceptions—abound in the endogenous-exogenous text.*

Exogenous variables are commonly attributed to forces outside economics, explained if at all by other disciplines; they constitute the data of economics. Thus in general equilibrium theory, tastes (the utility functions) are presumably physiological, cultural, and psychological in origin. The production functions of input-output relations maintain a physical science and engineering orientation (though the economist should admit more psychology). Resource-ownership has historical, legalistic, and institutional roots. As exogenous variables organized by the plaster of principles of utility maximization, cost minimization, and profit maximization, the *endogenous* variables of *relative* prices, output, input, and factor incomes emerge in the general equilibrium plots. On these tests, interest rates, rents, and *real* wages are also elicited as

---

* The exogenous-endogenous adjectives (corrupted by usage to exogeneity-endogeneity nouns) seem to have entered the literature with Friedrich Hayek, *Monetary Theory and the Trade Cycle* (New York: Harcourt, Brace, 1933), N. Kaldor and H. M. Croome translators. Lionel Robbins, in his methodologically influential *Essay on the Nature and Significance of Economic Science* (London: Macmillan, 1935), p. 127, credits R. Strigl of the Austrian school (of which Hayek is an illustrious member) with originating the terms for economics.

endogenous relative prices. The QTM injects an absolute price level dimension by entering exogenous money supplies.

As government behavior is less predictable, immune to the profit-maximizing calculus (though some want to substitute the spuriously precise "cost-benefit" calibration where both wings of the equation belong to the incalculable future), government is inscribed as an exogenous variable, lumped with earthquakes, floods, wars, and lesser political traumas, comprising haphazard shocks upsetting the data and provoking endogenous responses. A whit lower than exogenous status is accorded to those technological breakthroughs which are unrelated to immanent cost-price data: the technological disruptions carry the more beguiling name of *autonomous phenomena*—exogenous (or spontaneous) under another guise.* The Malthusian theory of population, with procreation functionally responsive to real wages, was an *endogenous* (or *induced*) theory. After Jevons read the riot act on a purely "economic" theory of population, Malthusianism tended to be among the more surreptitious entries in economic tracts.† Now the subject comes on as economic and sociological, camouflaged under the demographic mantle.

The technological and population illustrations contain an intriguing message. On that blissful day of "scientific" triumph, when all the secrets of change in the human existence are unlocked to comprise a glorious, all-embracing theory of society and its evolutionary-revolutionary transformation, *everything* would be endogenous, with events flowing naturally, explicably, from one historical exigency to another contingency in an inexorable sequence of events, all predictable in advance. The collection would be deterministic, omitting chance, impulse, or atavistic errata. Tolstoy, in filling his engrossing canvas in *War and Peace* with armies destined for the inevitable though unwanted clash, would be its prophet. All would be endogenous in a comprehensive science of society—if only we could piece the pattern together in advance.

To step back from this prescience, we call exogenous those events which defy prediction within the standards of fineness and timing that are critical for instrumental coping. Of course, by intuition, by historical experience, by reasonable surmise, we can predict that money emissions per annum in mature economies will generally be positive and below, say, 25, 15, maybe 10 percent. But we are neither sure nor comfortable within the range of potential flux: the molehill spread between 2 and 10 percent makes a mountain of difference

---

* Marx, and Joan Robinson (*Accumulation of Capital*), would stress the endogenous aspects of technology.

† It was W. Stanley Jevons, more than any other early writer, who started economics on the road to being an allocational theory under "Given, a certain population . . . : required, the mode of employing their labour which will maximize the utility of the product." See *The Theory of Political Economy* (New York: Augustus Kelley, Reprint 1965, 1st ed. 1871), p. 267.

in the Monetarist inflation parables or the WCM stagflation saga. *Some* part of the vital predictive sequence lies outside the economist's ken or econometrician's model: only by guessing can the endogenous portion be extracted from the affected network of equations.

At bottom, the conflict over money wages being exogenous or endogenous involves a dispute on whether $(\Delta w/w)$, year-to-year, reflects purely profit-making forces within a deterministic supply-demand model or whether the annual variations have a life of their own in a historic setting attuned to *extraeconomic*, i.e., exogenous or nonprofit maximizing forces, even though the bargaining agents conjure certain economic parameters which, on probing, dissolve into an inaccurate description of what they are about and what will transpire in the wider economic context. Thus we are left with historical indeterminacy unless possessed with exact information on motivations, pressures, posturing, political maneuvering, and ideological rationalization at each moment of time when wage bargains are being struck. History alone, in the sense of relevant knowledge of the train of events up to yesterday, and the reading of it for tomorrow's signals, can enable us to "predict" money-wage outcomes.

Some recital and assessment of the assorted bag of presumed endogenous *money*-wage theories will be attempted. Practically all of the views are sadly disjointed on the crucial link of Δw to ΔP. To reiterate, our study is preoccupied with *money*, not *real* wages. There has been an astonishing confusion of the two, with real-wage theories palmed off as an explanation of money wages.

Conceivably, there can be short-run indeterminacy and long-run determinacy. In the one context it may be possible to predicate endogeneity, in the other exogeneity. Involved, then, can be a matter of *timing* of functional responses. Generally, in matters of inflation or unemployment, periods of one to five years interest us—to put a calendar-time dimension on the subject (in some defiance of Marshall). For longer periods, too many other things can happen, and the analysis becomes largely a vapid exercise in logomachy. Timing, in economics as in life, is nearly everything.* To say "the lags are longer than expected," so that we must await an imponderable passage of time, is to add little to our understanding. Reactions may be imperceptible in a short period and of dubious compelling force in a longer time span. Despite *some* temporal interdependence there would be warrant for the exogenous designation in such instances. Looking back, even checking memories of participants, the historical prologue might have receded almost entirely as a psychological or cultural determinant of behavior, considering the interplay of other factors.

---

* This, I take it, is both the strength and weakness of the recent preoccupation with "disequilibrium" lagged responses of the sort that apparently intrigued Robert Clower, "Reflections on the Keynesian Perplex," *Zeitschrift für Nationalökonomie* (1975).

A "Compleat" Endogenous Wage Function

It is hardly a clever feat to write the money wage as an endogenous function of a basket of variables, as:

$$w_1 = w(w_0, w_{-1}, \ldots P_0, P_1^*, \ldots U_{-1}, U_0, U_1^*, \ldots A_0, A^*, \ldots R_0,$$
$$R^*, \ldots X, J_0, j_0, g_1, B_1, Z_0), \tag{5.1}$$

where subscripts refer to t_0, t_1, etc. Asterisks denote expectational variables. Newer symbols are:

R = profits

J = union leadership attitudes, including membership pressures, leadership personalities, and political posturing

j = union membership attitudes which may clash in militancy with union leadership over settlement terms

g = government attitudes, and nature of intervention in bargaining disputes

B = foreign trade and foreign exchange aspects

Z = public resentment of strikes and wage claims

Penetrating the mock precision of Eq. (5.1), it would correctly be derided as a "garbage-disposal" function, a sewer receptacle of unused "explanatory" variables. Some variables are unimportant, some are interacting and, for most, the sign or magnitude of functional variation is obscure. An intimate knowledge of history and personalities would be indispensable to solve the interdependencies which boggle *a priori* mathemization.

In the longer past, a safe surmise might hit, by history and intuitive feel, on a possible settlement in the 2 to 5 percent zone per annum. In the 1960s, a plausible guess would place the figures at from 4 to 8 percent. Since about 1970, numbers would have to range from a floor of about 10 to upwards of 25 percent in the United Kingdom, Canada, and Australia, with a shade below the lower end applying to the United States. Where "normalcy" will henceforth land us is the troublesome enigma.*

The Neoclassical Derived-Demand Theory

Most theories are somewhat of a compression of Eq. (5.1). The survey will reveal that economic analysis is bluffing when it purports to "explain" *money wages* in a market supply-demand model. Hit-and-run expositions trade on the credibility of other parts of economics to fantasize the state of the art, mesmerizing the reader to stare beyond the void in the money-wage paradigm,

---

* Under "normal" conditions most equational or functional formats are superfluous, with informed guesses performing with equal precision.

taking solace in some faith that the black cat must be prowling somewhere in the dark jungle of a bleak textbook-land.

As a prelude to the dominant neoclassical theory of derived demand, whose ramifications into the thought structure are often overlooked, it is well to retrace some Phillips curve concepts.

The Phillips curve as a disequilibrium structure

In its pristine elegance, before being cluttered with more variables in a progression toward the "compleat" function shown in Eq. (5.1), the Phillips curve reported:

$$(\Delta w/w) = w(U'), \tag{5.2}$$

where $U' =$ unemployment rate subject to: $[\Delta(\Delta w/w)/\Delta U'] < 0.$

Growing unemployment rates would thus temper $(\Delta w/w)$. Though the principle was latent in the theoretical literature dealing with *real* wages, and illicitly transferred too often to *money* wages, it was the latter empirical confirmation by Phillips that merited the encomiums until the sign of the derivative in the restraint on Eq. (5.2) was toppled by events.* Once outcomes of $[\Delta(\Delta w/w)/\Delta U'] > 0$ became commonplace, the shifting Phillips curve theory was born, transforming instantly a predictive "law" into a descriptive postmortem.

Some preferred to lag Eq. (5.2), with w_1 a function of U'_0. Others preferred a string of linear lags, as $w_1 = aU'_0 + bU'_{-1} + cU'_{-2} + \dots$. Others, in bending with the fashions, made the variables expectational. A stylized tracking of Phillips curve points responsible for its fall from grace appears in Fig. 5.1(b), showing the erratic numbered time path taken by money-wage changes, compared to the S.E. prediction. Figure 5.1(a) shows (the solid line)

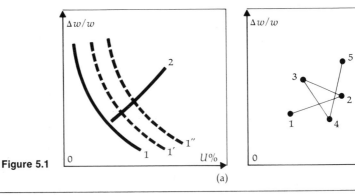

Figure 5.1

(a)　　　　　　　　　　(b)

---

* The remarkable paper was A. W. Phillips' "The Relation Between Unemployment and the Rate of Change of Money Wage Rates in the United Kingdom, 1861–1957," *Economica* (1958). An early effort to apply the ideas to United States data appeared in Paul A. Samuelson and Robert M. Solow, "Analytical Aspects of Anti-Inflation Policy," *American Economic Review* (May 1960).

the "normal" Phillips curve, lettered 1. Curves 1′ and 1″ comprise part of the family later tacked on as market money wage events traced path 2.

When applied to equilibrium theory, the soul of economics, Phillips curve unemployment implied an "excess" supply of labor compared to the demand. "Excess supply," to good Walrasians, spelled disequilibrium which would be relieved by dampened *real* wages. There was a ready disposition to interpret the Phillips curve inference of *tapered money-wage advances* as comporting with neoclassical *real*-wage analysis; it was an easy alliance consummated under unreflective textbook covers: everyone *knew* "excess" supply lowered prices! Consternation ensued as the Phillips curve broke out in a pathological wage rash.

The theory of derived demand

Neoclassical real-wage theory is lodged in derived demand. It stands alongside marginal utility doctrine in furnishing the substance of the revolt against the classical thesis that costs determine value, that values run out from factor costs in production to product prices. Jevons, Menger, and Walras knew what they were about: if utility determined value, productive factors were gauged as important only insofar as they contributed to final output; they reversed the classical saw to read not that costs determined value, but that the value of productive factors emanated from the value of their inputs in fashioning desired outputs. Despite Marshall's perception of the derived-demand thesis, the critical status of the idea has sometimes been lost in the modern teaching.*

Marshall sketched the gist of the theory in his celebrated illustration of the demand for knife handles and blades, showing that each was "derived" from the demand for knives: by arbitrarily holding the supply curve of handles constant, and then deducting the supply prices of handles from the demand prices for knives, a derived-demand function for blades was elicited.

Turning to wage theory, Fig. 5.2(a) measures the price of the product of industry X along the vertical axis, with output quantities ticked off horizontally. Usual industry demand and supply curves, such as D_1 and S_1, are imposed, intersecting at the P^*Q^* equilibrium. Suppose wages go up. Reverting (mentally) to the marginal cost curves in firms, the cost curves are pushed upward at each output volume. Proceeding to the industry adaptation, the product supply curve will also mount, say to S_2. Conversely, if money wages fall, then after the adaptations run their course within the firms, S_3 reveals

---

* For earlier bibliographical references, see my *Approach*, Chapter 1, or the updated statement (but hardly revised) in Martin Bronfenbrenner, *Income Distribution Theory* (Chicago: Aldine, 1971), especially pp. 144–159. J. R. Hicks, in his auspicious debut as a major figure, notes on the very first page the significance of derived demand. See *The Theory of Wages* (London: Macmillan, 1932). See also my essay on "Keynes and the Theory of Derived Demand," *KaM*.

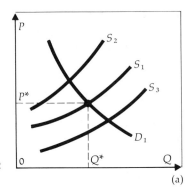
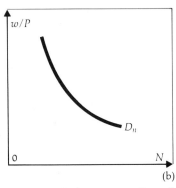

Figure 5.2

(a)　　　　　　　　　　　　(b)

supply offers. Higher money wages, the analysis concludes, raise P and lower Q, with opposite effects for lower money wages. It follows ineluctably that an implicit down-to-the-right demand curve for labor can be drawn, signifying that more labor will be hired at a lower money wage.* The demand for labor will resemble D_n (as in Fig. 5.2(b)) when the vertical axis is modified to read w or, better, w/P, while the horizontal denotes N rather than Q.

Leaving aside subtleties concerning (1) factor-substitution, (2) repercussions on the price of other factors, and (3) long- and short-run characteristics, the proposition is presented that regardless of wage events the product demand curve will sit stern, implacable, unwavering. The product demand curve holds as solid as the Rock of Gibraltar whether money wages nose-dive to one penny or zoom to $1 million an hour.

Interpreting the vertical axis as representing *money* wages is, of course, to bind the product analysis intimately with money income: aside from special assumptions, it *must* follow that (in consumer markets) whenever money wages rise in all industries and joust product supply curves to the left, the product demand curves will also take leave and climb, insofar as the markets cover the mass of consumer goods purchases by the mass consumers, specifically wage earners. A "sitting" product demand curve is a hoax under money-wage changes: *ceteris paribus* is a fictional artifice unable to depict the flow of events.†

---

* This assumes that the product demand curves are drawn on *money* income provisos. Friedman insists that Marshall intended *real* income—which would hardly make the theory suitable for an exposition of realistic market events. Despite Friedman's view, it is possible to interpret matters differently; as the analysis proceeds, the "real-income" interpretation hardly salvages neoclassical wage theory. See his "The Marshallian Demand Curve," *Essays in Positive Economics*, p. 50 *passim*. In some way his article is an answer to my earlier "Foundations of the Demand Curve," *American Economic Review* (Sept. 1942). Friedman wrongly assigns me "credit" for a view simply reported as stated by Henry Schulz and A. L. Bowley. For some criticism of the Friedman position by a generally sympathetic economist, see Leland B. Yeager, "*Methodenstreit* Over Demand Curves," *Journal of Political Economy* (Feb. 1960).

† Cf. my *Approach*, Chapter 1.

Rather than press on into the meticulous mathemized rendition of derived demand and the constraining elasticities, insofar as it directs its focus to real wages it is a signal detour along the quest for a theory of *money* wages. If it is tendered as a *money*-wage theory, it is a monumental confusion, remiss in skipping supply-demand interdependence: offsetting lifts in both product supply and demand curves might yield *no* change in output and thus maintain unchanged labor hire despite severe money-wage escalation. The money-wage labor-demand curve could stand rigid, perfectly inelastic.*

The marginal product curve refuge

It was the hollowness of this "theory," when used in a money-wage context, that really inspired Keynes' *General Theory*. Money-wage cuts were roundly prescribed as the cure for the Great Depression. If the principle was valid, as in some chaotic renditions of derived demand, a new theory would be otiose: cut money wages and jobs would magically appear. Keynes' answer was that the wage surgery would pull prices down precipitously and almost proportionately. What with bankruptcies and international beggar-my-neighbor repercussions, recovery would be postponed. Exacerbated worker suspicions would also damage industrial harmony and discipline. Pigou real-balance effects for full employment restoration came later to try to salvage the theory, though even Pigou (*Lapses from Full Employment*) despaired of the medicine, the cure possibly being more damaging than the disease.†

Yet it is not unusual to find "Keynesian" textbooks, after elaborating Keynesian concepts in 150 or more pages, casually drawing neoclassical labor-demand curves signifying more labor hired at lower money wages! One wonders what Keynes' *General Theory* was all about.

Short-cutting the product market underpinnings of derived demand are a plethora of elegant marginal productivity models which deal in *real* wages, and pretend to be about money wages. Marginal productivity theory (MPT) myths can be exposed succinctly.

In Fig. 5.2(b) the D-curve represents a labor-demand curve, where the vertical axis denotes real wages (w/P), while N is measured horizontally. Notationally, the demand equation is written and equated to labor supply, as $D_n = N(w/P; K) = S_n = N(w/P)$. The real wage thus travels in the light of day. Of course, K denotes the elusive "stock of capital," homogeneous no doubt, expressed in value terms—to explain values!

---

* Ibid., Chapter 6.

† The lack of reflection on Keynes is nowhere more lamentable than in the inattention to Chapter 19. This is titled *Changes In Money Wages*, with the first sentence referring to "the effects of a change in money wages." Surely, it must strike the eye that a book purporting to offer *a general theory* stepped back from constructing a theory of *money* wages. Keynes saw none, and he was content solely to unravel the effects of money-wage changes.

Granted $P = \bar{P}$, all is well: vary w against the P granite, real wages move proportionately; on the principle of profit-maximization less labor is hired at higher real wages. Thus the labor-demand locus follows the persuasive slope called for in stable equilibrium.

Suppose, however, that P does not stand tall and resolute while w wavers. The downward-demand curve serenity is pierced. For example, starting any-place in the chart field, if the wage-price elasticity $(E_{wp}) = 1$, where $E_{wp} = [P\Delta w/w\Delta P]$, so that the w and P rises are proportionate, labor demand is im-prisoned on a one-point demand curve!* If $E_{wp} < 1$ the labor-demand function might slope *upward*, as the underconsumptionist theorists would have it. Only $E_{wp} > 1$ redeems the neoclassical image.

Although the E_{wp} elasticity is crucial, the labor-demand locus is almost universally drawn with undue reticence of the Δw to ΔP kicks; a hush pre-vails, giving credence to the vertical axis being interpreted as of the form $w/\bar{P}$. Holding prices generally as unaffected by wages is singularly sterile for insight into the w and P link.

Mainly, the w/P or MPT theories—the "Good Old Theory" for Bronfen-brenner—repose on the QTM, and draw surreptitiously on the neoclassical theory of the firm in a facile and uncritical use. For example, from the theory of the purely competitive profit-maximizing firm, it follows for the one vari-able-factor case, as with labor added to equipment, that in equilibrium:

$$P = MC, \tag{5.3}$$

where MC = marginal cost

$$P = w/MP,$$

where MP = marginal product of labor. Rewriting Eq. (5.3), $MP = w/P$.

Diagrammatically, therefore, plotting a labor-demand curve, where (w/P) denotes the vertical axis, is tantamount—for the competitive cases which alone provide deterministic models (unless the economy-wide degree of monopoly is *assumed* constant)—to drawing an MP curve, imitating the practice of J. B. Clark in his "natural-law" distributive faith. Inscribing (w/P) on the vertical axis, with $P = \bar{P}$, maintains the marginal productivity *real*-wage theory afloat; the guiding proposition follows that under the static "law" of diminishing returns more labor will be hired only at lower real wages. It is as if to portray the entire economy as a vast farm, with diminishing returns exacting an inexorable toll. Swept under the rug are queries into diverse MP curves in various sectors and, above all, an evasion of an inquiry into differ-ent "laws" of return in industries producing Pigou's "wage-goods" (analogous

---

* Cf. "The Full Employment Model," in *KaM*. This also deals, aside from the wage-price elasticity, with real-balance effects, expectations and investment, and money supply in contrasting the theory to Patinkin's prestigious analysis. For some criticism, and some confusion, see N. Peera, "The Full Employment Model and the Implicit Employment Function," *Kyklos* (1974), pp. 610–612.

to Ricardian "corn" as labor sustenance) against industries catering to non-wage-earner luxury items. A more studied "big farm" monolith in macro-economic contexts takes refuge in Cobb-Douglas functions where output is a homogeneous good subject to diminishing returns in labor hire: J. B. Clark—who also identified MP as the ethical payment—survives without the perplexities of monopoly or changing output composites over time—or idle capacity in industry and technological progress in response to changes in labor hire which can *only* take place in time.

Equation (5.3) is peculiarly amenable to QTM macrotheory. For it is easy to slip into the position that $P = P(M)$, so that $P = \bar{P}$ with P determined by money supplies or (to invoke MV/Q) where Q denotes total output phenomena along the MP curve. With $(\Delta Q/\Delta N) > 0$ to signify positive marginal products, and $(\Delta^2 Q/\Delta N^2) < 0$ to insure diminishing returns, then Q *at full employment* establishes P at full employment. Thereafter, with $P = \bar{P}$ only one value of w is consistent with N_f and Q_f. Any attempt to raise money wages *and the real wage*, with $P = \bar{P}$, must prompt labor dismissals. The conclusion is inescapable that unemployment must ensue from higher real wages.

Unless P is predicated on this chain of hypotheses it is hard to know where or how the w/P theory originates. In any event, once it latches on to $P = \bar{P}$, whatever the supporting "theory," the neoclassical logic becomes quickly transported from a theory of *real* wages (of dubious marginal productivity ancestry) to one of *money* wages—which is a different subject entirely, one far more complex than the neoclassical probe. Admitting *some* feedback from Δw to ΔP, the analysis falters, with cases of $E_{wp} \gtrless 1$.* Too, there are implicit real-balance effects, money-supply *assumptions* (of $\Delta M \gtrless 0$), and anticipatory variables that mess up stationary designs for a dynamic front.

Redistributive shifts have been conspicuously ignored in the MP theory. Rewriting the WCM:

$$(A/k) = (w/P). \tag{5.4}$$

Thus as N varies, there are likely to be some A-perturbations. On static laws of return, a higher real wage signifies $\Delta A > 0$. Quickly, this carries an intimation of labor-demand *indeterminacy* inasmuch as a higher real wage, with a higher proportion of consumer output absorbed by wage earners, carries some buoyancy for the Keynesianism C-function, tending to *increase*—not decrease—labor demand and employment. All this is implicit in a multiplier theory which includes distributive phenomena.† In contrast to the orthodox

---

* Using the E_{wp} form is not a negation of w-causality; it would be as easy to use the reciprocal. E_{wp} has been chosen merely to illuminate the neoclassical theory within its own context.

† The usual formula for the *average* "multiplier" would be: $Q = I/s$, where $s = (S/Q)$, or the average propensity to consume. But $S = s_w \omega + s_r \pi$, where s_w and s_r are the average savings propensities out of wage and nonwage income. Thus:

position, real wages, and income distribution generally, are a *determining* variable in aggregate Q and N rather than one determined directly in the theory of "wages."

"The superstructure of the orthodox wage model has been erected with great care," as Keynes might have written. Unfortunately, its isolation of P from w is enough to demolish it and render it as an upstart theory of *money* wages regardless of its status as a theory of real wages.* The theoretical void is seldom acknowledged, with the (w/P) or MP diagram paraded out front where it is mercilessly indoctrinated, through textbooks, as purveying something about money wages. Disclaimers are rare as the leap from real to money phenomena is deemed successful by those who do not discern the impenetrable obstructions.†

A Potpourri of Money-Wage Misadventures

A hodgepodge of tenuous money-wage theories will be examined briefly. The nebulous explanations are rooted in a variety of contradictory premises.

General equilibrium sanctuaries

Faith in endogenous money-wage explanations sometimes draws sustenance from a presumed (still unrevealed) general equilibrium model (GEM) of

---

$Q = I/s_w\, \omega + s_r\, \pi$. In the latter statement distributional phenomena are a *determinant* of real income Q. These distributional aspects have endured a long neglect in macrotheory.

*   Cf. "Marginal Productivity and Macrodistribution Theory," *KaM*.

†   The rueful commentary is that outside of the Phillips curve offering, with a pocketful of extra variables, economic theorists have devoted little attention to the problem. For my own attempts at the formal resolution, see my *Approach*, Chapter 6, based on a 1956 *American Economic Review* article. Ultimately, in view of a union-oriented labor-supply curve perfectly elastic over the effective equilibrium range, the theory can be rendered as exogenous, relieved of the deterministic formalisms. In the modern textbook literature there is simply no movement beyond mathematical symbolism. T. F. Dernburg and D. M. McDougall, *Macroeconomics* (New York: McGraw-Hill, 1976, 5th ed.), Chapter 10, develop the (w/P) analysis and, for the "Keynesian" system, stipulate that "the money wage is fixed" (p. 205). This is a commonplace remark by Keynesian critics and supporters. It is surely a strange use of language to assign unemployment to wage rigidity in these days of upward flexibility! In Darby, pp. 85–86, the (w/P) theory is regurgitated in a form parallel to that outlined. W. H. Branson and J. M. Litvack, *Macroeconomics* (New York: Harper & Row, 1976), a textbook often selected for "graduate" courses, use the (w/P) formulation, and argue that the *IS-LM* system must be "solved" simultaneously—with money supply "given." This is a pseudo-model for it rests on the queer hypothesis of $M = \bar{M}$ regardless of Q and N, or w—surely Keynes never intended this perversion. They, too, tie unemployment to "wage rigidity." (See pp. 134, 157–166.)

    Apparently, Keynes never lived, nor wrote—or was unread.

    The sample can be extended to other widely used "textbooks," fresh with original "analysis."

Walrasian ancestry. Unfortunately, existing models foreclose a welcome sanctuary: as the theory has squirmed uneasily over the entry of money, it can hardly provide a register for money wages except by grafting on some uncritical QTM elements and returning us to square one on the Δw to ΔP interactions.

GEMs maintain their analytic aplomb in eliciting *relative* prices and, as observed by Friedman, extracting "wages" (real, not money) as "simply" another price—more on this shortly.

Within its own context the myriad GEM perplexities prevent its ready application for understanding the economy in which we happen to live. There is some amnesia in its omissions: (1) contractual obligations, stipulated in fixed money sums, are "outside" the model; (2) the admirably explicit Walrasian assumption of "neither profits nor losses" is stultifying for unravelling the vitality of the *capitalistic* system, or savoring the motivating forces of the market economy. The position is not urged very far along by Marshall's refuge in "normal" profits, as a euphemism for Walras' venture in excision;* (3) GEM's commitment to "certainty," or "perfect foresight," or "perfect information," or relief from error in market adaptation not only denies the human facts but eliminates money, banks, insurance companies, unions, and a vast array of real-world institutions. Then there is, of course, (4) perfect competition, while (by 3) it follows that (5) money is excluded.

How all this can build up to a theory of *money* wages remains a mystery except in the minds of those who tantalize us with the intimation of money wages being "simply another endogenous price."

GEMs also premise: (6) that "labor demand equals supply," after also imposing stability restrictions. Voluntary full employment is thereby *assumed* at the outset: small wonder then at the adeptness of the forthcoming "proofs" that the system grinds out automatic full employment—despite the obvious facts. Keynes, for example, observed unemployment in England (1921–1935) never below 9 and as high as 22 percent. A 15-year stretch of the miseries on the dole should condone the premise of *unemployment* "equilibrium" as more tuned to the realities. Recent unemployment, colossal again in Western economies, stigmatizes the N_f models.

Attempts to insert a "price level" in the Walrasian model, by Gustav Cassel in his *Theory of Social Economy* (1932), or by Patinkin or Friedman in more recent years, invariably intone a QTM illusion once they abide the GEM "full employment" hypothesis. Grafting a Fisher (or Cambridge) equation of exchange onto a "fixed Q," with V being explained by the "demand for real-money balances," a QTM conclusion is inescapable, even after allowing for Pigou-Patinkin "real-balance" effects. Inject more money and, presto, P bounds up—in the cut gem of a GEM. What else could possibly happen after the helicopter money rainmaker hovers over an economy of

---

* Cf. Joan Robinson, *Economic Heresies* (New York: Basic Books, 1973 edition).

"fixed Q"? Also, through it all w is at peace, moving in calm response to adapt simultaneously with P, without truculent impulses of its own.

The fixity of Q—at the Q_f position—predestines QTM conclusions as w behaves as an orderly equilibrating variable settling into its niche like any other price. Unfortunately, as Friedman has discovered in confronting the ΔP and ΔQ puzzle, events are more haphazard in an economy awash in unemployment or struggling with growing pains.

GEMs, as presently constituted, offer only stones as victuals to nourish the naive faith in an existing endogenous money-wage theory.

Wages as "simply" another price

Monetarist references to money wages in the inflation trauma are sparse. When they assure us that wages are simply another price, this is good GEM doctrine, with all its shortcomings. When more money is declared able to compress unemployment below the "natural" rate "in the short period," before culminating in inflation, this a Phillips curve anecdote, with w climbing along with "other" P's as the N's temporarily perk up. When they affirm that strong monetary restraint will burst the inflation balloon at the cost of short-period unemployment by imposing some discipline on labor or their union leaders, the Phillips curve soundings again are strident.

In some microtheories of Monetarists, either derived-demand theories are propounded or the MP (or w/P) real-wage "explanations" proliferate, with real-wage aspects scaffolding money-wage preconceptions.

To interpret money wages as "simply another price" is to mistake flies for elephants. A rise in the price of peanuts, or pins, or paper, will affect—fairly minutely—other prices from the cost side, as an industrial input. Incomes of peanut farmers, paper processors, or pin-makers will be enhanced. Yet in the vast price network it will not be unreasonable to assume other prices substantially constant, as a convenient fiction; there should not be too strong an input-cost disruption, or a market-demand upheaval due to enhanced incomes of those engaged in affected industries. *Ceteris paribus* is only gently teased.

A *general* wage rise, however, involves more than a difference in degree: money wages (and salaries) comprise about 55 percent of *gross* business costs, closer to 75 percent of *net* costs, and probably even more of *variable* costs. On the demand side, in consumer markets in the United States, for example, wage earners absorb about 85 percent of the purchase volume: in other countries the figures may be higher. There is thus a heavy cost and demand interaction bestirred by Δw which cannot be matched by any single "other price." Violence is done to the *ceteris paribus* of "unchanged demand for products," or cost curves being imperceptibly dislodged, when money wages ascend. Further, while there are good substitutes for pins, paper, and peanuts, and which appear fairly soon, there is at best only "long run" possible labor displacement—but this theory of technological displacement erects obstacles of its own for Walrasian models. Money wages constitute a unique "price" in the "m-price" model; they far overshadow any other price, and their exogenous perturbations under wage bargaining dislodge (practically) all other prices.

Competitive labor markets

When a general equilibrium theory of *money* income, *money* wages, and "equilibrium *involuntary* unemployment" comes wrigging out of its *real* income, perfect certainty, contractless, money-less, full-employment, and relative-price cocoon, it will undoubtedly also have to shed its competitive coating if it hopes to have explanatory relevance.

Some aver that money-wage inflation would dissolve if the labor market was competitive. This seems to make sense until the surface is scratched. It is to pine openly for some other world, without labor unions; others like to wish the giant corporations away. Manifestly, labor unions and collective bargaining sprinkle generous pinches of bilateral monopoly and game theory over the economy; exposition would be tidier by erasing their indeterminacies. Yet dreams of legerdemain cannot perform miracles without strife, inflation, and a facile nonexistent "competitive" *money* wage. The latter, as previous pages disclose, does *not* exist even in principle: it cannot be extracted from a GEM.

Fuss over labor-union "monopoly" can degenerate into a barrel of words. If the largest concentrated firm charged the "competitive" Pareto optimum price, the "monopoly" pejorative would lose its sting and become devoid of reproach except on grounds of bigness or on indisputable evidence of cost inefficiences. Welfare objections to monopoly ordinarily fault their excessive profit-maximizing prices.

Are unions "monopolists"? This is an old chestnut; if they are so charged, what do they maximize? Real wages? Employment? The wage bill? The relative wage share? Monopolist *behavior*, not firm size, is the usual target for condemnatory cross fire. Attacking unions as monopolists, without comparing union wage outcomes to those of the mythical "competitive" order, is an evasion unless we are apprised of the "competitive" outcome.

Sheerly for forensic fun, suppose unions were swiftly abolished. Overall, it is quite doubtful whether this would usher in a benign era since power relations would be dismantled, and the countervailing political power leading to democratic compromise and a tenuous but workable state, balanced between conflict and harmony, would be dismembered. Leaving aside the prospective powerful social upheaval, if the suppression of unions instituted an era of money-wage cuts, the result would hardly ensure full employment— there would also be bankruptcies and weak (money) sales markets, as Keynes tried to make plain.

Suppose that, somehow, full employment came to prevail as proponents of money-wage "flexibility" (with real-balance effects, to be sure) assure us would happen. As firms began to bid for more labor and other firms responded defensively to hold their staffs—as economics departments do in university faculties—the higher money-wage scenario would suspiciously begin to resemble the situation faced in 1968–1970. "Competition" would do nothing, so long as w outran A, to eradicate inflation despite the illusion of a "competitive" world.

Reference to "competitive" labor markets becomes a mystical subterfuge, with only a gloss of theoretical respectability; it would not be any more able to insure a stable P-trend—or society—than the prevailing union framework. There is in this infatuation with a mythical "competition" a yearning for a world that never was, nor will be, in democratic societies; even Adam Smith, writing when "combinations of workmen" were proscribed by law, well understood the proclivity of businessmen to collude in oligopoly price conspiracies and band together in oligopsony, forming labor-market ventures to suppress wages in a one-sided legal oppression.* Banning *all* labor-union activity would amount to outlawing collective associations, underwriting a wholesale—and unwholesome—concentration of economic and political power in nonlabor hands.

Unions are here to stay, as a vital countervailing force in a pluralistic society characterized by sometimes diverse, sometimes marginally overlapping, sometimes conformable interests. Seeds of harmony and sprouts of conflict coexist, sometimes the one overpowering the other. A more sanguine objective would be to act politically to temper those union actions which are often inimical to labor's interests as well as pernicious to the fortunes of other societal groups. But it is frivolous, idle, and deleterious to social order, while being unduly protective of business groups, to contemplate the political fragmentation, strangulation, or dismemberment of unions without simultaneously acting against "monopoly." One might guess that only chaos would follow from this abandonment of evolutionary experience.

As with Monetarists suggesting unemployment as a remedy for inflation—opting for an (unsuccessful) jump out of the frying pan and directly into the fire of closed job opportunities for others—a drive to abolish unions could carry an even more predictable outcome than monetary stringency: militant social strife, important output and income losses, human frustration, indignity, political turmoil, with even more sullenness at the beck of adventurers anxious to topple the market economy.

Catch-up and expectational theories

Monetarist theories often profess "catch-up" games, with $w(t_1) = aP(t_0)$, where a may be a coefficient generating more or less than proportional wage lurches. There is the Catch 22 in the lagged theory: it *assumes* that yesterday's money wage had little to do with yesterday's price level, and that

---

* *Wealth of Nations*, Book I, Chapter 8.

tomorrow's money wage will not carry a price-level kick tomorrow. The "catch-up" theory is a veritable son of derived demand, mimicking the unlagged parent. Obviously, it is a compressed one-variable relation extracted out of "ye-compleat functionné."*

Recently, erstwhile purveyors of the (w/P) or MP-labor-demand doctrines have been prone to insert some "expectational" content into the stationary conceptions for relevancy in this unstable age of inflation. Rather than presume that entrepreneurs predicate their labor hire on some simultaneously existing price level, they regard P^* as the effective denominator, as (w/P^*). Similarly, in bargaining, labor is endowed with analogous P^* images.

Effectively, each P^* will generate a different w/P curve, with each a largely scaled modular replica: also from $(w/P) = (A/k)$, with $A = A(N)$ it would entail some strange aberrations in k to think that P^* would be forthcoming independently of the *exogenous w*.

Overall, this is a pseudo-solution despite the new faith that at last an endogenous money-wage theory has been born; according to the new disciples, w can be most anything, depending on "expectations." This is a curious theory indeed to be promulgated by endogenous proponents for the exogeneity aspect is simply demoted from money wages and promoted in "expectations." Where the vague P^* guesses are inscribed as "adaptive," with today's P^* for tomorrow contingent on yesterday's P_{-1} results, then there is a fictitious bit of "catch-up" determinism injected. Clearly, on this "thinking" $(\Delta w/w)$ can in a time context be most any number.

Queries abound on the time horizon of P^* expectations, the conviction with which they are held, and the unanimity (or consensus) of expectations. Mostly, the P^* theory is an ingenious exercise in circumlocution to dress up an *exogenous* expectation, with vague roots in history past and history still to be made, all done to masquerade as an *endogenous* money-wage theory. It is a confession of MP-bankruptcy for, given the supporting P^*, money wages can be anything: the "expectational" theory is shinnying the exogenous money-wage tree. Neoclassicism, lapsing into its P^*, has turned up in the exogeneity nest.†

Of course, some still charm readers with models of Nirvana and perfect anticipation—where there is little reason to make anything happen in view of perfect certainty. Inflation, not unreasonably, offers no trouble on board the supersonic jet flight into stupefaction. It would be interesting to have the modellers reveal their personal $w(t)$ and $P(t)$ projections, say beginning

---

* The "catch-up" theory, if widely acted upon, would be a historical thesis, yet doomed to be shucked before it strangled the economy under productivity growth. Cf. below, the comments on "indexation," Chapter 8.

† Some adaptive models are literally extrapolations of the past, which is very nice if trends are neither disrupted nor broken. See, for some skepticism about the "unsettled state" by a Monetarist advocate, David Laidler, "Expectations and the Phillips Trade Off," *Scottish Journal of Political Economy* (Feb. 1976).

20 years back, report on them, and regale us with their prevision for P^* in the 1980s.

While the expectational theory spruces up the state of the art by *abandoning* the perfect certainty of the neoclassical orthodoxy, the expectational theory of w, and the grafted expectational "theory" of inflation, is rudderless at sea until it sights the connection of $P = P(w \ldots)$ and treads its way to Incomes Policy as the stabilizer of the P-vessel. Adherents of money policy, the proponents of the "new endogeneity," still languish in QTM models which are only thinly disguised by the chants of expectations. "Expectations" can be turned by operating on the $w(t)$ path; creating unemployment through the steady-money rule will not bring (w/A) to book without inflicting job instabilities and deferring the optimal resolution.

Penetrating the expectational smoke screens, the lesson of $P = P(w \ldots)$ is still befogged in the purported explanations of the "expectational" theory of inflation.

Bilateral or trilateral monopoly

Bilateral-monopoly theories of wage determination, of the union seller facing the management buyer, proliferate. As in product-market analysis, the same indeterminateness prevails within the ceilings set by management pondering strike costs and future settlement ramifications, and union floors weighted by reciprocal imponderables. The ceilings and floors can even be elastic as the days progress, given the turn of strategies and glimmers of victory and defeat. Too, as a third force, public attitudes and government intervention color the bargaining, whether through rubbery or stringent wage guidelines or through government insistence on quick settlement imparting a "trilateral" determinacy on at least a rough agreement date with vagueness on contract terms.

The issue of whether game theory is more suitable for analytic resolution of the battle of opposing forces can be put aside. However agreement is reached, the WCM must then take hold to outline the ramifications after the feints, parries, and blows struck by participants and reconciled by high-priced mediators or less income-minded bureaucrats standing in the wings or seated at the table.*

Keynesianism

For completeness, we merely mention the money-wage gap in *IS-LM* Keynesianism. This requires either: (1) recourse to Phillips curves, or (2) a confession of the void in the vital P and w center, which is the candid route mapped by

---

* J. Pen, *The Wage Rate Under Collective Bargaining* (Cambridge: Harvard University Press, 1959), T. S. Preston translator, is explicit in his intriguing and intricate models on $P = \bar{P}$ while $\Delta w > 0$. This is the abnegation of the WCM and the w to P interaction. For some approach of the bilateral monopoly aspects through game theory, see E. Roy Weintraub, *Conflict and Co-operation in Economics* (London: Macmillan, 1975).

Hicks in his *Crisis*, or (3) some sterile words on money-wage "rigidity," a rather perverse bit of semantics for talking about treatment of upward money-wage *flexibility*.

The Missing Theory and Some Misplaced Class Struggle

"One of our theories is missing." This is the communiqué that would have to be issued after the foregoing survey. The situation is this: we have a theory of inflation sited in money-wage changes but we lack a theory of money wages.

There is an impostor dwelling in the literature, surviving as a disguised MPT dressed in (w/P) and feeling its way by a question-begging $P = \overline{P}$ or entering P as supported in a QTM context, sometimes even with $Q = \overline{Q}$, which is a contrary display of reasoning for $\Delta N \gtrless 0$. Too, some sympathizers express nostalgic longings for "competitive" labor markets to resolve w. They wish away unions without the faintest intimation of how labor markets would perform in the euphoric other-world economy, yet they forego the necessary probe of the interactions of Δw on ΔP in that one-sided state of dubious bliss.

It would be possible, by inscribing w as a parameter of Aggregate Demand and Supply, to elicit a labor-demand function by linking each w to the accompanying equilibrium N.* The function would rest on: (1) the MA response by way of ΔM to each w where $P = P(w, \ldots)$ in the WCM equation; (2) the implicit income division for this becomes an Aggregate Demand determinate at each w for $(w/P) = (A/k)$: any real-wage variation can affect real C and, with any distributive shuffles, the multiplier; (3) expectations of future wages being tied to each Δw: ramifications will run out to the I function and to the demand for money.

Attaching a labor-supply function to the demand relation tends to negate the whole exercise in favor of the exogeneity postulate, especially if supply is almost perfectly elastic through labor-union stipulations of their supply offerings; supply can also become volatile over time to reflect membership belligerency and leadership adamancy at the bargaining table. As in Marshall's "scissors," the price (money wage) is determined by supply phenomena if the latter are perfectly elastic.

Analysis then can best start, as Keynes' did, with some prevailing $w(t_0)$ which is the current quantitative embodiment of past economic history, and all its twists: in this sense the theory is "institutionally" oriented. Thereafter, in face of the assaults and defense of union, management, and government attitudes and pressures, analysis must grapple with the system-wide repercussions of any $w(t_1) - w(t_0)$ discrepancy that comes to rule. The size of $\Delta w(t_1)$ tolls the inflation bell while the MA reaction, along with I and M^d behavioral patterns, will decide Q and N magnitudes.

---

* For further elaboration, see Chapter 10 below.

Some bitter-end resistance

Resistance to the exogenous money-wage postulate will come mainly from those who are either little-versed or well-trained in economic analysis. Both will face the distress of having to relinquish their preconception that demand and supply must be busy bees swarming in each labor-market hive.

While labor heterogeneity is implicit in these conceptions, our study has focused on the traditional homogeneous labor assumption or the fairly analogous case of a proportionate jump in w. Unfortunately for the faithful adherents of demand and supply conclusions, when the heterogeneity of labor is considered, their theories become even more wispy. They must still explain why, in each labor pocket, the money wage keeps advancing despite obvious unemployment within the sector or among outsiders beyond the gates but anxious to have work within them. For example, with many others wanting the jobs, the pay of government employees advances; the same is true for university professors, auto workers, construction employees, etc. Once we ask about the determinants of labor demand, the heterogeneity theory falters on the same bedrock diagnosed earlier; quickly we are back to either Phillips curves, derived demand, the MPT, or the like. The theory is hard to unglue.

It would be an act of theoretical heroism and acumen if the demand and supply holdouts would consider an across-the-board Δw, and explain how their old school tie explains the w to P tie, and the ascent of w under *growing* unemployment. Until a persuasive explanation is forthcoming the demand and supply appeal is merely a wish for a nonexistent logic. Future economists and economic policy would benefit from the explanation—if it could be fashioned rigorously.

The Misplaced Class Struggle

The WCM connection of $P = P(w, k, A)$ does rub against Marxian themes, especially the credo that every wage dispute represents another skirmish in the worker-capitalist class war. If the class struggle is the relentless issue, the war is fought over the wrong things in the wrong place and at wrong times. For insofar as $E_{pw} = 1$, a rise in w will fail to pull up real wages; it will only accomplish some intracapitalist income shift, from rent and interest recipients to entrepreneurial participants. After the smoke clears the only change is in P; labor wins nothing apart from injuring transfer recipients outside the GBP sector. More generally, so long as $k = \bar{k}$, despite the heat generated in collective bargaining, labor's real income is only enhanced by $(\Delta A/A)$, by productivity phenomena which largely (not entirely) go on unruffled despite labor's illusion that it is abetting its own real-income fortunes by grabbing off outsized pay increases. So long as k holds firm, only P is at stake, and not the wage share or real wages. While this conclusion pertains to the GBP sector, the real fortunes for transfer income recipients included within the PI (personal income) category may be impaired: a burden is

hrown on older and retired workers by the bellicosity over wrong means
xpressed by the younger, vigorous work force demanding higher w sym-
ools and escalating P skyward.

This analysis holds aggregatively. Nonetheless, within the wN (or W)
ggregate, some wage advances will outstrip the lot, and others will inevitably
un slower: there is thus always some income shuffle *within* the wage share.
This is the most palpable "class" victory celebrated by forays in the money-
wage race: the fight is an internecine war of labor against labor, rather than
abor against capital. Thus the Marxian prophets injure friends and foes
like.

Keynes perceived this a long time ago in the context of the Great Depres-
ion when the more obvious fact was the sectoral resistance to money-wage
uts. Keynes wrote (*General Theory*, pp. 13–14):

*. . though the struggle over money wages between individuals and groups is
ften believed to determine the general level of real wages, it is, in fact, con-
erned with a different object. Since . . . wages do not tend to an exact equality
f net advantages in different occupations, any . . . group . . . who consents
o a reduction of money wages relatively to others, will suffer a relative re-
luction in real wages which is a significant justification for them to resist it.
n other words, the struggle about money wages primarily affects the distri-
ution of the aggregate real wage (the real wage bill) between different labour
roups . . . . The effect of combination on the part of a group of workers is
o protect their relative real wage. The general level of real wages depends on
he other forces of the economic system.*

The assessment is no less true today than when Keynes wrote: the
ndustry- or occupational-union objective is to improve its relative position
n the income scale; "relativities" are being tested and broken as unions vie
ne with another. Only if a national labor organization bargained simultane-
usly for all labor, so that all wages moved proportionately, would the intra-
abor scuffle be avoided. Without unison in the *timing* of proportionate wage
argains, or some public policy compelling this outcome, labor-market anal-
sis must be a tale of group conflict and intralabor struggles. Whether a
niform wage advance would surpass annual ($\Delta A/A$) real norms (or arrest
eal-wage deterioration under natural-resource bottlenecks) hinges on k. A
ramatic turn in income shares will revolve about capitalist dexterity, ingenu-
ty, and political clout—or unprecedented generosity—when under assault.

Labor princes and paupers in conflict

here is hyperbole in the proposition that "all labor suffers in recession" and
n equating union strike militancy to a battle in the class struggle.

Surely, those who bear the scars of the depression ordeal are those who
re thrown on the unemployment pile. Only if *all* labor suffered job losses,
ay with work sharing and a collapsed workweek, would labor in general
e exposed to the recession shock. This partly happens as the duration of

unemployment per employee tends to fall evenly on employees. Concentrated unemployment, as was experienced in the construction and related industries in the United States over 1974–1977, victimizes a select group of employees in the systemic instability. Likewise, the Arab oil embargo severely hit workers in the automobile industry and in related sectors such as gas stations, motels, and supporting services. It is thus inflated rhetoric to consider all labor vulnerable in an economic downturn. It is, in fact, highly possible that those who remain employed may actually find their real income enhanced. In 1933, at the nadir of the Great Depression, those at work whose money wages were maintained while prices tumbled found their real-income fortunes improved. Their only hardships lay in their insecurity concerning where the job axe would hit next and in human sentiments of commiseration with friends and family frustrated by job losses.

Likewise, there are princes and paupers in the labor movement. Those who have more bargaining muscle as a result of vital economic placement and group militancy (and often political support) are able to stay ahead even during an inflationary sequel. Other labor groups are victimized by the aggressive hit-and-run tactics of other unions which distort relative wages. Again, labor versus labor is a more accurate description of the situation than Marxian class struggle. Ceaseless decentralized-command skirmishing among groups claiming to represent "the" worker not only aggravates the inflation predicament but damages erstwhile comrades.

Wage inflation under decentralized bargaining thus makes the normally disorderly bargaining process even more unruly. When most wage bargains are closed within the 3 to 5 percent per annum range, the spread of the "relativity fan" is constrained: inroads by one group eked out at the expense of another will be paltry. When some win annual increases of 25 percent, others 15, 10, or 5 percent, intralabor antagonisms will fester and the labor movement is likely to spoil for an intraclass fracas.

Considering the inherent clash of interests within decentralized labor, it is perhaps no accident that in economies beset by unemployment and inflation, and confronted by unconventional problems in terror weapons, terrorism, energy, ecology, urban chaos, inefficient transportation, discrimination, health, crime, and educational abandonment, a more *conservative* political tone has been brewing. Consider recent trends in the United States, Canada, the United Kingdom, Australia, and elsewhere. Part of this conservatism undoubtedly springs from the inflation disorder and an intuitive public awareness of output loss in the rash of strikes and exorbitant pay hikes which are an institutionalized invasion of real-income shares of other constituents.

The conservative bent is inherently a Marxian conclusion, premised on the protective-income mechanism which opposes change. The irony is that fate, in the form of interlabor group rivalry, has dismembered the Marxian monolithic class unity, utterly distorted simplistic political stances, and fostered intralabor class tensions. Victors and victims in inflation and unemployment become particularly hard to distinguish, leading to a fragmentation of political interests based on economic fortunes.

PART 3

Inflation Remedies: Income Gearing

Introduction: The Debut of Incomes Policy

Mindful of Mark Twain's wry observation on the weather, we spend much time in "analyzing" inflation, yet apart from rocking Q and N through futile, conventional remedies we do precious little about it. We wring our hands, we look properly grave, we consent to another turn of the monetary screw, and we solemnly denounce governmental largesse, monopoly opportunism, and maybe union bellicosity (some deplore its pusillanimous stance!). Yet a 30-year postwar history—to go back no farther—caricatures the ritualistic inbred faith in MA inflation deterrence: if monetary policy could have succeeded, the Fed long ago would have aborted inflation and gathered up the kudos of an eternally grateful population able to get on to other pressing problems of the age. To judge by the record, to put analytics aside, there is a 63-year history of wailing and flailing by the Fed, with each of its chairmen doggedly "fighting inflation," always proclaiming victory within grasp, seeing light at the end of the tunnel as the reward for vigilant steadfastness. Results disclose mainly an addiction to heroics in language as a refuge from perception as the economy has bathed in unemployment. Announcements of interest-rate freezes, defrosts, bills-only, twists, nudges, and money aggregates resemble superanimated cavalry officers chattering about another charge of the Light Brigade even as the battle has shifted to the air.

Unless we develop a new institutional strategy by way of Income Gearing we are doomed to a perpetual struggle with sometimes edging, sometimes zooming inflation. A nonmonetary plan must be drawn. Unlike the Fed, even a general staff would reconsider its weapons after so long, so spotted, and so unrewarding a P and N record.

Inflation is neither natural nor inevitable except to natural-law economic theologians who believe that events in the economic sphere are somehow predestined and beyond tampering, overlooking the part played by human behavior under prevailing institutions and the possible deflection of choices under altered institutional practices compatible with a substantially unrevised market economy. Most of our economic practices have evolved as technology and human events dictated; this is what business strategy and public policy are all about: to shape practices to new conditions as the interplay of relations warrants and ideological values condone. Surely, something has gone awry with respect to the price level, and it is this that must be corrected, rather than waiting, with Micawber, for some divine healing or staying with medicine that has proven so ineffective. Thought, allied with legislative sanction, should aim to hasten the stabilization process in democratic ways. Rationally, we must repair the control gap, while shelving a Monetarist stagflation solution. Economic policy must be extricated from its fetish of reliance on the MA as the inflation savior. Conveniently overlooked in the money dazzle is that P and Y (or w) are as tangled as a plate of spaghetti: it is money income that fixes the price fluff.

A malaise of capitalism?

Inflation, despite some obscurantist noise from the left, is not endemic to capitalism. This is a cultivated illusion, nurtured by the fact that dictatorial regimes can, with more impunity, mandate the wage and salary scales and simultaneously determine prices for consumer goods. Yet even dictatorial regimes are hampered in implementing onerous controls. Sporadic flare-ups in Poland and the Soviet Union attest to the need for some government sensitivity to public opinion lest a harsher turn of the real-income screw provoke a less manageable turbulence: sullenness is tolerable, mutiny is alarming. Inflation, however, can largely be suppressed by proscribing money incomes from the collectivist planning center.*

All money-income societies seeking price stability, whatever their organization in terms of property rights and production decisions—including the selection of industrial leaders and the scope for implementing decisions—must *gear Y to Q* so long as there is money "costing" of production accounts and market choice through money-income payouts representing generalized purchasing power. Any imbalance must mean rising price trends—or lengthening queues—when there is an ostrich-like refusal to synchronize money income and goods availability.

Democratic governments, abhorring totalitarian methods and relying on reason and the consent of the governed, must learn to achieve the same gen-

---

*   On inflation in the East bloc collectivist countries, see Michael Fogarty, "Fiscal Measures and Wage Settlements," in *Wage Determination* (OECD, 1974), Paris Conference, July 3–6, 1973.

eral ends of Income Gearing in ways compatible with their market economy and parliamentary framework. Methods must be oriented to the enterprise system operating within the customary rules of law. Only in obtuseness, diversionary sham, or studied error, can the inflation ordeal be assigned a status of systemic distinction contrasting socialism with capitalism. All money-income economies must wrestle with the balance of money incomes and available C-output. All economies *must* apply Incomes Policy, either deliberately or unconsciously, either aiming at the proper income equation for price steadiness or squirming before price eruptions by refusing to heed the imperatives of money-income discipline.

The refusal to shoal up the money-income factor in our stabilization technique has meant that P has been buffeted about by gusty Y and w winds. Our economies have suffered from "malign neglect." Enterprise societies must learn to close the income gap in "benign" ways to subdue the stagflation blight. Otherwise economic, social, and political disorders will be fitful, occasionally grave, and temporally incessant, with occasional respites in "livable," stable-price epochs.

Gearing Q and Y flows

The central proposition is that all economies must somehow gear money-income flows to production facts. In some idealization of the matter, assume an imaginary society charting its future production program. Assume also that it possesses the vital aggregative data on consumer desires to spend and to save, and that it was motivated to implement the information beneficently. Unknown are the purchase propensities of specific individuals, so there is scope for the use of money. Also, to simplify, assume that a social consensus prevails on the proper income distribution. Clearly, in projecting a steady $P(t)$ path, without queues and rationing, money income allotted per person (Y') could be augmented over time to accord with ΔA.

The hypothetical model presumes a *planned* gearing of Y' and A. A gearing process, imperfect and more calloused and casual toward consumer choice, already prevails in collectivist economies. The inflation plague mars those mixed-market economies which have overlooked the need for enforcing a money-income balance; sooner or later—and sooner as outsized money-income demands proliferate—market economies will have to devise measures compatible with their traditions to align w to A or Y' to A. The indirect monetary and fiscal subterfuges have been notorious price sieves, to judge by the statistics.

Realistically, wage negotiations lay the money-income foundations in the market economy, often with only a tenuous attachment to economy-wide productivity aspects. The battle of wits and wills shapes the lion's share of money incomes. One union's gains become a record to meet or beat in other settlements as each labor group vies to improve or protect its relative income standing. Negotiated wage trends spill over into nonunionized sectors and to government employees, as fairness concepts obtrude. Professional incomes, fed by the wage-salary purchasing-power enhancement, rise as if in emulation. Farmers report higher prices, and incomes, as the pay gains are pooled in buoyant market demand. Welfare claimants also assert their pleas for income rectification.

The money-income balloon can thus puff up far more than the limited productivity swell. Money income gains of 10, 15, 25 . . . percent per annum can become commonplace, although productivity only inches ahead in the 2–4 percent range.

The discrepancy between money income and productivity testifies to our relentless assault on the rules of reason and arithmetic. With the obstinate folly of those who pronounce that the world is flat, our policy-makers insist that the income-productivity mismatch can be conquered by conventional methods. We prize the obsession that despite the money income-output imbalance ΔP can be suppressed by fealty to ΔM stratagems.

Income Gearing

There is thus a paramount need for a conscious Incomes Policy to gear ΔY to ΔQ and allow monetary and fiscal policy to make their long-awaited contribution to the establishment of full employment without the policy timidity fostered by inflation fears.

An age of Incomes Policy must dawn. In the democratic societies the methods must be compatible with the prevailing concepts of freedom, cognizant of individuality and the rights of personal expression that do not trample the aspirations of others. The plan must be conformable with the market economy and protective of the spheres in which it is to be preserved and encouraged. The warden mentality of despotic police states, meting out jail sentences to nonconformists and replete with bureaucratic torpor, must be eschewed.

Too often the mere suggestion of Incomes Policy sparks a shopworn, ideological opposition to "controls," and "harassment" and a Patrick Henry-style pronouncement of defiance of an "abridgement of human rights," even before a concrete proposal is broached. Yet it is possible that the apoplectic responses are excessive inasmuch as they turn a deaf ear to the proposal to be submitted. Nothing to be advocated should in any way violate the democratic precepts and the maintenance of the entrenched market economy. The entire purpose of the specific Incomes Policy to be elaborated is to *sustain* the market system, to redeem it from its boom-bust cycle of despair or its stagflation mess. The end is salvation and retention: the entire thrust is thus conservative, for reform not replacement, in both intent and design.

Actually, it comes down to saving capitalism from its friends, the myopic apologists who see nothing wrong with it and thus obstruct measures to reduce its flaws and enhance its enduring status. For the inflation-unemployment cancer of modern-market economies must be eradicated if the system is to have a chance to survive in calm. With a flat P-trend, and reasonably full employment, it could best show its capacity for producing goods in abundance, without frustrating millions of job seekers, while relieving daily life of attendant inequities, anguish, and allocational irrationalities where even economic sophisticates do a poor job of anticipating the P-lurches or devising protective screens to shield their real position.

There will be some words on price and wage controls later. The general attitude toward them is distinctly negative: they smack of the jailer extending the list of venal crimes to cover voluntary agreements, and they are an incongruity in a democratic society and a market economy. They diminish individuals by transferring to government judgments that can best be resolved by personal agreements. They traduce Mill's precept of the learning experience from diffusing decisions to private hands when the possible margin of difference is small, at best or worst.* We should want to encourage a system that gives scope to spontaneous urges, the well-spring of freedom, rather than embracing bureaucratic rule, steeped in the custody of caution and "crimes against the state." Extensive controls must block the innovative spirit of individuality, and even of eccentricity, to deprive us of the riches of diversity and coloration of nonconformity as relief from humdrum monolithic monotony.† (To be sure, many of the same criticisms apply to the giant corporation. At the moment, however, the issue is inflation and price controls.)

Price and wage controls, replete with legalisms, dilatory bureaucrats, snoopers ferreting out price "crimes," and business harassment provide a stage for diversionary political posturing and a setting for pompous legal briefs; they must inevitably be busy with small potatoes. The program is born dwarfish, encumbered by legislative trivia concerning whether the agencies are to be comprised of 3, 5, 7 or . . . members, how political affiliation is to be rewarded, terms of appointment, whether there is to be a separate pay and price board, modes of enforcement, legal appeals, etc. Most of the dialogue is a cacophony of procedural noises unrelated to substantial w and P matters. Of course, the human maneuverings dish up delectable news tidbits on political meanderings, undergoing journalistic inflation as a report on one of the great struggles of human existence. Attention is riveted on small matters in national life, and distracted from large and novel issues.

---

* John Stuart Mill remarked that: "The business of life is an essential part of the practical education of a people." *Principles* (Ashley, ed.) pp. 948.

† Quoting Mill on "the ultimate form of human society," and the choice between private property or socialism: "the decision will probably depend mainly on one consideration, viz., which of the two systems is consistent with the greatest amount of human liberty and spontaneity." Ibid., p. 210.

Friedrich Hayek devotes considerable attention to this aspect in his welcome though overdrawn reminder opposing many ameliorative measures without which the unfettered market economy would lose adherents. The provocative matters concern the preservation of the vital core of the market system, viz., of product market, occupational, and input choices and not necessarily condoning and suffering its fringe disorders. See *The Road to Serfdom* (University of Chicago, 1944 edition).

These remarks are obviously disdainful of controls; they should comfort every ideologue who lives in mortal dread of government action—about anything. Nonetheless, controls have an *occasional* place. There is the adage that the best time to repair the roof is when the sun is shining. Thus when the time is ripe to institute a serious and durable Incomes Policy, temporary controls can fill the interlude. They can impart some breathing space to block an anticipatory overreaction until the more permanent method to hold the income line is enacted. In the interim they can abate further inflationary damage. Whether the controls are a wage and price *freeze*, penalizing any further advance, or a pause, allowing some upcreep is a judgment best appraised in the particular historical context.

In mid-August 1971, in the first of the Nixon Phases of price and wage controls, a 90-day freeze was ordered. Despite some prophecies of the imminent collapse of civilization, they seem to have "worked": economic life went on. A not unreasonable inference, however, is that the economy can stand practically anything for a short period, much like the human body under extraordinary tension. Nothing resembling the Nixon Phases, for any stretch of time, is advocated here.

A compatible Incomes Policy

It is suggested that a mode of Income Gearing compatible with the market economy is the proper objective. The proposal to be elaborated draws on the corporate tax mechanism to police Y and P restraint. To allay premature negativism, the purpose is *not* to collect tax revenue but to deter inflationary conduct. The plan can be likened to a posted speed limit where the objective is not to amass revenue but to outlaw suicidal road conduct threatening the life, limb, and property of others. If all of us drive sanely and cautiously, observing safe speeds, posted "rules of the road" need not be legislated. Because of noncompliance, voluntary observance has been superseded by mandatory restrictions on road speed.

Conceivably, it may be possible to secure voluntary incomes compliance without the coercive intervention of government. In the harmonious community, only a meeting of minds is necessary for social discipline: consensual democracy strives to realize the same type of community of interest. While results may be achieved by moral suasion, in a vast and complex society a policy must generally have legal sanction to command obedience. In smaller economies containing a handful of 5 to 10 labor unions (perhaps in the Scandinavian countries, or Israel, or like economies, where most of the dominant union and business leaders can be gathered in a small room), persuasion may yield a voluntary "Social Compact."* In the larger economy of the United Kingdom, reeling under high inflation, there has been much talk by the Labour

---

* And sometimes Social Contract—but this might be better reserved for its broader reference in political theory.

government of an entente whereby the labor movement would practice wage restraint in return for assurances of government pursuit of welfare-state programs. In the United States, too, there is frequent reference to the need for a Social Compact, less formal than law, to induce moderated wage and price conduct. Considering circumstances in the United States, it is naive to think that voluntary restraint can supplant legislative enactment.* The Kennedy Guideposts depended on moral suasion to slow the wage drift from 5 and 6 percent down to about 3 percent. But we are long past these low numbers and the economy may again cross the double-digit inflation zone. Social Compact, yes; but it will have to be legally enforced.

The foregoing remarks imply a variety of imaginable approaches to Income Gearing. We begin first with a method that promises compatibility with the market economy, designed to protect it from itself, its inflationary failings, and its unemployment byproducts. Thereafter, we consider some alternative modes of enforcing Incomes Policy. Before the close, the recent passion for indexing will be appraised.

---

* Early 1977 reports indicate the Carter administration is dusting off appeals for restraint, i.e., jaw-boning for its initial approach, although there is a studied refusal to use the words to a cynical audience.

CHAPTER SIX

A Tax-Based
Incomes Policy:
TIP-CAP

One promising approach to Income Gearing builds on the corporate income tax mechanism in a tax-based Incomes Policy (hereafter designated as TIP).* Only the major principles will be amplified; if the proposal is feasible tax administrators will know how to draft it for effective implementation. Just as a corporate income tax requires definitional safeguards to eliminate legal loopholes, TIP will have to be hedged by supplementary criteria to thwart abuses

---

* The TIP proposal—the Wallich-Weintraub plan—was developed jointly with Dr. Henry Wallich. See *KaM*, Chapter 6. My early version of TIP appeared in *Lloyds Bank Review* (Jan. 1971). Some variations to surmount some tricky obstacles are offered below. For evaluations of TIP, generally confirming the inflation-deterrent aspects, see Peter Isard, "The Effectiveness of Using the Tax System to Curb Inflationary Collective Bargains: An Analysis of the Wallich-Weintraub Plan," *Journal of Political Economy* (May 1974); Y. Kotowitz and R. Portes, "The 'Tax On Wage Increases,'" *Journal of Public Economics* (May 1974); Michael Fogarty, "Fiscal Measures and Wage Settlements," in *Wage Determination* (OECD, 1974, Conference Papers, Paris, July 3–6, 1973). Also, Lawrence S. Seidman, "A Microeconomic Approach to the Control of Inflation" (Philadelphia: University of Pennsylvania, October 1975) xerox.

Dr. Fogarty points out that a close parallel to TIP has been applied in Hungary, with relatively high success compared to other economies. (I might add that this was totally unknown to me at the time of my writing on the subject; letters after publication from Peter Wiles and Richard Portes informed me of the Hungarian experiment.) The article by Fogarty contains a good bibliography, and some analysis of several Incomes Policies, with the balance leaning toward TIP as "a workable basis." (p. 311)

and avenues of uneconomic resource use; it appears that the main provisions can be fairly straightforward without erecting an administrative nightmare.

Elements of a solution

The free-world economies are essentially incentive-deterrent systems which use the price mechanism to induce labor and capitalist-resource owners to cooperate in producing the goods and services wanted by the population. High prices relative to costs encourage specific production flows. Low price-cost ratios for individual products erect a deterrent, stifling outputs. (Note that the stress is on *relative* price-cost ratios, rather than the absolute levels conjured in discussions of inflation.)

Rather than emulating the methods of the collectivist societies which issue commands to "do it or else," free societies must combat inflation by replicating the *incentives* and *deterrents* of the price mechanism. An effective instrument is already at hand in the traditional tax powers; they need not be exercised in an onerous way, especially since revenue is *not* the objective. As in most good law, the tax regulations must allow *legal* circumvention to impart flexibility; evasion can be permitted—but at a price, in the manner of a traffic fine for conscious speeding, maybe under emergency contingencies. This notion of the normal "rule of the road" contains the moral that we must seek to apply.

What follows then is a new perspective, though not a new principle, of taxation. But the focus is innovative enough to transform the macroeconomic impacts of our tax system. Prior to the Great Depression it was not uncommon to view the cyclical trough as a "natural," inherently inescapable phenomenon. In conducting its financial affairs the Treasury usually aimed for a balanced budget. Taxes were envisaged as necessary to enable governments to acquire the resources for implementing their programs. Fealty to the balanced-budget dogma hampered recovery in the early 1930s by depriving the economy of constructive fiscal action to ameliorate the squeeze in job markets.

Revision in fiscal-policy precepts accompanied the Keynesian revolution. Budgetary policy has since veered toward shaping taxes and expenditures to attain high employment levels. Acting on the Keynesian insight, governments have largely succeeded in averting deep unemployment catastrophes since the Second World War, at least until the more recent exasperation over inflation. In some intellectual retreat and confusion, many are now sympathetic toward abandoning the N_f goal to hammer down inflation. Yet the Monetarist and fiscal-austerity antidotes have led to the fiasco of superimposing the indignity of lost jobs and the misery of lost income on the anguish of inflation, consummating the "stagflation" tangle.

The tax mechanism can furnish a viable alternative to the ineffectual and costly mess of monetary and fiscal orthodoxy once we apprehend the correspondence of taxes to price-cost relations. For example, favorable price-cost ratios dangle the profit carrot and unfavorable ratios wave the menacing stick, thus smiting the pocketbook rather than physically violating the person. To Adam Smith the carrot-stick price mechanism was the "invisible hand" impelling a rational use of resources without bureaucratic intervention or tyranny. Avoidable taxes possess the same dual nature: firms will avert actions that magnify the corporate tax burden, thereby avoiding the stick; and they will undertake market actions that minimize the tax toll, thereby seeking the carrot (posttax income). Tax literature is replete with incentive-deterrent ramifications of personal and corporate income taxes.

Taxes are a pervasive and commonplace part of our democratic order where individuals work out their own life patterns in jobs and purchases under the protection of known laws designed (imperfectly, to be sure) to benefit the community at large. An Incomes Policy enforced through the tax mechanism can thus be compatible with a market economy and the broader attributes of freedom.

Ingredients of a Solution

Using the tax mechanism to accomplish Incomes Policy can therefore harmonize with the market economy in an evolutionary fashion while pursuing the "revolutionary" ideal of an inflation-free, full-employment economy. Before sketching the details, we consider first some emotional tirades that are apt to be provoked when any program breaks with tradition and renounces the stereotyped posturing of labor and management in vying for public support.

Antiinflation, not antilabor

In the economic arena, big gains are rarely achieved without some pain. Whenever our conventional modes are altered some group will feel aggrieved. Reforms, however, are inevitable, and can be sanctioned whenever they are consistent with democratic principles and in conformity with the market system blend of private and government action. Wage earners surely would be better served by measures designed to promote a stable price level and full employment. For the United States, especially, its ability to live and inspire emulation of its successes in the world economy in competition with the Soviets would be enhanced. The ends of reduced inflation and full employment can never be seriously construed as antilabor or anticapitalist when they promise to stop attendant job disorders and augment real income.

Some contend that inflation will not abate unless unions are either destroyed or so fragmented as to sap them of their bargaining power. This is an extremist, partisan attitude certain to generate heated—and irrelevant—debate. Unions are here to stay. There is no way of eliminating them in a democracy. Most people will view this as a good and healthy manifestation of a free society; well-run unions, and even some not so well run, accomplish many worthwhile purposes. They are the counterweight to the unbridled economic power of industry. Few can in good conscience lament the passage of the age that gave credence to the prediction of Karl Marx on capitalism's demise. Unions have literally saved capitalism from its own crudities; it is no accident that union leaders are often more stalwart champions of freedom and the enterprise system than are some unreconciled capitalists who flirt with political charlatans in support of ventures inimical to even their own class and freedom.*

Stiffening resistance

Nevertheless, it is with the unhampered power of unions to eke out excessive wage settlements that we must deal. Individual business firms are too often impotent to neutralize the ability of unions to impose inflationary settlements, even when these settlements are to the disadvantage of other wage earners as all seek to protect their own position by making counterclaims for wage increases. The upshot is that all are penalized by the ensuing general inflation. All run faster to stay pretty much in the same relative place.

The solution must consist of measures to stiffen the backbone of industrialists. Currently, industrialists are prone to settle rather than endure costly strikes; the ritual involves first protest, then submission to union pressure, then passing the bill on in the form of higher prices. Each is trapped in the jungle of inflation because others have been caged there before. None can be blamed for the plight, yet everyone is culpable for the outcome.

Individual businesses will be encouraged to resist unreasonable demands only when they are convinced that there will be resistance in other firms and industries. Also, when each labor union understands that employers are no longer easy targets who will just pass on price increases to consumers to rescue themselves from extravagant settlements, unions can be expected to become less demanding at the bargaining table. The hapless sitting-duck image of management officials must be erased before any plan can succeed as a defense against inflation.

Hence, we must change matters so that it is in their self-interest, their own preservation, for industrialists to reject inflationary wage settlements. Penalties must be attached to abject surrender. Also, if defeat does come, it will be only partial; the terms of surrender *must not* be *too* onerous. Partial cave-ins and prudent compromise must thereby contain some safety-valve to avert a chain reaction and a business collapse; neither bankruptcy nor punitive levies should be engendered. But the price of submission must be made high enough to dissuade management from easy surrender.

---

* There is the cynical attribution to Lenin that "on the day of the revolution" capitalists will sell the collectivists the rope for their own hanging.

Policing the program

The assignment for policing the program and enforcing the Incomes Policy would thus be handed to the business corporations, but relieved of any aid and comfort to the adamant union "busters" who would attack labor head-on. Inevitably, the latter sequel would rear the ugly conflict of "capital" versus "labor," with all sorts of extraneous, divisive, and disruptive rhetoric, most of it hackneyed and without bearing on the virus of inflation. Price-level stability is the issue, not socialism versus capitalism, nor class warfare and antagonistic bitterness. It is silly to pretend that if only ownership and control rights were abrogated inflation would be dispelled. Conflicts over income distribution and resource organization must be resolved on other grounds after weighing the social, economic, and political ramifications. To inject the abstractions of social systems into the inflation analysis serves only to confuse and deflect resolution rather than to enlighten understanding in order to eradicate the blight.

Reasonable wage-salary norms

Rather than individual incomes, it would be the *average* increase of wages and salaries, or of all incomes generally, that would be the concern of an antiinflation Incomes Policy. The key word is *average*; some individual incomes might advance faster and others slower. The aim would be to contain increases in money wages, on the average, to the gains in average labor productivity in the economy which, in the past, have tended to approximate 3 percent a year. With little inflationary cost, an average increase of 3 percent or so, or even of 4 to 5 percent a year, could be ceded without inviting a corrosive price bulge. For calculating ease, we will assume a 5 percent pay gain as a reasonable Incomes Policy norm.*

An average increase of 4 percent would mean that in ten years the *typical* wage income would mount by nearly 50 percent. All wage incomes would, on average, double in about eighteen years; prices might mount at a pace of 0.5 to 1 percent a year. An average annual gain of 5 percent in wages would mean wages doubling every fourteen years. Price trends would build up at a rate of about 2 percent a year. Either pace would protect labor, and the economy, from the explosive events of recent years; rational economic life-planning could proceed without the complications of erratic price upheavals. With the P nearly steady, monetary and fiscal policy could drop their abortive antiinflationary defensive stance and the economy could be led closer to full employment.

Thus there are real advantages to an average wage climb of 4 to 5 percent per annum. It would add up to be a prolabor, probusiness program.

---

* My own preference would be for 3 percent—though I would compromise at 5 percent.

A Corporate Tax on Excessive Wage Settlements: TIP

We consider now the broad principles of a plan to curb excessive pay boosts by placing the policing responsibility by means of a tax onus on offending corporations.

The principle and an illustration

The business corporation is always acutely conscious of the corporate tax bite. Posttax profits, after all, are the measure of its market success. A penalty tax could well dissuade firms from acquiescing in inflationary wage-salary concessions: an added tax on corporate income could be imposed whenever, say, *average* annual pay boosts were granted in excess of a norm of, say, 5 percent. The tax impost could be stepped progressively according to the degree of violation.

An illustration can clarify the idea. Suppose the firm's income tax amounted to $5,000,000. Based on its data on the number of employees and its wage and salary bill, the firm would be obliged to compute its *average* wage-salary payment. Suppose this came to $7,500 in 1975 and to $7,875 in 1976, denoting exactly a 5 percent annual increase. No further tax levy beyond the normal $5,000,000 due would be invoked. Suppose, however, that its average pay boost was 10 percent, amounting to $8,250. The firm might then be subject to 10 percent more taxes, or $5,500,000; a 55 percent, rather than a hypothetical 50 percent corporate tax rate would apply.

More will be said about the size and progressiveness of the penalty rate. What should be noted is that the tax base would carry an added dimension: the usual tax on profits would be supplemented by a superimposed levy determined by the firm's inflationary pay behavior compared to the general norm.

Protests that the firm's actions are not inflationary if it has not raised prices may be anticipated. Clearly, the counterargument is that if it had observed the economy-wide pay norm it may have been able to cut prices as a result of its superior cost-reduction productivity improvement. By and large, an optimal price mechanism would report prices holding constant in stationary productivity sectors, rising for industries under declining productivity, and falling in the progressive area of the industrial system. If pay boosts were tied solely to productivity within the industry or firm, the pay scale would very quickly run berserk with arbitrary and discriminatory outbreaks, with earnings generally detached from skills, and a matter of luck and chance in being located in industry sectors where progress was speedy. Earnings, for example, for pumping gas into airplanes would shoot up by 10 percent per annum and be stagnant at the local garage. The entire wage structure would become distorted; equity standards would be shattered, with vociferous dissents. A fair wage policy must aim at equal pay for commensurate skills as assessed in the market.

Definition and coverage

Administratively, compared to wage and price controls, the simplicity of TIP commends it; it demands only a few more tax calculations by the firm and which are already contained in the wage bill and employment data which it reports on income tax statements and on payroll tax withholding forms. For the Internal Revenue Service the TIP proposal carries only some review of a few extra lines in a tax audit. Very few additional government employees need to be engaged. Coercion and court hassles should be minimized. Also, for the firm in appraising its particular circumstances, pay norms can be abrogated—at a price. Just as the speed limit can be flouted (as under emergency conditions but at a penalty), the firm can likewise surpass the stipulated average pay ceiling. This "safety-valve" adjunct is a valuable, properly inviolable, aspect of a judicious system of laws which must accommodate diverse special round pegs that can be squeezed only awkwardly into square pigeon-holes.

For the first tryout, undertaken tentatively to garner experience, TIP might be limited to a list of the 1,000 largest firms in the economy, with the size of firms defined either in sales volume or employment, with the latter presumably the best reference point. The 1,000 largest employers would constitute a substantial portion of GBP.

In computing the average wage-salary figure, the wage bill would include the total wages, salaries, bonuses, fringes, and related payments customarily identified in calculating business wage costs for corporate tax purposes. To derive the pay average, and thereafter the annual increase, may be a trace more formidable. Tallying merely the numbers reported for tax purposes might open the door to some fudging: to limit the average increase the firm might engage more part-time employees, lowering the computed average pay scale. A definition of "full-time" employees, and "full-time equivalents," would be requisite with, say, ten employees working three days per week counted as six full-time employees. As an initial hurdle, some thought would have to be given to part-time and full-time employee classification with manifold possible resolutions.

Consultants, hired on a daily or job basis, could obscure the average pay results. As independent contractors, their compensation might be separated from the wage-salary aggregate, and their number dropped from the employee category. The figures might be subject to a special rule if experience reveals some distortion on the score of inflation or equity. While the ordinary progressive personal income tax would capture excess income gains, for the special instances any rule is likely to be imperfect, to be tested, improved, or abandoned, in the crucible of pragmatism. At the moment the search must not be for a policy to cover all contingencies, but one that meets the pressing need. The philosophic divining rod tapping for an "ideal" slate could be the enemy of a "good" solution.

A weighted average job classification

Legal evasion, and some uneconomic resource use, could also spring from reliance on the computation of a simple pay average for 1976 compared with 1975. For example, if a firm hired another $100,000 vice-president the boost in *average* pay might jeopardize its tax status; likewise, if the top officer was granted a $250,000 bonus. The firm would come under tax pressure to add unskilled employees in income brackets below its average pay scale. Using our earlier illustration of a prospective tax penalty of $500,000, the sum could be expended on 100 employees at $5,000 per annum for menial services to camouflage the reported "average" increase.

In some circumstances this absorption of "unskilled" marginal labor can be viewed with equanimity: jobs would be provided which may be less wasteful than having the same 100 people unemployed. Under fuller employment, and envisaging an optimal rather than the actual underemployment economy, the behavior can be a wasteful and frivolous distortion induced by TIP.

Yet Lawrence Seidman has argued that this distortion may be less ominous than it appears to be at first sight: it would be a valid objection if TIP were merely a one-year impost. With TIP serving as a durable tax adjunct, "wasteful" labor hire would continue on the payroll into the next year when, presumably, neither a new executive would be hired nor would the top officers add generously to their own pay. Thus the average pay jump will be better contained, relieved of a TIP-tax penalty: if the firm tried to release its wasteful labor hire, it would be subject to tax. Avoiding the tax would thus involve condoning excessive wage costs. In the long view, then, a profit-maximizing firm would be unlikely to resort to the tax escape hatch now for it would merely postpone tax or profit penalties to the future.*

On the assumption of deeper validity to this tax dodge (which I also held originally) to clog the escape route Dr. Wallich (formerly Professor at Yale University and now a U.S. Federal Reserve Governor) conjectured the calculation of a *weighted* average pay rate. Conceivably, the firm would be required to classify employees as: A—managerial and executive, B—clerical and staff, and C—production. The average pay for successive years for each group could be computed, and the weight attached would come from the number of employees in each group as a ratio of the total number in the base year. The sum

---

* Seidman, "A Microeconomic Approach." It is the microanalogies of Seidman, who likens TIP to a tax on pollution, that have led Professor A. P. Lerner to favor the proposal in the light of the need and in lieu of the lack of feasible alternatives. See his "From Pre-Keynes to Post-Keynes," (mimeo, March 1977).

of the weighted pay averages would yield a comparative value for the annual pay changes.*

Inserting a weighted average may push the proposal over the brink from pristine simplicity to uncivil complexity. Disputes over weights and classification could become contentious and interminable, impairing the constructive aspects of the TIP program, and relegating it to the "long-run" sphere of infinite academic conjecture rather than practical application.

There may be an easy way out to preserve the logic of the weighting principle. Resolution will be facilitated by recalling its purpose—to limit legal evasion of a penalty tax through hiring redundant labor at pay scales below the firm's prospective penalty average.

Value added per employee

One simple resolution would direct the firm to compute the net value added per (full-time equivalent) employee. That is, the firm would deduct the cost of materials purchased from suppliers from its sales proceeds. Then, net sales (= value added) would be divided by the number of employees. If this dollar figure *rose*, while the firm's average pay hike remained within the permissible (5 percent) norm, the firm would be exempt from the TIP.

If the calculated value added per employee (hereafter AP) fell, the firm would be subject to tax. To derive its tax liability the firm would be required to compute its average pay on the hypothesis that a *smaller* number of employees—derived by assuming the former AP prevailed—was actually used. To illustrate, if value added per employee *fell* from $20,000 to $18,000, the number of *effective* employees would be reduced by 10 percent ($20,000 − $18,000 divided by $20,000) for purposes of computing the average annual pay boost and TIP liability.

---

* A simple illustration may clarify the concept of a weighted average. We assume labor classes A, B, and C.

	(1) Wage bill	(2) Numbers	(3) Average pay	(4) Weights (Number of employees to total employees)
A	$ 20,000,000	1,000	$20,000	1/16
B	40,000,000	5,000	8,000	5/16
C	100,000,000	10,000	10,000	10/16
Totals	$160,000,000	16,000	3 ÷ $38,000 = $13,000 approx.	

Unweighted average: $160,000,000 ÷ 16,000 = $10,000
Weighted average: (3) × (4)   = $10,000

Note: In subsequent years, despite relative shifts in the A, B, and C numbers, the same weights would apply so that the weighted and unweighted averages would differ.

Utilizing the concept of "net value of sales per employee" as a presumptive test to ban legal tax-dodging through redundant labor hire would seem to derive sustenance from economic analysis. Not only would the AP calculation tend to mitigate some conceivable wasteful employment abuses, but it also duplicates the results of a progressive growth economy in which employee output improves per annum. If output per employee is generally declining, standards of living are doomed to fall. The supplementary value-added calculation would go far to preserve the simpler TIP version involving a direct annual pay average; the required computation of a second simple average (of net sales* per employee) is a minor complexity which possesses the virtue of applying pressure on firms to maintain at least their previous standards of efficiency. Failing to pass the latter test, they are likely to deliberate more finely before granting excessive executive self-compensation.

Other variants for calculating changes in employee productivity to discourage TIP evasion may be forthcoming. Joining AP to TIP can thus block a potential source of economic mischief without the bog of controversy over a "proper" weighted average. Using the AP concept the simplicity of TIP is preserved and, simultaneously, economic efficiency is promoted or, at least, unconscionable inefficiency is discouraged rather than rewarded.

A deflated AP:CAP

Matters are not yet complete; there is added complication caused by inflation that poses a problem requiring remedy.

If the price level and the reporting firm's prices were stable the direct AP computation would suffice. Conversely, in an inflationary environment where prices rose by 5 percent or more the AP would almost certainly climb regardless of superfluous labor hire. "Value-added in constant dollars" is the obvious answer; that is, sales prices of 1976 would have to be reduced to a 1975 price equivalence.

Considering the delay in the published price statistics, the firm could be required to *deflate* its sales figures by resort to the general GNP deflator, or consumer price index, or any accepted index of prices for particular industries, using the price data for a twelve-month (or annual) period in any fifteen months *preceding* the tax fiscal year. To illustrate, if the tax return covers July 1, 1975 to June 30, 1976, and is submitted (say) in August, the firm's accountants would either use price indexes covering the report period, if available, or an index for twelve months running anywhere in the period April 1, 1975 to July 1, 1976. The leeway would ensure availability of reasonable price indexes.

---

* As productivity is the objective, the sales or operating revenue would also include any increase in inventories (valued at market prices) or impose a deduction from revenues of inventory decreases. Definitionally, these matters should not pose major new problems despite some imprecision in accounting methods; small imperfections are not a substantial drawback to the thrust of the computation when performed consistently over time.

Thus if, on the index chosen, prices averaged 8 percent higher, the firm would deflate its total sales figures to 92 percent of the reported value to derive a "corrected" or deflated AP (hereafter CAP). Thereafter, if the deflated CAP showed an *increase* the firm's direct calculation of its average wage-salary for TIP purposes would be entered: further computations would cease. If CAP revealed a productivity relapse, carrying a presumptive design of wasteful hire with intent to escape the TIP tax penalty, the firm would have to recalculate its average wage-salary on the assumption that its employee real productivity was constant, and that its use of labor per dollar of deflated sales held up unchanged from year to year. Its average wage increase would then be computed on the basis of its wage bill divided by the fewer employees for its sales volume disclosed by CAP.

CAP and upgrading skills

A continued TIP-CAP mechanism should also stimulate productivity improvements and technological gains which often require an upgrading of personnel skills: rather than merely forestalling productivity retreat or relapse, TIP-CAP can foster an advance in labor efficiency. For just as TIP alone might encourage inefficiency through redundant labor hire, it might carry the onus of obstructing some technological progress.

An illustration will lend concreteness. A firm may contemplate replacing thirty payroll or office clerks, at $8,000 each per annum, by ten computer programmers at $16,000 per annum. Or it may be shifting its product mix to more capital-intensive items. Innumerable prospects for raising the capital-labor ratio to higher paid, higher skilled employees can be envisaged as in motion in the world of fact.

An undiluted TIP would undoubtedly place an extra tax burden on the firm, at least in the first year or two when it altered its technological plant requiring personnel upgrading. TIP would not usually prevent the change but the TIP tax might defer the date of highest profit a year or so inasmuch as the TIP penalty tax would pertain only in the transition years when lower paid employees were replaced by higher skilled people. Surely TIP cannot be tarred by a blanket indictment of "blocking" technological change; mainly, it would alter the time pattern of after-tax profit accrued by the year or two during which staff skills were reshuffled.

Even this (probably) minor source of obstruction of technological improvement could be allayed, either partially or totally. Considering the less inflationary environment and more stable high employment, the economic balance should swing to more, and more rapid, technological modernization. More directly, in computing CAP, the firm would perceive its prospective real-output growth. Suppose it estimates a CAP or deflated value-added growth of 10 percent between 1975 and 1976 while the economy-wide average approximates a 3 percent swing. Then to encourage industries of superior productivity, it might be feasible to permit the firm to surpass the basic TIP 5 percent average pay norm for wage-salary increments by a permissive sweetener of 1 percent for every 3 percent superior showing in CAP.

Thus if in a particular firm CAP grew by 9 percent, as compared to a "normal" economy-wide figure of 3 percent, the extra 6 percent improvement could allow the firm to reward its employees with an average pay increase of 2 percent above the 5 percent norm: an average pay boost of 7 percent would be free of the TIP impost.

The prospect of tying minor extra wage gains to superior productivity might tap a welcome nerve by alerting employees to their stake in trimming operating costs, injecting a pecuniary reason to discard defensive work rules which impede the orderly cost reductions which remain the key to higher living standards.

The TIP tax schedule

For the first year or two, the inception of TIP might be relieved of the CAP calculation. For, insofar as there is unemployment, the absorption of the lower skilled labor might be less costly than the support of idle labor by unemployment compensation. Likewise, monetary and fiscal policy could render the climate propitious for investment. Over the longer term the CAP aspects would be commended as a TIP supplement. (Under stable prices AP = CAP.)

The computational steps necessary to establish the TIP-CAP wage-salary changes subject to penalty might be enumerated.

TIP computational steps

1 The firm would first calculate its average wage-salary in 1975 and 1976 by dividing its total wage-salary bill by the number of employees, with each aggregate suitably defined.

While past trends suggest that to stabilize the price level the annual average wage-salary advance would approximate 3 percent, we shall use an illustrative norm of 5 percent, although this will usually propagate a 2 to 3 percent inflation per annum.

2 If the firm reported its average pay hike under (1) as being of the order of 5 percent or less, the presumption would be that the firm was conforming to the noninflationary pay norm.

As proof of compliance, the firm would have to demonstrate that efficiency was not sacrificed, or that it did not resort to inefficient labor hire practices to evade, legally, the TIP rate schedule. Thus it would have to submit a CAP computation.

3 By deducting the cost of materials from its operating revenues in, say, 1975 and 1976, the firm would ascertain its undeflated "value-added." Correcting the 1976 figure for the price-level change would yield comparable deflated value-added totals. By dividing the latter by the number of employees in the respective years the CAP 1976 statistic would result.

a) So long as CAP 1976 exceeded AP 1975, and so long as the firm's average pay boost was 5 percent or less, it would be relieved of all TIP liability.

b) If the CAP 1976 was *less* than the AP 1975, the presumption is of labor-hire inefficiency. It would then be necessary for the firm to recalculate its average pay hike of 1976 on the assumption that it used the same number of employees per dollar of deflated sales in 1976 as in 1975. Thus if in 1976 the CAP was 10 percent below 1975 the number of employees in 1976 would be reduced by 10 percent in calculating the average pay increase. Tax vulnerability under TIP would thus emerge.

4 If the average pay hike over the two years exceeded 5 percent the firm could still be relieved of tax liability under TIP.

a) CAP would be calculated. So long as the CAP 1976 exceeded AP 1975 by more than 3 percent, the firm could be permitted some leeway in calculating its TIP liability.

b) For example, if CAP growth was 7 percent, compared to a normal 3 percent, the excess 4 percent could qualify for some TIP relief as a reward for efficiency.

1) One-third the gain, or ⅓ of 4 percent (= 1.3 percent), could be added on to the permissible pay hike of 5 percent. The particular firm would be able to regard an average pay increase of 6.3 percent (or less) as immune from TIP. Only if its average pay hike exceeded 6.3 percent would it be subject to a TIP penalty tax.

Limited complexity

At first reading, the CAP addendum impairs the unique charm of a child's TIP exercise. But the supplemental CAP calculations are themselves elementary: the alternative still remains one of either: (1) inflation, (2) a more permanently depressed economy, reduced profits, or (3) wage and price controls.

It has been suggested that the CAP features could be postponed for a year or two. Further, TIP would apply to only the largest 1,000 employers. On this perspective, with the calculations confined to a narrow group of firms hiring certified accountants, there appears nothing in TIP-CAP that transcends the comprehension of commonsense accounting skills. If TIP were applied to more firms, small as well as large, the CAP feature could be reserved (at least for several years) to pertain only to the very largest businesses.

The TIP-CAP tax schedule

After establishing the tax base subject to tax penalty—or relief—the thorny issue of the tax schedule instantly obtrudes. Before tackling this, we might consider the connection between wage increases and corporate profits for it is in these magnitudes that we should find the clue to tax rates that will prove light or heavy, onerous or incidental.

Arguments run both ways, for lenient as against oppressive TIP tax rates. Leniency, at least for small transgressions, conforms to the legal principle of light punishment for minor offenses. Militating against this is the cutting edge of harshness as a strong deterrent. While the best argument for a light tax blow lies in TIP's novelty, a heavy tax hand draws sustenance from the imperative to stop inflation. At this juncture, the latter consideration might be deemed paramount. On either appraisal, analysis can point up the relations with which the rate schedule will have to wrestle.

Profits and wage increases

In an inflationary era, if the profit growth lags money incomes generally, profit recipients will have good reason to strive to restore the normal balance or remain spectators at their income demise. Consider the explicit profit (R) relations:

$$R = PQ - wN = \pi PQ, \tag{6.1}$$
$$(\Delta R/R) = (\Delta P/P) + (\Delta Q/Q) + (\Delta \pi/\pi). \tag{6.2}$$

The relative change in profits thus involves relative changes in the profit share $\Delta \pi$, prices, and output. If $\Delta \pi = 0$ (or $\Delta k = 0$) $= \Delta Q$, the P and R rise will be proportionate. Likewise, if the relative P and w rise match, then:

$$(\Delta R/R) = (\Delta P/P) = (\Delta w/w), \tag{6.3}$$

if $\Delta k = \Delta Q = \Delta N = 0$.

To suppose these relations hold is tantamount to the supposition that Q, A, and π are unaffected by the w and P bounces. After all, this *is* the tacit assumption of those who hold that "real" phenomena are settled in the "Walrasian" real sector and dependent wholly on relative price phenomena.*

---

*   If we consider $\Delta N > 0$, the approximation loses the term $(\Delta N/N)$ thus:

a) $R = kwN - wN = wN(k - 1)$

b) $\Delta R = (w\Delta N + N\Delta w)(k - 1) + wN\Delta k$

c) $\dfrac{\Delta R}{kwN} = \dfrac{1}{k}\left(\dfrac{\Delta N}{N} + \dfrac{\Delta w}{w}\right)(k - 1) + \dfrac{\Delta k}{k}$

d) $\dfrac{\pi \Delta R}{R} = \dfrac{1}{k}\left(\dfrac{\Delta N}{N} + \dfrac{\Delta w}{w}\right)(k - 1) + \dfrac{\Delta k}{k}$

e) $\dfrac{\Delta R}{R} = \dfrac{\omega}{\pi}\left(\dfrac{\Delta N}{N} + \dfrac{\Delta w}{w}\right)\left(\dfrac{\pi}{\omega}\right) + \dfrac{\Delta k}{\pi k}$, where $\omega = 1/k$, or the wage share

f) $\dfrac{\Delta R}{R} = \left(\dfrac{\Delta N}{N} + \dfrac{\Delta w}{w}\right) + \dfrac{\Delta k}{\pi k} = \dfrac{\Delta N}{N} + \dfrac{\Delta w}{w} + \dfrac{\omega \Delta k}{\pi}$

Thus with $\Delta k = 0$, the profit share in an employment advance matches the relative wage and employment growth. As in the labor theory of value, the profits growth depends on the growth in labor hire: with $\Delta w = 0$, employment levels (with $\Delta k = 0$) determine the profit magnitudes. Allowing for $\Delta k \lessgtr 0$, and $\omega \simeq \pi$, changes in Δk affect the profit position. For TIP calculations positing $(\Delta R/R) = (\Delta w/w)$ is not unreasonable though it probably understates the profit growth. A steeper TIP schedule would overcome this omission.

If we write $N = N(Q)$, and $Q = Q(I)$, where $I =$ investment, then the implicit assumptions of theories which stress the dependence of profit levels on investment become apparent.

In applying the TIP rate schedule on these suppositions (of k constant), the pre- and posttax profit *share* after the wage hike is constant. As absolute aggregate profits, however, are higher ($\Delta R > 0$), so long as the capital stock has not grown proportionately the average profit rate will be higher. To impose a TIP tax penalty to stifle the growth in *absolute* profits (i.e., for $\Delta R = 0$) for the totality of business firms, we can work through on the supposition that Eq. (6.4) is valid. Thus we require:

$$(1 - T - \Delta T)\,(R + \Delta R) = (1 - T)\,R, \qquad (6.4a)$$

where T = corporate tax rate

$$\frac{\Delta R}{R} = \frac{T'}{T'_2} - 1 = \frac{\Delta T'}{T'_2} \qquad (6.4b)$$

where $T' = (1 - T)$ = income retention rate, T'_2 = retention rates originally applied to R and $R + \Delta R$, with $T'_1 > T'_2$.

According to Eq. (6.4), if profits rise (before taxes) by 4 percent because of a 4 percent hike in w and P, TIP will have to escalate the corporate tax rate up by approximately 4 percent. Thus:

$$(\Delta R/R) = (\Delta T)(1 - T - \Delta T) = (\Delta T/T'_2). \qquad (6.5)$$

From the relation between w and R, given the desired stiffness intended for TIP, the normal corporate income tax (T) and the TIP surtax (ΔT) can be combined schematically:*

Normal Corporate Tax plus TIP:

$$(T + \Delta T) = T + a[(\Delta w/w) - (\Delta w^*/w)], \qquad (6.6)$$

where $(\Delta w^*/w)$ = guidepost norm (say 5 percent).

Thus if $(\Delta w/w) = 7$ percent, and $(\Delta w^*/w) = 5$ percent, by setting the coefficient $a = 1$, the TIP surtax would be 2 percent for a 48 percent tax bite, assuming 46 percent as normal corporate tax rate. Judged in severity, a TIP schedule of $a > 1$ will lean to the onerous, and $a < 1$ will inflict a diluted blow.

Surtax on immediate or highest past profits?

Opinions will differ on a proper setting of a or on a scale of progression for a, depending on judgments concerning the wisdom of moderation in enacting a novel tax measure, against the conviction of a need to strike a peremptory warning against inflation. A compromise might envisage low TIP rates for 1 to 3 percent wage transgressions over the 5 percent threshold, with steep progressivity for average corporate pay boosts over 8 percent per annum.

Some firms with low current-year profits, but with large past and prospective profits, might be ripe candidates to be victimized by wage and salary raids far beyond the 5 percent target, for the TIP surtax on them would be

---

* This mode of expression has been suggested by Seidman.

(practically) nil. To close this angle of egress to defeat the program, the TIP surcharge might be levied on the *highest* pretax profit of the last three (or five) years. This should erect a sufficient barrier to block union concentration on firms whose immediate profits and tax liability would not be hindered by a TIP levy on current profits.

Shifting the TIP Surtax

The theory on whether the corporate income tax is, or is not, shifted is one of the more amorphous topics in economics. At most, there is imperfect and incomplete shifting.* Gauged by a profit-maximizing hypothesis, in either a competitive or a monopoly framework, tax shifting is precluded outside the nebulous "long-run" context. Even under the long-run mystique, if TIP fostered a flatter P-trend, higher Q through higher N and lower interest rates, the long-run thrust of tax shifting through restricted capital formation as the vehicle would be suspect.

Shifting is most plausible in a situation of unexploited monopoly power where a firm, or an oligopoly cluster of firms, have for a variety of reasons acted to pursue "fair" or "satisfactory," rather than maximum, profit goals. The possible inroads of TIP in reducing after-tax income through poking through the pay norms might provide a convenient opportunity for lifting prices while maintaining a stable posttax profit. This case provides the best scenario for the shifting thesis.

Still, the conclusion should not be pressed too far. As the TIP surtax is not a universal impost, firms who are subject to it will face competition by firms either fully immune or only mildly vulnerable to TIP. Imports will also open competitive doors. As other firms contain their wage costs to escape the TIP penalty, more competitive market forces will be brought into play.

Ultimately, the degree of tax shifting revolves around the rate schedule. Positing complete shifting regardless of the rate is based on a view that firms would fare as well in posttax profits under a corporate income tax as they would on its abolition. This would make it a painless tax! Nobody can really believe that firms taxed at 100 percent rates would be equally as profitable as at a zero levy.

Corporate alarms of steeper tax rates probably derive from the facts and fears of profit compression rather than from theories which presume limitless latent monopoly power in each firm. Conceding only *partial* shifting, a higher a-coefficient in the TIP surtax schedule would rack up an urgent profit squeeze to halt abnormal average pay jumps. With the ordinary corporate income tax at 46 percent, a surtax would deliver a cogent message to intrepid firms defying the pay norms.

---

* Cf. L. Seidman, "Tax Shifting and TIP" (Philadelphia: *University of Pennsylvania*, Xerox, 1976).

Tax shifting: a once-over phenomenon

Suppose that with *full* shifting TIP drove the corporate tax up by 5 to 10 percent and prices rose proportionately. Manifestly, this would be a "once-over," one-shot price bulge. Once the higher tax rates prevailed over time, subsequent price increases could not be assigned to TIP. Better wage behavior over time would lower the tax penalty and, on shifting arguments, reduce prices for the two reasons: (1) a lower TIP rate, and (2) a restrained wage pace.

With incomplete shifting, say of one-half the TIP surtax, or of a 1 percent price rise for every 2 percent increase in taxes, the TIP penalty should induce wage restraint. Even a 5 percent "one-shot" price rise—an excessive estimate, to be sure—would be minimal if TIP checked money wages by 2 percent *each* year. Over a ten-year period, the 22 percent price containment would vastly counterbalance the 5 percent TIP price boost, chopping 17 percent off the higher ranges of the price ladder.

The shifting argument is less devastating than critics pretend. *If normal tax rates were initially lowered to counteract prospective TIP collections, the shifting argument would disintegrate.*

Unions and Collective Bargaining

What of labor unions' behavior under TIP? Obviously, it would be disappointing to the prospects for democratic survival if a program that promises to protect the price level, improve job prospects, and block the erosion of savings and pension rights is rejected summarily. Ordinarily, there is some fragmentation of labor thinking on money wages and inflation: union officials, at times, are almost wistful for laws which would ease their task in pursuing moderate settlements which they envisage as beneficial to their group interests when membership recalcitrance forces them to adopt a more extreme stance. Sometimes leadership flamboyance dominates membership desires. Considering the dismal inflation experience, a TIP program, aiming at uniformity in *all* wage and salary advances, might win support: there is already widespread perception of the wage-price spiral, and the awareness that as all unions grab roughly equivalent big bundles each ends up in nearly the same relative place, with P and U becoming the traumatic casualties.

Whether unions would resort to mass protests to defeat the TIP proposal is a matter of political judgment, and the degree of commitment to democratic will and respect of the law. So long as the purposes are explained, the equities elaborated, the inexpensive enforcement attributes stressed, TIP should not rear any more formidable obstacles than any other antiinflation measure. Jobs, steady prices, foreign-exchange real-income advantages, equity, inexpensiveness, and maintenance of free institutions without overzealous government harassment comprise a solid list of rational political debating points.

Collective bargaining

Collective bargaining would not be entirely throttled under TIP although some of the more fantastic settlements, and the even more whimsical demands of the past, would be precluded. After all, this *is* its objective. With strong price-level stability the inglorious outsized "victories" would, in any event, lose the mete of legitimacy hitherto attached to them.

Only an unduly prolonged digression could explore the almost infinite variety of collective-bargaining strategies that TIP might encounter: all of the several studies have concluded that TIP would be effective in moderating wage demands.* On a general plane, presuming prudence and wisdom rather than exercises in brute political power, unions will discern the more limited capacity of firms to transgress the pay norm under the TIP bludgeon. Relenting would be costly to the firm; it could not surrender frequently. Weighing the odds on the firm's reluctance to submit, unions should taper their claims.

The bargaining zone

The inclusion of executive and managerial salaries in the average-compensation figure would open a little more margin to unions as a bargaining wedge; wages could rise by a bit more than 5 percent if, say, executive salaries rose by less, and without tax penalty to the firm; for example, unions could win 7 percent if other employees were held at about a 2 percent figure.

This leeway for negotiations could serve a healthy purpose in checking indiscriminate managerial pay while the firm was pleading poverty to the unions. A more wary eye would be placed on *all* business incomes, with the not unlaudable result of curbing corporate executive compensation which is often vastly in excess of the President of the United States, Governors, Supreme Court Justices, etc., for tasks far less exacting or significant for social or economic well-being.

The corporation could continue to be magnanimous to employees or executives, but it would have to answer to the tax collector.† The tax aspect would be a traffic signal: look, stop, advance with caution—or answer to the shareholders. In a small way the corporation would be returned closer to its shareholders and there might be inculcated a higher sense of executive responsibility.

Collective bargaining thus could proceed as before—almost. The ceiling on pay increases would not be absolute; more might be squeezed out occasionally, at executive expense or through subjecting the firm to higher taxes.

---

* This seems to be the general conclusion of all the existing analyses alluded to earlier, i.e., Isard, Kotowitz-Portes, Fogarty, and Seidman.

† Thus even as unemployment approaches "reasonably" full employment, with $U = 3$ to 4 percent, TIP conforms to allocational criteria: the most profitable firms can (in anticipation of higher relative profitability) bid more for labor to augment their staff than less profitable firms.

Unions could not justly complain about the program. Their status would be preserved. Their membership could be promised a doubling of pay almost every fifteen years, and about 60 percent per decade. Labor could not protest "exploitation." But groups would no longer be as untrammeled or licensed to injure other groups of society, including other wage earners and former members, the retired workers. Public posturing might lead unions to oppose TIP. Tactically, it would place them in the anomalous position of opposing a *corporate income tax*. Traditionally, unions have advocated higher corporate taxes in protesting higher income taxes.

Along with everybody else, union members have a stake in the battle against inflation. TIP would permit them to carry on practically unhampered. It would serve their own long-run interests, unlike the futile game of leapfrog in wages and prices, where excess wage gains end up mainly as an optical illusion while the value of money dwindles.

The demagogic might contend that the proposal attempts to restrain wages but not profits; this is to misconstrue it totally. If wages and salaries are moderated, prices will be contained so that profits could not skyrocket. This has been amply argued earlier. If in fact profits became unduly large there is an obvious corporate tax remedy. But to draw visions of a profit windfall under TIP before experience under its enactment and in defiance of analysis is a smokescreen, and not a valid objection on the critical damage to labor of stagflation.

Safety-valve aspects

The plan would not entirely prevent higher wage increases any more than fines for violations eliminate traffic speeders; mainly, they forestall the frequency of offenses. Where the pay norm is breached, the burden would be borne by the transgressing firm: the penalties would involve money, rather than criminal charges, bureaucratic harassment, and the moral disapprobation attached to price-wage control evasion.

The safety-valve feature of penalty taxes has even more in its favor. Where firms required especially talented people they could still pay more to obtain them; while the practice would become somewhat more costly, the firm's operations would not be unduly obstructed. The institutional TIP impediment for small trespasses would not be onerous.

The plan thus features the necessary flexibility. It cannot be seriously contended that an added tax on *some* firms would herald the end of capitalism. Lowering the *normal* corporate tax rate on the expectation of some TIP revenues would dispel this tedious refrain.

Salaries

Common equity requires that salaries and executive pay be included in calculating the average employee compensation. It would be distinctly unfair to limit ordinary workers while executives remained free to raise their own incomes munificently on the pretext that their earnings were noninflationary. The market system would not be handicapped for larger individual merit increases could still be granted: TIP liability attaches to the average increment and not to any individual allotment.

With respect to stock options, retirement plans, or other fringe benefits that executives have arrogated to themselves, these can be treated under TIP as they are currently, under the corporate and personal income tax laws. Although these intricate and delicate instances are a subject of chronic reinterpretation, overall, for TIP calculations, they are a marginal influence that should not deter the implementation of TIP even though regulations, over time, may warrant modification.

There is nothing in the TIP proposal to dilute managerial incentives. There is enough reward in opportunity, status, work interest, or the power aspects of being "boss" to assure a flow of aspirants for executive posts.

Some Technicalities and Omissions

Some technical problems and TIP omissions require comment; none appear to erect insuperable impediments though they warrant deliberation in any legislative enactment.* Remarks will be brief and mainly concerned with aspects on which judgments can differ.

1 *Coverage.* If the TIP features are directed to apply only to the largest 500, 1,000 . . . firms, smaller firms might conceivably become union targets primarily for bargaining levers. If successful, repercussions would flow to larger firms whose pay practices would be condemned as unrealistic, even exploitative.

To close this threat, perhaps after an experimental year or two of restricting TIP to the largest firms, the plan could cover most firms, or firms with over 50, 100, 200 . . . employees, as judgment dictates.

Essentially, the basic TIP plan without CAP should suffice in smaller firms where the potential of wasteful labor hire appears less foreboding: the limited ownership base of the firm is unlikely to condone profit dilution through excessive executive pay boosts subsequently neutralized through excesses in unskilled labor hire to elude TIP.

The CAP provisions would probably also be superfluous considering the limited scale of capital equipment. At worst, the short interim period of an adverse profit outcome (compared to present tax law) would only defer by a year or so the higher earnings potential of new equipment. Actually, if the normal corporate tax rate was reduced, small firms would not be hampered.

2 *Trucking and Construction.* In trucking and construction, the typical firms

---

*   Cf. Wallich-Weintraub, from which the enumeration has been drawn.

are small. Yet the industries have been prominent in inflationary income gains. Either they can be included in a comprehensive TIP coverage, or special measures to stabilize pay in this area may be required. The matter may become less urgent if other unions behave with more restraint.

3 *Government Employees.* Government employees, or employees in universities, hospitals, and various eleemosynary institutions receiving operating grants from government, could be allowed the normal guidepost advance. Every two or three years pay scales could be appraised against industrial pay trends and revised where appropriate.

4 *Agricultural and Professional Incomes.* Omitted are small farmers, small businessmen, and self-employed technicians and professional people. Largely, their tax obligations would not extend beyond the personal income tax. Between the forces of substitution between self-employment and industrial hire, and the contained pace of wage-earner purchasing power, there is a reasonable expectation that earnings in these sectors will mainly hold the pace.

Earlier, in the theoretical formulation of the consumer price level, we observed its dependence on the average money-wage level. Events in the self-employed sector should confirm this analysis. It would be frivolous to oppose TIP because it does not *directly,* and in one swoop, embrace all activities—even those which are peripheral in the total national income evolution.

5 *New Firms.* Special provisions would be required for new firms without a previous year's experience for computing TIP liability. If the new firm is a successor to identifiable former firms, the previous pay experience could be invoked. Otherwise, either some published "normal" data by the income tax service could be applied as a guide or, alternatively, new firms could be relieved of TIP liability—the waiver would mean a one-year respite.

6 *Existing Contracts.* Some contractual wage agreements providing for increases will have been written in the past to extend into the future. Either they may be rendered subject to TIP or relieved from tax onus for a year or so.

7 *The Transitional Period.* Needless to say, there would be transitional problems in implementing TIP for firms adopting different fiscal years for reporting. Precedents abound in instances accompanying the imposition of almost every new tax.

Supplements to Facilitate TIP Compliance

Some may foresee the need for supplemental measures to assure TIP compliance. For example, suppose a firm (or industry) offers a guidepost 5 percent increase, and this is rejected by the union. Confronted with potential losses through a strike shutdown, bankruptcy may be a greater menace to the firm than submission. The fear could be a potent club inviting a penetration of the pay norm: the tax cost may be a pittance compared to the impending financial disaster.

Conceivably, loan guarantees might be contemplated to cover fixed contractual costs to firms which offer a 5 percent pay boost which is then spurned by unions clamoring for larger hikes. The availability of a loan fund guarantee could set the bargaining range more immutably near the 5 percent zone as the capacity of firms to resist was augmented; the loans would have to be carefully monitored to obviate collusion and abuse. This aspect may be left to legal minds.

Alternatively, harsher provisions capable of provoking charges of "slave labor" would be a denial of union recognition, or curtailed unemployment benefits to those striking for, say, pay boosts in excess of 8 percent. Agitation might be partly defused by adopting a sliding-scale reduction, such as a 10 percent cut in unemployment compensation during the strike interval for demands running between 8 and 9 percent, 15 percent for 9 to 10 percent, etc.*

Some political flack would undoubtedly greet even a discussion of these measures. There may be other promising alternatives to assist firms striving to abide the pay norm.

The Administrative Feasibility of TIP

The aphorism that "the power to tax is the power to destroy" may be revived to castigate TIP. While the phrase has the ring of authenticity, it is mainly half true: the power to tax is also an instrument for making social, political, and economic life more tolerable. Ultimately, this is what taxation should be about, to accomplish worthwhile ends that would not otherwise evolve in the business sector without government direction. As TIP aims to curb inflation, it is compatible with the greater freedom; it is designed to expand it through job opportunities in a more stable price milieu; it cannot remotely be identified as an inhibitor of democratic values.

The tax burden of TIP

Whenever a stage is reached that warrants lower taxes, there is nothing in TIP to jeopardize or defer such a move. The ordinary corporate tax rate could be lowered so long as the inflation premium was retained. If and when business and union wage conduct became more responsible with respect to inflation, TIP could be abandoned. But by then the penalty aspect of the tax would be a dead letter anyway.

---

* The Incomes Policy of James E. Meade builds on this penalty. Cf. *Wages and Prices in a Mixed Economy* (Institute of Economic Affairs, 1971). The London *Economist* (April 10, 24, 1971) would impose higher Social Security contributions from union members ripping the wage norms.

TIP, to reiterate, is not designed to recoup tax revenue: its purpose is to stop inflation; totally effective, it would yield no revenue, with full analogy to perfectly observed speed limits on the highway. Inevitably, until more restrained income behavior became rooted, TIP would yield some tax revenue. So long as Treasury needs did not warrant higher tax collections, the normal corporate tax rate could be cut in contemplation of TIP receipts. Thus in projecting a TIP tax yield of 3 percent, the normal corporate tax rate could be dropped by 3 percent. With total tax collections constant, it would be specious to allege that firms were deprived of "capital," or that they were exposed to punitive tax measures, etc.

Administrative feasibility

TIP might encounter opposition at the administrative level mainly because of its novelty. To administrators, old taxes are mostly best—even after a recital of their catalog of woes. Yet TIP should not really compound the administration enigmas. Existing definitions of wages, and the wage-salary bill for the corporate income tax return, should suffice for TIP computations without redefinition. On the two new definitional categories, even imperfect resolution is unlikely to hinder the outcome on almost any "reasonable" classification of "full-time" equivalent employees and "consultants." Data on both categories are already tabulated according to Department of Labor concepts.

On the CAP adjunct to TIP to block legal evasion through inefficient labor hire, the complexities can be exaggerated. For if the concept is limited to, say, the 1,000 largest firms, neither calculations nor personnel for administration appear overwhelming. Entailed would be a few more lines on the tax form, for CAP and for TIP, perhaps reported on a separate page. Assuming one tax officer checking only TIP computations, while the other audits remain as before, 100 forms per tax expert per annum would not constitute an excessive workload. For 1,000 firms this comes to an IRS personnel enlargement of 10! Even doubling or tripling the number entails minimal cost, a pittance compared to the benefits of a stable price level and more nearly full employment; the total GNP advance might be of the order of $100 to $150 billion per annum (in 1977 prices). Extra administrative cost would be less than the proverbial drop in the bucket.*

Automatic policing

It is in policing that TIP has unassailable advantages over either persistent stagflation or the costs incident to price and wage controls. A thorough control program in the United States, for example, might require 50,000 to 100,000

---

* The conclusion would not be altered by including man-hours in firms preparing TIP data. The cost would be evaluated against the profit losses through reduced employment under recent stagflation, and against the costs and vexations of compliance with price and wage controls.

employees and cost $1 billion. TIP is minimal in cost, and far less interventionist in design and scope. As it utilizes the familiar tax mechanism, it has a market-economy flavor, with marginal interference in private decisions. The corporate tax is not exactly a novel phenomenon in business decision making.

Even a pessimistic assessment would concede that TIP *may* work; economic analysis suggests that it should be effective. Based on the most gloomy prevision of failure, the risks in an experimental venture would be nominal; TIP would not shelter a vast and vested bureaucracy. It could be shelved quickly if experience condemned it. It does not entail any basic new data from firms, and it relieves them of noxious wage-price controls. Neither the scope nor the organizational structure of trade unions will be affected, although the ceiling in collective bargaining becomes more clearly defined. In no wise does it embark on radical paths in economic control. It harmonizes with the traditions of a market economy and its vaunted freedom.

Industrial monopoly and labor's interest

Beyond TIP-CAP, if it still happens that prices continue to rise despite the maintenance of unit-wage costs, it will be time enough to look at the industries or special monopoly sectors that upset the stability. Then we shall know that business is at fault through an enlargement in k, the markup factor. All the present evidence points to excessive wage and salary gains, and to their translation into costs, as the primary cause that requires immediate correction. The overriding problem has been that each labor group strives to protect its own "relativity," only to contribute to inflation. This has been the tragedy of our inflationary era: relative wage gains have been mostly illusory while the unemployed have become sacrificial lambs on the bumpy price ride.

The "relativity" dimensions cannot be explored here. Rational discussion must commence among union representatives. But the economy should not be destabilized in the largely futile and abortive struggle of each labor group to gain the upper hand.

Labor generally has a manifest stake in the size of its relative share, in k. With TIP-CAP in place, monopoly industrial practices could become subject to clearer attention and probe. Untoward pricing phenomena have been obscured by wage inflation; they can be scrutinized more clearly in an era of price-level stability. But those who indict "monopoly" and "oligopoly" as the source of inflationary mischief in recent years are engaged in a diversionary attack by not confronting the overwhelming facts of immoderate money-income gains.

CHAPTER SEVEN

Profit Margins and Personal Income: TIP-M and TIP-P

For completeness, some alternative tax-based Incomes Policies are considered: (1) tax-rate concessions for lower profit margins (TIP-M); and (2) a personal income tax impost to suppress income inflation (TIP-P).

By and large, any attempt to compress profit margins will have scant price leverage. For $P(t)$'s mounting at a low 1 to 3 percent progression per annum, TIP-M might slow the pace a bit. Thus the proposal might be reserved for a more distant day; it can, however, have distributive significance. TIP-P, on the other hand, could be a powerful lever to choke high double-digit inflation. Yet the timing of a tax penalty might touch off some unfathomable ramifications, obscure to a priori analysis pitched to usual income tax models. For a period of a few years, however, the effects might be endurable, measured against the distributional distortions and the massive (output) losses of stagflation. Conceivably, TIP-P might quickly restore noninflationary expectations of normal money-income advances.

Others may see deeper merit in TIP-M and TIP-P, especially for hitting special inflationary situations. Hence, for evaluation or rejection, an examination holds more than casual interest.

Tax Benefits for Lowering Profit Margins

If tax incentives are to be granted to induce firms to reduce prices, the tax bounty must center on *profit margins*, suitably defined. Making prices the object of tax relief would arouse perplexing quandaries in quality control and product variation: firms would try to fob off deteriorated products at lower prices to qualify for price rebates. To add to the administrative quagmire, most large manufacturing firms produce multiple products, and in a confusing array. On top of policing quality, tax stipulations would have to qualify in terms of a "weighted" price. Undoubtedly, this would create enigmatic definitional nightmares to boggle the minds and torment the souls of tax administrators. New products and product innovation, both part of the story of progress, might undergo some harrowing adventures in tax review in the firm's quest for tax breaks instead of risking venture capital on substantively original product byways.

One other factor militates in favor of rewarding firms that lower profit margins rather than prices. Otherwise, the tax break could open a bonanza to monopoly firms showing productivity improvement and who should be lowering prices in the normal course of events. They would become tax beneficiaries for doing what they should be doing, and what they are likely to do anyway.

Tax rebates rather than penalties

Under TIP only a penalty tax was considered; if a tax bounty was granted for holding pay increments to the norm increment, labor might legitimately protest that premiums were being paid "to beat down wages." With the penalty attached only to average pay increases beyond the 5 percent "fair" norm, the sting of opprobrium for "exploiting" labor would be blunted, as deluded and demagogic.

Conversely, if a penalty is attached to a rise in profit margins, numerous cases of perfectly rational and optimal private decision making will be subject to corrosive tax harassment. Profit margins, previously too low and responsible for losses in the past, may be in the throes of more normal recovery: they would now be subject to penalty. Changes in sales volume may invite higher margins, on wholly defensible grounds. Other instances can be conjured, suggesting that a tax penalty on uplifts in profit margins would be harassing and unworkable.

Cutting taxes for firms that reduce profit margins might foster some reduction in k and thus enhance real wages, i.e., fractionally lower prices for any level of money wages.* Labor could thus be a beneficiary, with firms recouping through lower taxes some proceeds lost through narrower profit margins.

Abuses and a potential tax rebate schedule

Tax benefits for lower profit margins could also be abused by playing games for a tax prize. In years in which the tax liability promised to be small, the firm could raise prices and profit margins sharply, prior to slashing them in the next fiscal period. Monopoly-oligopoly market power, or tacit seller col-

---

*   For the real wage relation, from $P = kw/A$, then $(w/P) = (A/k)$.

lusion, would have to be allied to facilitate the market conduct. Thus TIP-M would have to be stringently chained to past and future profit-margin behavior, with tax returns opened up for scrutiny several years after they were filed to forestall strategic loopholes.

TIP-M might function better in a fairly stable productivity environment. Profit margins would have to be defined consistently over time, probably as the difference between sales proceeds minus all other costs to derive pretax profits, with the difference related to sales proceeds to provide a ratio.* In assessing possible magnitudes of tax relief, the limitations of TIP-M in providing assistance against the type of inflation of recent years become acutely apparent.

Suppose that the current *pre*tax profit per unit of corporate output is ten cents per dollar of sales price: this is close enough to the facts, and is convenient for the arithmetic. With a corporate tax rate of, say, 50 percent, to encourage a firm to cut its profit margin by one cent, from 0.10 to 0.09, would require a compensatory tax cut of 10 percent, from 50 to 45 percent. For a cut of two cents, from 0.10 to 0.08, the tax rate would have to drop to 37.5 percent. Yet despite the precipitous tax relief prices would edge down by just 2 percent or less inasmuch as the tax relief would not be universal. A 5 percent price level descent would call for a zero tax rate!†

Thus, even huge corporate tax cuts would yield indiscernible price abatement. Obviously, TIP-M lacks muscle in containing (in the illustration) nonprofit portions of sales price or gross money incomes comprising 90 percent of the price-level components; TIP-M could only play a miniscule part against inflation.

Using the Personal Income Tax Lever

The personal income tax provides a sturdier defense for subduing money-income inflation, especially in a severe price storm caused by spectacular pay boosts: TIP-P could either supplant or supplement price and wage controls. Like administered controls, however, TIP-P is best conceived as a short-lived expedient rather than a permanent stabilization fixture. Its chances for longer survival seem to be confined to a most rational, dispassionate, noncontentious world, with a high ideological consensus on objectives, and uniform support by market participants eager to comply. These are ideal circumstances that belong to some never-never land in which personal incomes occasion neither envy nor dispute, and where the income-division decision has only a minor functional bearing on occupational choice and resource allocation.

Nonetheless, despite this cursory disparagement, TIP-P can have a propitious short-run application, with shortcomings no worse, and results maybe

---

* Thus: $(PQ - \text{nonwage costs})/PQ$.
† The tax formula would be: $t = (10x - 0.5)/(10x - 1)$, where x ranges from a price cut of one to five cents.

better, than either inflexible or capricious administered price and wage controls.

Stumbling blocks in TIP-P

In using the personal income tax to abort inflation the key objective is to make inordinate annual income gains less valuable, after taxes, than an income advance that complied with the designated norm. A stumbling block in application would be that the blunt TIP-P methods might be unable to distinguish between excessive ordinary income advances and income gains through promotions which carry heavier responsibilities and merit abnormal income jumps. Also, there are a variety of puzzles in instances of erratic income changes for the self-employed, where the plus and minus abnormal and subnormal annual earnings might cancel out for individuals over time. Professional, erratic, and random income fluctuations, and small business activities, might be jeopardized by tax impositions bearing heavily on one year's income gains.

TIP-P would have to hit the annual incremental income gain to supplement normal income tax levies. As with TIP-CAP, if Treasury revenues promised to rise unduly, normal income tax rates could be cut so as to keep the total intake no larger than the sums targeted by usual fiscal objectives.

Wage and salary incomes that conformed to the stipulated norm increase would have to be made more valuable than an abnormal income increment: income increases of 5 percent would have to leave as a residue higher *after* tax take-home pay than advances of 10 or 15 percent, or more. To check higher wages from entering business costs initially, or to stop the ascent at its origin, the pretax income increase would comprise the base for TIP-P calculation.

One fairly simple way to limit pay demands would be to grant—after first *raising* the normal income tax rate—a tax break of 25 percent or so to everybody reporting an annual income increase of 5 percent or less. The computation could be made on a separate page of the tax form, or on some separate lines.

Simultaneously, a punitive tax levy, and exclusion from the tax cut, could be imposed on all annual income advances exceeding 5 percent so that, after tax, the individual experiencing the inflationary booty would be worse off than with a lesser pretax income gain. For example, in calculating the annual income advance, there would be an addition to the tax bill, computed at normal rates, of all income increases in excess of the 5 percent norm. For those whose income advanced by 10 percent, the *incremental* income would be taxed by 50 percent, for a 25 percent increase the incremental tax rate would be 80 percent, etc. A progressive scale along these lines should go far toward inducing ambivalence to rapid income gains. Unless TIP-P was expected to be a fairly permanent feature, however, it would undoubtedly encourage some income postponement. Considering the heavy tax penalties, legislatures are likely to shrink from voting such harsh levies, except in extreme emergencies, even though the imposts differ only in form from wage controls that freeze incomes.

Averaging features

Hence it would be theoretically possible through TIP-P to get individuals to abide by the pay norms. Equity, however, would compel modification of any straightforward application; opposition would crystallize quickly against any tax rebate on high incomes complying with the increment rule. Obviously, tax relief of 25 percent for foregoing an annual income increase would be very lucrative for incomes of $50,000 or higher and paltry at the lower end, so some absolute ceilings on tax relief would be widely urged. As in most tax matters, the volume of complaints and the wisdom of compromise will condition the legislative outcome.

Perplexing instances abound in cases where disproportionate annual increases have recently occurred. Some taxpayers will have amassed huge advances in the last year or two, and will be willing, under TIP-P, to settle for the more moderate norm in the current year. Others with more limited past advances will have legitimate grievances at the TIP-P timing. Averaging income gains—over the last three or five years—would attend more fairly to "relativity" inequities. Tax reductions might be reserved only for those whose incomes have grown by less than 35 percent (or some other figure) over the last five years, permitting some "catch-up" by laggards in the money-income chase. After a year or two of experience with the law, the "backward-looking" average could be depressed to a 6, and then to a 5, percent norm.

Averaging provisions would be practically imperative to prevent abuse if TIP-P was designed as a permanent tax feature: otherwise, unions could exact whopping increases in Year 1, followed by moderation in subsequent years to qualify for tax rebates. Averaging could negate a "hit-and-play-dead" strategy.

New employees and irregular incomes

Joint returns, where one income substantially outweighs the other, would probably best be treated largely according to the growth in the separate incomes. Some vexation would occur where a person is employed for the first time: one resolution would be an exemption for "first-job" certification.* Otherwise, definitional controversies might generate higher public heat and administrative turmoil than lenient tax treatment. Government employees adhering to the normal annual increment would qualify for tax remissions. Promotions, which we discuss shortly, constitute a harder nut to crack.

Recipients of irregular incomes, where the immediate trend is downward,

---

* Definitions would probably have to exclude early after-school employment, or summer jobs, etc.

would opt against averaging, and would welcome the one-year tax treatment. However, on the upswing averaging would mitigate hardship for moderate income gains. Sharply ascending income fortunes would undoubtedly suffer from the harsh tax bite.

In general, TIP-P would be a feasible approach for those employed by large business firms, whether in blue-collar job categories or in executive boardrooms. Certification of employment within an establishment of over 5, 10, 25, or 50 employees, or whatever figure is selected for administrative convenience, would facilitate the TIP-P program. The complications lie in employment outside the large firm.

Promotions and abnormal pay increases

Bona fide promotions with substantial income boosts provide a test for TIP-P. Still, the difficulty might not be insurmountable: by paying a formidable tax in the first year after receiving the promotion the individual would, in effect, have to wait until the second year before deriving any real financial benefit from the climb up the achievement ladder. Averaging would mean an income wait of more nearly three years than one.

Again, a certification of the facts might be submitted along with the tax return in the first year following the promotion. Based on past data of promotions within firms, industries, or the economy generally, certifications might be confined to a fixed percentage of the total number of employees. Favorable tax treatment, however, would probably have to be restricted to only once in every three or five years to block avenues of abuse.

A one-year delay before reaping the full income gains of promotions is not wholly intolerable nor impractical; at worst, it would temporarily separate new responsibilities from pecuniary rewards. While others may devise better solutions, promotions confront TIP-P with a genuine conundrum, involving equity and the efficient functioning of the system through nourishing ambition for greater economic benefit.

Self-employment

Tax treatment of the self-employed is always a nettlesome complication in a structure of industrial capitalism: it is bound to fit awkwardly, as a fish among fowl. Even definition is fuzzy; whether to confine the definition of self-employed merely to individuals or to establishments of 5, 10, or whatever small number of employees, either to be excluded from coverage under TIP-P or to be subject to alternative tax rules.

Incomes below $15,000, and certified as emanating from small firms or professional sources, might be granted blanket exemption from the punitive features of TIP-P, with little loss in the inflation struggle. Union protests could be countered by the reminder that union members could obtain the same tax treatment by relinquishing their job security and fringe benefits for employment in smaller firms. With the same treatment open to everyone in the small business category, a defense against the discriminatory tax criticism would be sustainable.

On self-employed and small business incomes above $15,000, TIP-P could be supplemented not only by some averaging back to cover, say, the last five years, but an averaging *forward:* reopening earlier tax computations in later years could operate to equalize the tax obligation. Thus if Year 2 entails a heavy impost because of a substantial income rise, a more level income path in subsequent years would refund some of the earlier TIP-P tax charge and iron out some tax discrepancies because of bumpy income trends. To equate erratic income swings to steady income progress is notoriously unfair.

Persons shifting employment from the "small" to the "large" firm category might be allowed the option of electing the most favorable TIP schedule with some limitation on treatment to "small" firm status every three (or five) years, to plug a possible loophole to those with more opportunities to pick the better shelter. Entering the "large" firm, the usual TIP rules would pertain. Where, on balance, TIP-P induced shifts toward smaller enterprise, social policy would condone the favored tax status. Recoiling from special provisions for the self-employed would probably render TIP-P uneconomic and impair market efficiency. Forces of substitution and competition should operate (imperfectly, to be sure) to align small business and professional incomes to those evolving in the large-firm industrial structure. With government and large-firm employment incomes in tow, self-employed and professional earnings are also likely to display less spectacular swings than under general income inflation.

Alternative Incomes Policy Proposals

TIP-M is likely to aid in throttling "small" inflations; TIP-P could act as a bulwark against "big" inflations. Considering that TIP-P would be tied to the personal income tax, which already has its myriad provisions couched in "legalese," only a "quiet" society—largely innocent of legalistic contention—is likely to embrace it permanently. Nevertheless, to reverse "inflationary expectations" in one quick slash, and to encourage money-income restraint, it would have some virtues. Whether present circumstances are propitious for adoption is doubtful.*

Many other versions of Incomes Policy can undoubtedly be concocted. Many would aim at chopping unions down to size by curbing their powers

---

* TIP-CAP could provide a school for educating income recipients of the need for restraint, and pave the way for TIP-P to recapture the gains that have eluded the TIP-CAP net.

or by compromising bargaining practices, perhaps injecting compulsory government mediation and approval of bargaining settlements. Interpreted widely as antiunion, they would undoubtedly engender an arduous political struggle, exacerbating class conflicts and creating social turmoil, with incessant controversy endangering evolutionary political systems.

Our objective is a steady price level. Unless we are to be deflected by tiresome skirmishes for ideological debating points, the perspective must focus on antiinflation, and not antiunion policies. Inciting new power struggles will only perpetuate inflation and impair the operation of the mixed economy, to the detriment of all participants.

Union sharing of an income aggregate

Also suggested for controlling the money-income aggregate is the idea that labor unions be informed of a total sum prospectively available for wage increases, permitting unions to divide the total at their discretion among competing unions.*

Jumping over the hurdles for illustrative purposes only, suppose that *all* labor was unionized and that the prevailing wage bill amounted to $1 trillion, say, in 1974. For the purpose of limiting the average increase to about 5 percent, unions might be told that there is a $50 billion sum available for allocation among the respective unions in autos, steel, trucking, dock workers, retail trade, construction, etc. Where unions comprise only 30 percent of the labor force, the sum might be cut proportionately.

It may be that the unions could resolve the matter internally and "amicably" by their own organization procedures. But one might suspect that a cruel game of fraternal warfare, not between labor and management but between union and union, would surface quickly: the conflict of interests bodes ill for domestic and industrial tranquillity. Despite the simplistic charm of the proposal, considering the troubles humanity already has in living harmoniously, the union membership would be sorely tested. Predictions of success for the arrangement could be harbored only by a breed of optimists on human nature.

Payroll Tax Cuts and Wage Restraint

Judgment is thus largely adverse to using the personal income tax mechanism, except in an extreme emergency, to force wage restraint. If this format is to be used, the incentive of tax cuts in return for moderated conduct seems to

---

* Cf. A. Cairncross, "Incomes Policy: Retrospect and Prospects," *Three Banks Review* (Dec. 1973). A. P. Lerner, in some analogy to ideas on pollution control, would sell "coupons," open to bidding, against this sum. See his "From Pre-Keynes to Post-Keynes."

be the stronger hand compared to punitive levies to capture extreme gains.*

Sometimes it is suggested that payroll taxes be sliced in the thought that this might fatten pay envelopes and encourage a more moderate bargaining stance. Three aspects of this deserve attention: (1) whether the possible take-home pay increments will induce better wage behavior; (2) what to do for an encore, after the payroll tax falls to about the vanishing point; and (3) how to finance the Social Security program. It would probably reopen a rancorous debate that will make the bitterness of the New Deal appear in retrospect as a model of gentlemanly discourse, especially with the trend in the age composition toward an older population. One can agree that their income fate is linked closely to current income and output facts, but some harmless fictions, such as the creation of a Social Security "fund," do make it easier to relate a just social program to ordinary lives, of people paying through their working years to recoup during their retirement days. Financing Social Security benefits through general taxation, as would be incumbent if payroll taxes were lowered, would incite perennial acerbic quarrels over even this portion of the revenue process. Expediency in maintaining the payroll fiction, despite its regressive features, may be conducive to the greater good in a demagogic era.

Alternatively, rather than using the payroll mechanism it may be possible, especially in more parliamentarian systems and smaller market economies, for the Prime Minister to meet with labor leaders and extract from them a pledge of wage restraint; thereafter the government would propose tax reductions covering income ranges of working people. The same gambit may work on occasion in the United States. Practiced too frequently, it translates into staking the prestige of the office of the head of state on ongoing economic practices, with less than unanimous assurance that the efforts to achieve industrial "detente" will succeed.

Measures of this sort rely on goodwill, as in an appeal to motorists to drive safely, with the difference that the number of possible transgressors is fewer and readily identifiable. Democracy is likely to work best under known laws rather than under a flashy series of *ad hoc* back-room bargains.

Various tactics of the one sort or another, as in marking payroll taxes down, meeting with labor and management, trading wage restraint as the price of tax cuts, and the like, may be useful to supplement TIP-CAP. But mostly they are more ephemeral, more appropriate to episodic outbreaks rather than to the chronic imperative of Income Gearing. The need is for a durable, long-term program, for the decade rather than the day.

---

* Cf. Laurence Seidman, "A Payroll Tax-Credit to Restrain Inflation," *National Tax Journal* (Dec. 1976) for a more favorable evaluation of the personal income tax mechanism as an adjunct to TIP.

CHAPTER EIGHT

A Summing Up: Controls, Indexation, and TIP

The lack of viable alternatives is almost enough to crack the case for Incomes Policy; the unhappy record discloses that monetary and fiscal policies are either powerless to arrest the disorderly money-income increases or, to succeed even temporarily, they must invite a job relapse. Once the recovery cycle is resumed, we are back to the starting gate on inflation, in a dog-chasing-its-tail syndrome.

As an alternative to a conscious Incomes Policy there is the either innocent or mad draconian tactic of price and wage controls. Then there is the sophisticated toy of "indexation," designed to make "living with inflation" more tolerable. Both proposals are discussed briefly.

Price and Wage Controls

Pervasive and meticulous price and wage controls are inimical to the functioning of the market economy. At best, they are a form of shock therapy to force a healthier frame of mind on "inflationary expectations" as a temporary remission interlude. Unless innocuously applied as a toothless bark, they must end up in diverting innumerable—mostly trivial—private decisions into public forums for tedious hearings before committees under political aegis. Whether Orwellian prisons of monitored freedom are realized or not, small transactions which inflict no harm on others are constantly elevated to public scrutiny, gossip, and review.

Rather than develop a scary story of horrendous damage to the democratic order (which is unlikely to materialize as revocation and sober judgment prevail), a list of price and wage control mishaps is presented. Nonetheless, this is not to denounce controls in all circumstances; once imposed they can serve as a short-lived defense line while a more rational and permanent strategy is enacted. This is their redeeming virtue. They can serve temporarily, a circumlocution for saying that for a short period the economy can survive most anything.

1 The price system provides signals of goods availability. Presumably, those best positioned to send and intercept the message are people engaged in the purchase and sale decisions. Yet controls entail intervention and intermediation by a bureaucratic layer. Time is wasted, and costs are lavished, in seeking a price decision before the act or in securing later approval.

2 Powers granted to a control agency can mean unnecessary exposure to abrasive and contumacious and harassing behavior affecting the livelihood and fortunes of a business, large or small. Vying for debating points or political laurels can outweigh economic judgment.

3 There are often interminable and contentious controversies over inherently nontestable, metaphysical matters, such as whether to have a board of twelve members or five, of appropriate representation; on staffing; over public versus private hearings; on legal representation and appeal; on technical as opposed to substantive violation in bureaucratic litigation.

4 Price-making protests provide an Olympic haven for lawyers as contestants in price actions. Dialogues absorbing small costs and occupying little time in a market economy become expensive and dilatory debates. Costs mount, ultimately to be borne by consumers. Legal wrangles can be as frustrating and oppressive as dictatorial regulations.

5 The bid for newspaper headlines becomes irresistible to individuals suddenly catapulted into prominence as price and wage "czars." Essentially, trivial price issues assume monumental national significance by public announcement. The play becomes more predictable if there is a human-interest angle that can be appreciated by practically everybody despite its inherent economic unimportance.

6 Human-interest issues are bound to be seized upon by political partisans, so that the limited time span of public attention becomes riveted upon small matters, while deeper issues of the age go unattended by ordinary citizens.

There is a Gresham's law at work: relatively well-understood insignificant matters drive out concern with substantial problems, for the former are easily grasped in some thought-escape from complex disorders. Even now our democratic society pays dearly for permitting inflation and unemployment to linger because of a past refusal to discuss the wage-salary issue outside the specific individual context of spectacular wage agreements. The problem is looked at piecemeal.

7 The wider the network of controls, the larger the array of administrators, investigators, enforcers. Court calendars are likely to become clogged, with a new breed of criminals tracked down by a new species of police officers wearing the badge of price detectives. Administrative costs can become sizable.*

8 Individuals agreeing to pay a few pennies, or dollars, more than the stipulated legal price are subjected to criminal or civil penalties, or both. A new kind of black-market "crime" will undoubtedly become rife if the administered prices drive out supplies and leave shelves bare.

It can be a perversion of the democratic ideal to make criminals out of consenting adults whose agreement affects others adversely only in some dictatorial and philosophical casuistry. To compound the dilemma, if violators are *not* prosecuted there is disdain for other laws more essential to a civil, and civilized, society.

This catalogue of defects runs more in political than economic terms. Involved, however, are the "politics"—meaning the human relations—of the economic system. Implicit in the control machinery is an economic rerouting of output, employment, and pricing decisions from private to bureaucratic hands, with egregious overtones for rational resource use. With the best intentions in the world, with the most democratic and wisest administrators, excessive cost and production delay will mar the usual control program. Orders from the top trickle down in the administrative hierarchy; it is not farfetched to conjure visions of Captain Queeg on the trail of a missing plate of strawberries—while the more vital war mission waits. Costs, time, losses, can have their repercussions in business investment and plant modernization. Ultimately, as pricing and production troubles brew, outside of the legion of confirmed controllers who smell jobs, while reveling in the sense of power and publicity in their functions, the controls will have to be dismantled as more members of the market economy are touched by their officious iniquities and disruptions.

Suppose this scenario of stormy weather ahead is a poor harbinger of events, and that despite past fiascos the controls are successful. If so, there will be clamor for their abandonment: they are foul weather gear. Following the Oliver Twist script in sounding for "more"—more money income—we shall again have to confront the inflation-unemployment tangle. And then go back again to controls, for another fling? The on and off cycle has already had too frequent a replay; if controls were feasible, and if they were compatible with the market economy, they would not have been scuttled so eagerly once the price emergencies had passed.

---

* Presumably, nobody will defend the controls as a medium for creating jobs, even for economists and lawyers!

Indexation and Corrections

As an alternative to controls, many suggest the institution of "indexation," whereby changes in money wages, mainly, are tied to movements in, say, the consumer price index. Some suggest wider indexation to cover all income, including interest payments on bonds.

Nothing in the skeptical ensuing remarks should be interpreted as a criticism of adjustments in old age pensions, or in unemployment payments, or in government salaries when these have become unbalanced compared to wage and salary trends in the private sector: these "corrections" are the equivalent of private sector proportionate wage boosts to the affected participants. Most people regard it as unfair that incomes of these groups should lag indecently behind incomes in the private sector.

It is private sector general wage and salary indexation that is in mind. It is not too farfetched to describe the central indexation thesis as zeroed in on a "mission impossible," that of "trying to catch up tomorrow, to events that happened yesterday, by consummating a strategic decision today." Basically, after observing the movement in the $P_c(t-1)$ index covering a (recent) past period, indexation contemplates that $[w(t+1)/w(t-1)]$ be moved upward proportionately, to rule in the future period until the new P_c report.

However described, indexation is merely one way, and not a good way, to seize on a figure to settle the size of the (exogenous!) wage increase to rule over a future period of time. Suppose the price index rose in the previous year by 10 percent and that this is the number chosen for $(\Delta w/w)$ for the subsequent year. We can surmise, with a high degree of confidence in the prediction, that the price drift will approximate the excess of the number selected minus 3 percent—or 10 minus 3—where the latter gauges the likely *forthcoming* productivity gain. The closer the indexed number is to 3 percent, the stronger the chance of a flat price trend. The more the indexed wage increment deviates from 3 percent, the higher the inflation pace.*

By happenstance, the indexation may work well—if it starts in a favorable price climate. Suppose it succeeds, suppose prices are constant. Would labor be content with zero wage increases? If the price level falls, will labor acquiesce in a money-wage reduction?

Merely on these considerations it is doubtful that indexing is a definitive solution; it would be jettisoned as soon as it succeeded in stabilizing the price level—if ever it did. Off to a bad start, it may well build in cumulative inflation. Either way, we would have to confront seriously Incomes Policy proposals when once the thinness of the index method became transparent.†

---

* Keynes remarked: "That money-wages should be more stable than real wages is a condition of the system possessing inherent stability." *General Theory*, p. 239. See also pp. 269–271.

† For theoretical evaluation, and further references, with the not unexpected mixed bag of conclusions, see the recent American Economic Association discussion: David

Taming the tiger

What index numbers? This will arouse new disputes, labor tending to be grieved that the number selected understates past price phenomena, while managerial groups will protest on opposite grounds. Also, index numbers are somewhat delayed, one, two, three months. While this lag may be over-come—at a cost—are wage and salary agreements to be revised immediately? To prevail for how long? Would the indexation occur weekly, monthly, an-nually?

Besides the laconic details of the mechanics by indexation proponents, how would indexation be enforced? Suppose several labor unions rejected the prescribed pay boost? Or suppose industry refuses to meet the terms? How will compliance be assured? In short, how is the tiger to be tamed?

To change the metaphor, there is much loose talk of cooking rabbit stew, according to recipe, but precious little by way of a guide on how to catch the rabbit, maybe in a country uninhabited by the little creatures. One con-ceivable method, to be sure, is via TIP: but this would reveal indexation to be one way of coming up with a wage norm. Although references to Brazil, which has adopted the idea, are commonplace, this is hardly a felicitous work-ing model for democracies; with its military government, without free labor unions, and with a labor force suffering real wage deprivation, it instantly arouses distaste to those committed to freedom. Likewise, the recent chaotic experience in Iceland (in a nation of some 200,000 dependent on fisheries) does not sparkle as an experiment that begs replication.*

Wise enough to implement a complicated indexation scheme, we should be able to do better in devising an antiinflation policy for, ultimately, indexa-tion is an injunction to "live with inflation" and—mainly in vivid imagina-tion—to "correct" for its harsher income distribution inequities; to be sure, these are corrections for recently *past* price levels rather than future egali-tarian directives. Yet "correction" is something a market economy does badly, and the likelihood of indexation improving its performance is dubious. Those concerned with more fundamental distributive "correction" will do a

---

Levhari and Nissan Liviatan, "Government Intermediation in the Indexed Bond Markets"; Henry Aaron, "Inflation and the Income Tax"; William Poole, "Indexing and the Capital Markets," in *American Economic Review* (May 1976). Also, Her-mann Albeck, "Inflation, Income Distribution and the Economic Cycle: On the Discussion of Index-Linked Wages," and Otto Pfleider, "Index Clauses in Long-Term Capital Transactions as an Aid to Inflation Control," in *The German Economic Review* (Number 3/4, 1975). Omitted generally in these analyses are the extreme cases, where indexation finally stabilized the price path or led to an explosive trend.

* In Australia the Labour party was rejected on the inflation issue in 1975. Having adopted indexation with sorry results the country now appears to be headed first for "partial" indexation while the Prime Minister requests a wage and price "freeze"—the venerable experiment of futile controls is being revived once more in this mindless merry-go-round. See *New York Times* (May 8, 1977), p. 3.

far more sensible job of achieving their social ideals under a flat price trend.

If indexation promotes inflation—as it may—government will be charged with designing the vehicle; if indexation succeeds in lowering the rate of price ascent, its barrenness as an enduring Incomes Policy will be apparent for, in theory, by requiring continuously *lower* money incomes (in response to a consecutive annual sequence of price-level falls) we would be left without money incomes, without money—and without money prices!*

An out-of-step policy

The very tenor of the indexation advice is suspect; it is predicated on a view of wages "catching up" to prices, as if the past price rise were independent of the prior money-incomes increase so that, now, money incomes can play "catch-up" while prices hold firm. The feedback of wages to prices is a neo-classical omission. But higher money-wage-salary incomes, however the figure is arrived at, whether by peering at price charts with indexation intent or not, will hardly depress prices if the grants exceed 3 percent: from both the demand and cost side, inflation pressures will be in motion. Presumably, at the bottom of the theoretical distortion is some mystic belief that in $(t-1)$ k has risen, and that prices can hold firm in $(t+1)$, while wages-salaries mount in $(t+1)$, with k-collapsing in the second period. Yet no evidence has been forthcoming on the variability of k, or the "profit-inflation" that is waiting to be "corrected" by indexation.

Going beyond indexation of wages and salaries, some proponents suggest a "tabular" standard in which contracts for rent, or interest and principal on bonds, are specified in dollars of constant purchasing power. The theme goes back about a century, to Alfred Marshall and Irving Fisher. Yet businesses have generally shunned "indexed" contracts; and there must be a reason. Yet the lack of enthusiasm for indexed contracts is obvious and basic for the very function of contractual agreements is to obviate uncertainty about future dollar payments or commitments: businessmen want to know their obligatory cash flow of payments in advance; lenders also want to anticipate their money flows with exactitude in *money* terms. Indexation would endow contractual payment uncertainty as a fact of life. It would be hard to persuade business-men whose prices have fallen, or have lagged behind the average, that their payment commitments must be honored according to average results, rather than conforming to their individual experience.

---

* Professor Friedman has been a proponent of indexation in recent years. Exam-ining his slender pamphlet on the subject, it comes to an advocacy of tax cuts and an exhortation to businessmen, apparently against their better judgment, to index contracts. The recommendation is a departure from Professor Friedman's confident espousal heretofore of subduing inflation by his simple "steady" rule. *Monetary Correction: A Proposal for Escalator Clauses to Reduce the Costs of Ending Inflation* (The Institute of Economic Affairs, 1974).

What the effect of indexation of interest on a new capital market series of bonds would mean to capital markets dealing in old obligations is a vast and dimly discerned subject which indexation proponents have scarcely surveyed. It would undoubtedly thrust a wrench into the functioning of the vital financial center of the market economy by playing egregious tricks on balance sheets, and solvency, in an inflationary era.

Flowing from the indexation theory has been the idea that income taxes be "indexed," with tax brackets lowered on inflation advances. Stripped of the resonant verbiage, this is a recommendation for *lower* taxes under inflation. This proposition can be considered on its merits, without the mystique of respectability attributed to it on incompletely analysed indexation grounds; there may, or may not be, a good case for lowering tax rates under inflation. In a sense, it seemingly contradicts the orthodox Keynesian fiscal policy precepts. But substantially the arguments pro and con are only remotely connected to indexation. If the tax cuts are an employment boon, or a price-level stabilizer—though the mechanics are obscure—we may want even deeper tax cuts than indexation intends.

Little to Lose, and Much to Gain

Commitment to the market economy rests heavily on the incentive-deterrent features of price-cost ratios, with widening bands stimulating output and narrowing ratios impeding particular production volumes. Implicit is the "invisible hand" organizing and coordinating resource use without the unwieldy harassment-prone bureaucracy in government intervention.

Well before Marshall, and at least since Cournot, excise taxes have been understood to lift costs and supply, operating to contract output and elevate price. Marshall likewise interpreted subsidies (per output unit) to be a "negative" excise tax, and thus a potentially useful incentive for stimulating industries of increasing returns.

Tax literature is replete with incentive-deterrent aspects of the personal and corporate income tax. Steeper rates of personal income tax progression are reputed to deter individuals from "moonlighting" or extra effort on their main job to amass income, compared to lighter marginal imposts. Likewise, the complexity of the corporate income tax attaches ponderable incentive-deterrent aspects to business decisions, with the tax wizards endowed with the wisdom of a modern sage in executive boardrooms. Tax minimization becomes a paramount corporate objective with profound ramifications for the economy.

While analyses may differ on the precise outcome of TIP, its incentive and deterrent aspects are less suspect, and they should be conducive to more salutary wage and salary settlements in the effort to stem inflation.

The deterrent aspect

The TIP-CAP tax revision is presented as an inflation deterrent, rather than a surreptitious measure to derive a new source of Treasury revenue. Revenue enhancement is purely secondary. The proposals require some modification in the conception of tax policy from: (1) a Treasury budget balancer; and (2) an employment antidote, to (3) a conditioner of stable price-level conduct. The evolution of doctrine is from the balanced-budget dogma in (1), to Keynesian fiscalism in (2), to Income Gearing in (3). The main idea is not new; sumptuary taxes have been imposed since early days to discourage liquor, cigarette, and drug use or, if the demands are inelastic, to make the items costly and to amass revenues from the purchase. The same thought motivates taxation on the purchase of "luxuries," such as cosmetics, jewelry, appliances, perfumes, etc. Clearly, in some instances moral disapprobation rationalizes revenue expediency. TIP-CAP is motivated purely by its wage-salary deterrent attributes in facilitating a price-level stabilization objective.

The 1975 United Kingdom income policy

On July 13, 1975, Price Minister Harold Wilson announced an Incomes Policy for the United Kingdom which is a more rigid, coercive, and egalitarian cousin of TIP. Essentially, there is a maximum limit of £6 (approximately $12.00 at the time) per week as a ceiling on pay increases; this is reserved only for incomes up to £8,500 (= $17,000) per annum.* In the event of non-compliance, employers are prohibited from raising prices; public authorities who defied the wage mandate were to be denied government grants and subsidies.

The egalitarian accent is unmistakable: $12 on $100 per week is 12 percent; on $200, just 6 percent. "Relativity" controversies would, sooner or later, surely boil over, with the physicians' strike of late 1975 being a case in point. One can suspect, too, that able employees will somehow fashion a variety of perquisites as a surreptitious income gain, in kind, or in promises for the future, or in conditions of work, as a human response to circumvent the brittleness of the scheme which was bound to hamstring even minor and innocuous decisions of the firm in executing its functional operations. In small ways, the inflexibility is a costly source of production inefficiency.

Likewise, the adamant rejection of all price increases for wage violations, regardless of the size of the discrepancy, is a harsh exercise in sanctions, affronting common sense in its totalitarian antecedents. Abundant reasons may occur for *some* price relief, with little detriment to the price level and without an inflation snowball. Neither the wisdom nor the transitory nature of the United Kingdom model makes it attractive for emulation.† It can be

---

* At the time, £1 = $2 approximately.

† In 1976 Prime Minister Callaghan was driven to the next phase, limiting pay increases while promising tax relief. In mid-1977 unions appear ready to test the pay limits.

commended mostly for acknowledging (at last) the connection between the enormous wage leaps and the egregious price bounce.

Resolving the Crisis

Quite in contrast to the United Kingdom version, TIP is inherently noninterventionist; it should be able to resolve the crisis of the market economy and block more testy forms of statism by those who are disenchanted by the existing order and who would replace it by a bureaucratic hand, without comprehending either sytem. TIP would, to be sure, make the Invisible Hand a good deal more obvious in assuring greater money-income stability and a more rational macroeconomic performance. The effort to temper money-income advances is intended to assure the steady accrual of the real-income benefits of productivity improvements which should emerge more handily in a steady-price and full-employment climate.

TIP would appear to be serviceable in the present inflation environment and, in two to three years of its enactment, be able to deflect the price level to a flat track. Definitionally, legally, administratively, it should prove neither costly nor too complex. It should exhibit far fewer snarls than the bureaucratic and politically oriented controls.

Success in containing the money income and price development could permit monetary and fiscal policy—the Keynesian stabilizers—to make their potent contribution to full employment. Incomes Policy would thus supplement and reinforce the existing macroeconomic stabilizers which have been effective in improving the job climate, compared to the older depression era, though lacking a direct means of controlling the average-income ingredient of inflation. While the TIP technique is evolutionary, it draws on the familiar tax mechanism so that it can coincide with decision-making in a market economy.

Labor should be able to count plusses: more jobs, and more secure jobs, with enhanced *real* income. What will be required of labor is to cease confusing universal, outsized money-wage improvements with real-income achievement. A rational economic society would then take a large step forward, released to deal with the novel and profound issues that confront us in this groping technological age.

A way out

In still another reflection on the ongoing sinking spell of the market economy, Nordhaus has concluded:

Given the increasingly cruel dilemma and the unsatisfactory response of policy-makers . . . it is tempting to search for new ways of controlling inflation. The ideal form . . . is one which reduces all denominated values by the same percent without changing any relative prices or real magnitudes. The Achilles heel of past price-wage policies (except the relatively innocuous guideposts) has been that they confused inflation policy with income redistribution. By concentrating on individual sectors, they have attempted to change relative prices and aroused the fierce resentment of individual groups.

There is probably no such ideal antiinflation policy, but economists have shown little inventiveness in designing durable antidotes to inflation other than recessions. One serious suggestion is an inflation tax which would penalize firms or workers to the extent that they deviated from a national norm. Such a mechanism would allow the decentralized decisions of which economists (and some politicians) are so fond. It would allow adjustment of relative prices, and when [the] inflation rate is at the norm it would leave relative prices unchanged. Most important, such a measure would directly affect the [societal] bad—inflation—rather than first pummeling [societal] goods like output and employment.*

Others will best comment on the "inventiveness" of the general Wallich-Weintraub proposal. Nordhaus seems to have TIP—or something like it—in mind, though reference is lacking. In any event, TIP-CAP does conform to the criteria that he identifies with a "good" outcome.

There is the matter of a transition period to a new policy era. Temporary controls would have a place as a TIP-CAP program is debated, improved, enacted. For a period of a year, for other than grave inequities, labor might be asked to forego wage increases and business, to drop prices of the order of 2 percent on average. The new program could start in an auspicious climate.

As timidity will not win the fair maiden, a timorous attachment to orthodoxy will only bury us in the stagflation morass, or lurch the system from price instability to job instability, drunk on the one or soused with the other, or bleary-eyed from both. Probationary reprieves from the double mess will come in the repetitive boom-bust or job-price cycles. The crisis of capitalism, of a long sinking spell to the edge of disaster, will endure.

Maintaining commitment to democratic ways, and consensual scope to the private and public sectors of the workable mixed economy, there is a better economic world to win. There is only inflation and unemployment to lose.

---

*   William D. Nordhaus, "Inflation Theory and Policy," *American Economic Association* (May 1976), p. 64.

PART 4

Other Inflation Themes

Introduction: Some Omitted Analyses

Several other theories of inflation have been bypassed in order to develop the WCM concept and its associated money and money-wage corollaries with minimal interruption or impediment in examination of either subsidiary or deficient ideas. For a more rounded survey some major theories prominent in the professional literature or purveyed in more popular writings are presented at this point.*

Chapter 4 above concentrated mainly on the money supply and demand aspects more immediately pertinent to the WCM analysis, including some account of Monetarist doctrine. Chapter 9 embellishes the earlier discussion in elaborating further strands in Monetarist thought, often by quotation from established writers, and makes explicit the innate contrasts with the WCM perspective. Between Chapter 9 and the earlier chapter a reasonably comprehensive statement of the analytical differences which become vital in policy application can be garnered.

Keynes versus the Keynesian interpretation—which is really Hicksianism —is the focus of Chapter 10. Hicks has recently acknowledged the inadequacy of his earlier model which, nonetheless, is still widely taught and which

---

* In classroom use some instructors may want to consider these chapters for reading and discussion either before or after Chapter 5 above. The arrangement will probably depend on student preparation, especially with respect to textbook Keynesianism. While I think that the early argument can be understood with little or no previous course work, Chapter 10 may require at least an introductory economics course in which the Keynesian macroeconomics flourishes.

abounds in high-priced and bulky textbooks. Students will once again have to unlearn what they have laboriously mastered if we are ever to overcome our analytical and policy muddles. Keynes would have been a far better mentor than the proliferating books conveying models that bore his name. An Aggregate Demand and Aggregate Supply approach much closer to the spirit and tenor of Keynes' work appears as a supplementary note.

Protests about ignoring and omitting monopoly pricing as the inflationary beast are predictable, so it is discussed in Chapter 11. The brief account will do little, it may be surmised, to allay the conviction—relieved of fact—that monopoly is the overweening culprit; yet profits simply cannot account for the kind of chronic inflationary binge that has been experienced in the United States over the last decade, and even less so in the United Kingdom and elsewhere. Yet the WCM theory in no wise underrates the importance of the monopoly overhang *but it is not the paramount actor in the context of inflation.* Once the average level of money wages was brought into reasonable alignment with productivity through time, it would be far easier to isolate either the relative price level disruptions engendered by monopoly and oligopoly pricing practices, or the failure of prices in industries of administered prices to reflect amply the productivity gains won through technological advances. Just as the WCM analysis is neither pro nor antilabor, none of it is pro or antibusiness. Its implications and proposals are simply antiinflation and the associated direct distress of unanticipated price eruptions compounded by the indirect pains and burdens of unemployment.

Government profligacy and the "tax-eater" aspects of bureaucracy comprise the content of Chapter 12. Public discussion generally attaches an exaggerated significance to government budget policy in inflation: a more correct line of criticism inquires about the degree to which fiscal actions coincide with the democratic consensus on what we want government to perform. It is more than a mite inconsistent to advocate expenditure programs and then oppose the outlays and the tax imposts. The more valid propositions on the budget as an inflation-maker will be shown to be already implicit in the WCM view: the theory is broad enough to encompass the legitimate points in popular and political flailing of our imperfect instruments of democratic self-governance.

CHAPTER NINE

More
on Money

Numerous supplementary issues abound in the discernible gap in money-wage theory, and from the WCM conception of monetary theory and policy. It might be illuminating, therefore, to assemble a series of notes in large part dealing with the theory of money-demand and, hence, the stability of m or V. Further, various aspects of their theory that Monetarists deem significant invite comment.* Considered earlier they might have deflected us from the main theme.

The mélange can be served first with the intriguing thought that the affluent Western bloc, whether it likes it or not, has stumbled into wedlock with an effective money-wage standard.

---

* On this chapter generally, see the very fine exposition of Monetarism, and a less sensitive evaluation of other views, in J. A. Trevithick and Charles Mulvey, *The Economics of Inflation* (New York: Wiley, 1975). The book leans heavily to the NQTM, exposing in an unintended way its shortcomings by invoking the Monetarist "long-run equilibrium" without penetrating the static mystique of the "long-run" conception. Shocks along the path, and thus investment, labor force, monopoly, government, or other "exogenous" deflections are bypassed. Likewise, they do not offer a "guess" on "how long" before the "equilibrium" actually evolves—if ever. Above all, there is only a glance at instances where labor does not comply with Monetarist stipulations, and thus whether the Monetarist "equilibrium" cannot be hastened through a feasible Incomes Policy. To be sure, the authors curtsey to a "temporary" Incomes Policy to break "inflationary" expectations "for a short period" (pp. 170–171).

At many places they discern the trade-union "bias" toward wage inflation but rather than pursue the logic they opt for the subtleties of M^d theory and policy. It is a case of looking at unpalatable facts and then recessing them in the mind—and omitting them from the model.

The Money-Wage Standard: The Pivotal w Price

The money wage has been described as an exogenous P, capable of leading a derelict life of its own and not immediately answerable to unfolding U data, or past P-history, or any determinate market forces. Overtly, there are innumerable occasions when it is clearly a price born outside the markets: governments, as in the collectivist economies or intermittently in most democratic economies, intervene to impose terms of pay settlements in key labor bargains and thereby set the tone for other bargains.

Money wages have been described as the *pivotal* WCM price, an anchor for costs and a sail for purchasing power. A reborn classicist might judge it to be the "natural" magnetic center around which other money prices cluster or gravitate. Hence it is not farfetched to describe the modern economy as on a *money-wage standard*, with the average wage performing the *numéraire* function of gold in a bygone era.

The gold standard

In the Walrasian model *any* item can serve as a *numéraire* (or standard, or common denominator of value), whether it be a pound of sugar, loaf of bread, or particular automobile; the standard might also be a mythical unit, a rock, a piece of paper, or a more fascinating *objet d'art*. Where the *numéraire* possesses a high market value, such as a house, other items such as bread, newspapers, or milk will be quoted in minute fractions of the *numéraire*. Where the *numéraire* item has a small value, *numéraire* multiples will abound.

For most of the history of capitalism, at least until about 25 or 50 years back—some may prefer the earlier, some the later date—the developed economies were on a gold standard, with varying flaws in the bind. Under the operating mechanics of the system, the price of gold was fixed, in the United States (up until March 1933) at $20.67 per ounce. In the United Kingdom (up until September 1931) the comparable number was £3, 17 shillings, 9 pence. Hence the schoolboy examples of $4.86 = £1, or roughly $5 = £1. All this was long ago; later history became more chaotic, with revaluation in the price of gold and restrictions on private gold holdings and dealings. The history is fascinating, though not our concern here.*

Under the older "automatic" gold standard the Treasury was prepared always to buy and sell gold at the stipulated price. (In the United Kingdom the selling price added one and a half pence to the buying figure.) Thus it is an exaggeration to say that governments "never" fixed prices in the glory days of the market system: *one* price was always fixed, the price of gold. Under the bimetallic standard there was a simultaneous fixing of the price of silver, at $1.29 (and some decimal points) in the United States, leading to the historic 16:1 ratio.

---

* For a very readable history, see Galbraith, *Money: Whence It Came, Where It Went* (Boston: Houghton Mifflin, 1975).

With the price of gold fixed, it was possible, as in index-number calculations, to say that when a larger basket of goods was sold for $20.67 either the price level _fell_ or the value of gold _rose:_ this was commonplace during the long price deflation from about 1875 to 1900. Or from about 1900 on, one could speak of the inflation or the depreciation of gold: as prices rose an ounce of gold would buy proportionately fewer goods. In general, it was possible to declare that causal responsibility belonged "on the side of goods or of gold." Only if the amount of available gold (and other money fixed in fairly rigid ratio to gold) was invariant, could the _P_-events be identified as "on the side of goods, not gold." Implicit, too, was a stable money-demand function. With discoveries and a gold rush, the inflation cause "on the side of money" was apparent.

After about 1925, in the interval before its dramatic demise, the gold standard was a more or less managed currency system governed by the central bankers obeying the "rules of the game"—or misgoverned by violating the rules—which called for the central bank to deflate currency and deposits when gold was shipped out of the open economy or to expand money supplies under gold inflows.

This thumbnail sketch of gold-standard history and analysis is all we need indulge in here.* The point is that under the gold standard there was a legal, and a conventional, _numéraire;_ consciously or not, individuals were quoting prices in terms of gold. A money wage of roughly $42 per week was equal to 2 ounces of gold, a house for $2167 amounted to 100 ounces, though the quotation did not dwell on the gold terms. To be sure, most bond indentures, mindful of legalisms and historic pitfalls of coin debasement and paper money, generally stipulated that interest and principal were payable in "gold dollars of the present weight and fineness"—in memory of Civil War currency depreciation on the cessation of specie payments.†

With money supplies linked indissolubly to the stock of gold, on QTM perceptions inflation was assigned to gold production outpacing goods production. There was the cyclonic California gold rush, the Klondike discoveries, and the Australian and South African booms. Over long periods, however, gold and goods production kept a reasonably uniform pace.

It takes only little imagination to envision our current system as a money-wage standard. Money wages are our effective standard of value, as individuals calculate how much of their year's salary will go for a car, or how much monthly income is needed to cover rent or home payments, etc. Business firms also calculate their price and output actions about unit labor costs.

---

* Cf. Keynes, _Treatise,_ or Harrod, _Money,_ for the historical and analytic perspective. See also Arthur Bloomfield, _Monetary Policy Under the International Gold Standard_ (Federal Reserve Bank of New York, 1959).

† The _ex post_ abrogation of these contract terms led to the historic 1930s Supreme Court gold decisions upholding the FDR gold-standard departure, largely on (specious?) grounds that personal damage could not be proved.

There is this difference. Under the gold standard a rise in money wages would entail pressure on the demand for money which was rather tightly circumscribed by the amount of gold: cyclical recession would set in. Currently, the M total is managed by the MA, limited only by flexible laws permitting the exercise of its discretionary mission. Thus it is not necessary, even with higher w, Q, and N in a growth economy, for the economy to be stifled back into unemployment, reduced output, and lower prices as in the recessions during gold-standard days where the toppled price cards would signal the creation of relatively more abundant real money balances. Greater amounts of money can be generated currently through MA open-market operations.

Nostalgia for a gold standard would be misspent. It is an expensive standard; gold must be mined or imported, either way involving high cost in human labor and materials only to establish a quantity of money to end buried in MA coffers and in mystique-laden shuffles to generate MA behavior to facilitate exchanges. Building up a gold stock also entails some shadow boxing with an illusory foe to defend the metal holdings; they are at best a fair-weather friend: the pretense is always discarded in emergencies. To say that gold "backs up" the money is to play on words: in football we have a good picture of where the linebackers stand. In gold, whenever there is a strong demand for it—a "run"—countries flee from the standard to arrest the gold drain: this would conform to the period of "bust" in the boom-bust cycle. It is as if the linebacker were so valuable to the team, and so fragile, that he was never put into the lineup for fear he would get hurt! Above all, the P, Q, and N magnitudes were vulnerable to the vagaries of gold production and gold demand. The gold-standard system invoked symbols to live by; it is more sensible to devise a more rational and less costly money order.

The money-wage standard

Foreshadowing the WCM and the idea of the money-wage standard are the following passages from Jørgen Pedersen, a Danish economist and clear precursor of the ideas.

The equilibrium price of, say, potatoes is determined by the condition that demand in a market economy must equal supply. The price of labour, w, does not equilibrate the demand and supply of labour. On the contrary . . . the system may be in equilibrium with any value of w. (p. 233)

It is clear that when w and P are interdependent . . . w cannot equilibrate the market. The demand and supply of labour depend on real wages, w/P, and the real price of labour from the point of view of the entrepreneur, also w/P. (pp. 233–234)

The level of w does not affect the equilibrium level of w/P, which is therefore indifferent to the equilibrium level of both employment and aggregate real income. (p. 234)

During many decades the government fixed the price of a commodity, gold. This was an indirect way of fixing w, and it proved to be a very irrational method. It led to many serious results detrimental to human welfare, and finally resulted in a collapse of the system. Why not fix the price of a certain quality of labour, thus adopting a wage standard instead of a gold standard. (p. 244)

It is widely agreed that the general level of w does not affect relative prices or the allocation of productive factors, and that . . . prices adapt themselves readily to changes in w. A "wage standard" would therefore seem to be the ideal method of controlling the monetary system.* (p. 245)

Pedersen is clear on *money* wages as an exogenous price, rather than a market-determined price. Too, he is careful to dissociate real and money wages. In the further step there is the advocacy of a controlled average money-wage level, or the deliberate adoption of a money-wage standard. Whether this step is or is not announced belongs to the arena of metaphysical discourse: relative money-wage patterns in the affluent countries affect their price levels and, over time, cast their strong influence on foreign-exchange rates. The adoption of an Incomes Policy would alter MA behavior, the P-experience, and the growth pattern of the economy, with full employment being persistently attainable compared to the stop-go of the present or the boom-bust of gold-standard days.

In a parallel insight, Hicks wrote:

So long as wages were being determined within a given [gold standard] monetary framework, there was some sense in saying that there was an "equilibrium wage," a wage that was in line with the monetary conditions that were laid down from outside. But the world we now live in is one in which the monetary system has become relatively elastic, so that it can accommodate itself to changes in wages, rather than the other way about.

It is hardly an exaggeration to say that instead of being on a Gold Standard [in 1956], we are on a Labour Standard.†

---

*   Jørgen Pedersen, "Wages and Inflation," in *Inflation*, Proceedings of the International Economic Association (London: Macmillan, 1962), edited by D. C. Hague. The late Professor Pedersen seems to have promulgated a WCM theory as early as 1930, tying his formulation to marginal productivity theory, as in $P = w/MP$, where MP = labor's marginal product. In view of the more restricted prospects of measuring MP as against A, and the presumption in the MP formula of competitive pricing, this is less satisfactory (in my view) than $P = kw/A$. Also, I am not aware of his stress on the demand aspects of money wages. Nonetheless, Pedersen's early commitment to a WCM theory is an instance of imagination, courage, and early priority. Through his influence Scandinavian economists show a greater willingness to examine a WCM theory. (I have taken the liberty in quoting to reduce Pedersen's W to w.)

†   J. R. Hicks, "Economic Foundations of Wage Policy," *Economic Journal* (September 1955), p. 391. Most of the article subsequently assesses not the average wage level but issues arising out of disproportionate relative wage discrepancies under collective bargaining.

This was written over 20 years ago when money wages were still prone to bound upward though confined within a modest range at about a 5 percent trend-like bar.

With w able to float skyward almost anywhere on the grid, depending on human passions of workers, government, and management, P will continue to bounce around. Like it or not, by the WCM lights we are on a money-wage standard: w is the pivotal price and money supplies, in some lag, will respond to unemployment as the MA tacitly concedes its inflation impotence. Better that money wages be tempered to near-optimal size rather than mushroom under chance storm conditions.

The EOE and WCM as Predictive Theories

Friedman has emphasized the worth of the EOE for its predictive value for P because of the stability of m. It is of interest to juxtapose the WCM and EOE for some contrast and arbitration. The showing should also pave the way for some rapprochement between the two conceptions.

From $(MV/Q) = P = (kw/A)$, we can write:

$$(M'V/A) = (kw/A), \tag{9.1a}$$

where $M' = M/N$.

$$MV' = kw \text{ or } (V/k) = (w/P) \tag{9.1b}$$

Form (9.1b) makes apparent the predictive base of the two theories.* For EOE disciples, it becomes necessary to predict: (1) M' and (2) V. In predicting M' there are the two projections, of MA action and of future N figures. For V, despite assurances on its "long-run" stability under "permanent" income conjectures, there is short-run variability.† In using the WCM elements, and an A-component common to both the EOE and WCM, there is the need to foresee: (1) k, and (2) w.

Enough has been said on k; it appears decidedly more predictable, in the short or long view, than V. Likewise, projecting w entails less of a guessing game than M', for over a substantial portion of the economy labor contracts are written 1, 2, and 3 years ahead. On this basis, there is some reasonable foundation available in existent facts to guess w ahead for far longer than the quarterly forecasts which engage contemporary econometric models.

In view of Friedman's zeal in reporting $(\Delta V/V)$ "stability"—constancy?— it is instructive to contrast relative annual changes in velocity to those in

---

*   Friedman has been the authority for testing a theory by its predictive results. He writes: "The ultimate goal of a positive science is the development of a 'theory,' or 'hypothesis' that yields valid and meaningful (i.e., not truistic) predictions about phenomena not yet observed." *Essays in Positive Economics* (University of Chicago, 1953), p. 7. Despite the title, there is a strong dose of "normative" economics in this book and, to the general benefit, in practically all of Friedman's writings.

†   Cf. Cagan, below.

($\Delta k/k$) over the period since 1950. The results are collected in Table 9.1 with k tracings in the accompanying figure just under one-third those in V_1. On the longer trend, k has dropped about 11 percent while V_1 has nearly doubled.

Year-to-year relative changes show better constancy in V but still not matching the lesser pace in k.

Some rapprochement?

If largely $MV = PQ$ is dropped in favor of $MV = kwN$, in a time profile the relation $[m(\Delta M/M) = (\Delta k/k) + (\Delta w/w) + (\Delta N/N)]$ emerges. Dropping k from consideration, and m on surmises of "reasonable" trend "constancy," the EOE looks a bit better in longer-run prediction. The reasons are fairly obvious: so long as ($\Delta N/N$) grew along a long-run trend path, and where

Table 9.1

Relative Changes in Markups and Money Velocity,
1950–1976*

	1950 = 100		Annual changes	
	k	V_1	$k(t_2/t_1)$	$V_1(t_2/t_1)$
1950	100	100	—	—
51	100	109	1.00	1.09
52	97	108	0.97	0.99
53	95	112	0.98	1.03
54	95	110	1.00	0.98
55	94	117	1.02	1.06
56	93	121	0.97	1.04
57	93	127	1.00	1.04
58	93	126	1.00	0.99
59	93	132	1.00	1.05
1960	92	136	0.98	1.04
61	93	137	1.01	1.01
62	93	145	1.01	1.06
63	93	148	·1.00	1.02
64	93	152	0.99	1.03
65	93	158	1.01	1.04
66	92	164	0.99	1.04
67	91	167	0.99	1.01
68	91	169	0.99	1.01
69	90	171	0.98	1.01
1970	89	172	0.99	1.00
71	91	173	1.01	1.01
72	91	180	1.00	1.04
73	89	187	0.99	1.04
74	87	191	0.98	1.02
75	89	196	1.02	1.03

*   For k: (GBP/W). For V_1: (GBP/M_1).

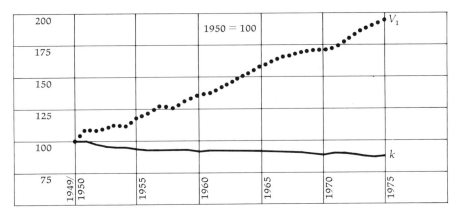

Fig. 9.1(a)

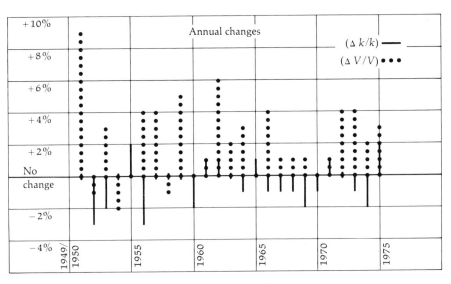

Fig. 9.1(b) Percentage Deviations from Year-to-Year
Constancy in k and V_1

the pace of change of w hovered about a long-run "normal" as in times past,
the EOE was able to achieve the success that has inspired Monetarist confidence for predicting Y and its P and Q components.

All this seems to hinge upon good behavior in $(\Delta w/w)$ over time. Under
an effective Incomes Policy the QTM might once more enjoy a venerated
place for predictive application.*

---

* If a successful Incomes Policy was implemented to stabilize P, so that $(\Delta M/M)$
thereafter approached 5 percent per annum, hard-core Monetarists would be apt
to allege that monetary policy did the price stabilization trick! Cf. the astonished
and incredulous response to such "reasoning" in a letter to the editor by Lord Kaldor
(dated April 11, 1977) to a *London Times* article of April 7.

Monetary Policy Under Full Employment

Earlier WCM analysis, for the most part, assumed a reservoir of unemployment—Marx's "reserve army"—at any date t, or some labor-force growth in the economy moving over time as the MA conjectured ΔM action. Full employment (N_f) aspects of MA concern were omitted.

Full employment

In order to retain the time perspective, we might suppose that either the labor force shows nil (or negligible) growth over time, or that for some extenuating reasons, valid or not, the objective is to hold N constant, as $N(t_0) = N(t_1) = N(t_2) = \ldots$, where the time intervals cover perhaps quarter-years or years. In the progressive economy where the $(\Delta L/L) \approx 1.2$ percent per annum, the MA should—must?—aim for at least commensurate Q and N gains.

The ΔM implications for $(\Delta N/N)$ are embodied in Eq. (4.8): MA maneuvering must balance $m(\Delta M/M) = (\Delta w/w) - (\Delta A/A)$. Whether ΔQ is enlarged depends on ΔA. Confining $(\Delta w/w)$ to about 3 or 4 percent, as through Incomes Policy, and with m short of 2, the MA machinations could occasionally drop even below the 3 percent "steady-rule."

Nonetheless, becoming engrossed solely in tests of aggregate M-totals could engender some sectoral disequilibrium. Recalling the P_c equation, and the multiplicative N/N_c term, a Wicksellian-Hayekian drama may be afoot, with an excess of funds deflected into the I-sector and impelling a P_c breakout in the C-sector (or vice versa).* Some structural disequilibrium may be set in motion through imbalance in *intended* savings compared to investment decisions.

To abort a sectoral disequilibrium process, the MA would have to project the volume of prospective savings at N_f and try to jiggle the interest-rate structure by dealing more in long-term open-market securities and less in shorts (or the other way around) to achieve actual $I =$ intended S: long interest rates could be raised and short rates lowered (or vice versa). Any mistakes committed in a stable general (GBP) P-environment, by virtue of a (w/A) alignment, need never entail a gross imbalance. Through shuffles in its Treasury bonds and Treasury bill portfolio the MA could implement its sectoral balance designs. Market swaps of one obligation for the other, and their purpose, would be comprehended by the money markets in a fairly stable general P-framework.

---

*   Cf. Chapter 3. Wicksell saw the cumulative inflation process emanating from central bank depression of interest rates through excessive money supply creation. Later he was led to renounce the inflationary theme in recognition of productivity improvements which tempered his essentially stationary thesis dynamized only via the money creation. Hayek, building on Wicksell, saw first an investment bulge and then a consumption binge as income recipients moved to spend their earnings; resource flows would then rush pell-mell, first into I and then to C. See Friedrich Hayek, *Prices and Production*.

Monetarist thinking which, for the full-employment case, concentrates only on money aggregates thus appears to oversimplify the MA task. The lot of the MA can never be made so easy except under the most fortuitous circumstances. Still, considering the constant M-aggregate, and reasonable obedience to the steady-rule violated only to account for $(\Delta w/w)$ variations, any Monetarist protests of discretionary MA portfolio swaps would lose most of their sting.

Unbounded pathological Wicksellian-Hayekian cases can be discounted, though some minor (*tatonnement*) imbalances are inevitable. Attainable MA deftness should be able to cope with disequilibrating tendencies in a calm P-sea.

The Open Economy

The necessary amendments for the open economy, and the implications for MA behavior, are also fairly straightforward: the extra complication is the n-term denoting the domestic content of GNP exclusive of imports. Recalling Eq. (3.18), the modification becomes:

$$m(\Delta M/M) = (\Delta n/n) + (\Delta P/P) + (\Delta Q/Q) \tag{9.2}$$

In Eq. (9.2) both P and Q refer to magnitudes *inclusive* of import content; alternative equational terms would be: $n(P_d + P_f Q_f/Q_d)(Q_d) = nPQ$. Probing m, n, P, and Q in an open economy swept by changing import prices and structural shifts in trade will occupy staff experts in intricate calculations and projections for MA reflection.

Even this n-addendum leaves the MA vexed with the other set of great worries of the open economy, namely, the capital flows that are often only tenuously connected to trade winds. To simplify, suppose the foreign balance is finely attuned, with imports and exports in a neat equality. An inflow of capital funds will, in effect, mean that the MA (or banks) will be acquiring foreign currencies as assets, and enlarging deposit liabilities by paying out domestic moneys. Insofar as the growth of bank demand deposits coincides with MA designs, the acquisition of foreign funds instead of domestic promissory notes or domestic bonds merely inserts a different money market asset account growing on bank ledgers. However, depending on the activity of these funds, compared to loans to business firms, the value of m (or $\Delta V/V$) may be subject to some unusual flux. The MA will thus have to assess capital inflows in its deliberations.

Insofar as the MA acquires the foreign currencies by intervening directly in foreign-exchange markets, the dealings serve as another form of open-market policy, perhaps requiring other offsetting swaps to achieve its interest-rate goals in an economy under full employment. Capital outflows, on the other hand, may require some reverse neutralization, with the MA undertaking open-market bill or bond purchases to bolster commercial banks' reserve balances and to prevent a distortion of the ΔM_s directives through the capital outflows.

Currency speculation, international interest-rate differentials, and political alarms at home or abroad can spark capital flows, posing a series of worries to disturb MA equanimity. In a regime of floating exchange rates, foreign-exchange market adjustments should help minimize capital movements, though, through exchange-rate effects on import prices and quantities, the possible ramifications extend to n, P_f, and Q_f. While the total incidence may be fairly small, the tracing of impacts can be a maze for full-time preoccupation of MA staffs in the more open economies.

Adherence to the steady-rule could thus be a prescription for unemployment disasters in conditions where there are flash spurts in $(\Delta w/w)$ compounded by a wave of capital outflows tending to depress the foreign-exchange rate and raise import prices: the contingency is not an inaccurate description of events in Italy, the United Kingdom, and elsewhere in recent years. The country experiencing the flight of funds and outsized wage movements is struck a double blow: exchange-rate depreciation is superimposed on the wage outbreak to elevate the home price level. Adherence to an adamant steady-rule would, in the circumstances, induce substantial home unemployment. While the lower exchange rate will stimulate exports (after some lag), the constrained finance would immediately handicap job expansion.

Lags: A Less Intimidating Perception

The endless complications thrust forward by Monetarists over lags can become the plot of a scary tale, in the manner of sensational newspaper accounts of gruesome killings which, fortunately, do not afflict the daily lives of most people. Likewise, the MA is attuned to the hazards of its daily existence and is able to roll with events as part of its operating routine: it is only the whirlwinds of an abnormal few days of crisis that breed consternation. In a world of P-calm, and free of alarms of war, the MA life can be fairly tranquil. Further, MA decisions and errors are rarely irrevocable; a few hectic days are seldom cataclysmic and beyond salvage once the disorder is intuitively apprehended and the original shock waves are absorbed. Like a fighter restored by a second wind after being struck some hard blows, the MA is capable of returning to the fray for a spirited rejoinder.

Much has been made by Monetarists of the lags between monetary policy and systemic responses, of the time discrepancy between open-market operations in financial markets and the percolation of the money moves down to job and output markets.

Largely, the warnings are sounded that departures from a steady-rule will predestine inflation, after a short or longer interval once the 4 percent line is breached: the MA courts the perils of Pauline after 3, 6, 16, or 34 months— or longer. Where the predicted apocalypse is averted after the dates expire, there are solemn Monetarist pronouncements that the "lags are longer than expected." It is never that the forecasts of the world's end in inflation are awry, but that the doom awaiting the sinful ΔM emissions has merely been postponed. Given enough time, and a misbehaving (w/A) ratio, the predictions must ultimately be confirmed—there were those who predicted inflation in daily bulletins in 1932 and 1933 at the depths of the Great Depression. Of course, it took World War II and postwar wage inflation to verify the daily diatribes at President Roosevelt. In some gesture of amnesty, President Lincoln is now seldom vilified for his greenback venture "causing" the contemporary inflation.

At bottom, the somber tidings of inflation are predicated on the QTM, new and old, mixed with the Phillips curve, after the lag subtleties are decomposed. If the WCM theory comprises the frame of reference, and if most of the ΔM emissions serve mainly to sustain Q and N along the $w(t)$ and $P(t)$ paths, the Monetarist premonitions become less ominous. Instead, given an exogenous escalation in $w(t)$ the pertinent concern with lags becomes transformed into a question of how fast the MA can nudge Q and N onto a full-employment track reflecting the economy's potential, while precluding unbalanced profit rates and a Wicksell-Hayek disequilibrium between C and I sectors.

So long as the monetary lags affect mainly $Q(t)$ and $N(t)$, as in $\Delta M(t_0)$ inducing $\Delta Q(t_1)$ or $\Delta Q(t_2)$ enlargements, the delayed inflation time bombs pictured by Monetarists instill fewer forebodings of future inflation, whether in $P(t_1)$, $P(t_3, t_6, t_{16}, t_{34}, \ldots)$. Inflation remains a (w/A), and not a ΔM phenomenon. If the (w/A) ratio threatens to become disjointed, it is an incomes, not a Monetarist, remedy that should be prescribed. To validate their P-theme, Monetarists would have to marshal persuasive evidence on smooth Phillips curve concatenations, or jumps in k after ΔN advances induced by money emissions. Evidence has not been forthcoming.

Natural Unemployment, Money Transmission, and Wage "Catch-Up"

Monetarist doctrine dominated journals, textbooks, and the press, even intimidating public policy designs, since the late 1960s.* The doctrine has currently lapsed into a more settled, less strident phase, its momentum shaken by its

---

* Monetarist literature has, as observed, grown like Topsy over the last decade. For a sizable bibliography, see Richard Selden, "Monetarism," in *Modern Economic Thought*. Readings volumes, with copious references, are Richard S. Thorn, *Monetary Theory and Policy* and William E. Gibson and George G. Kaufman, *Monetary Economics: Readings on Current Issues*. See also, Patinkin, for citations to the older literature. An insightful and playful account of the "inevitability" of the Monetarist wave appears in Harry G. Johnson, "The Keynesian Revolution and the Monetarist Counter-Revolution," *American Economic Review* (May 1971).

noxious—and ineffective—inflation cure of tighter money and more unemployment.

Nonetheless, one should not begrudge the Monetarists due credit for stimulating study on the inflation crisis in contrast to Keynesians who fiddled —while economies were being seared—with doctrines of "living with inflation" and proceeding (as Keynesians) to neoclassical "equilibrium" growth models, *sans* price levels, ecology, and distributive phenomena, and without a serious government sector, even as the growth path *assumed* full employment. Despite their insensitivity to unemployment, Monetarists nudged the economics profession back to the here and now by exposing the ominous threat to stability released by the cutting edge of inflation.*

We consider now some further doctrines prominent in the Monetarist vision.

"Natural" unemployment

Mixed in with the NQT distillation, in Friedman's renditions especially and filtering through to the legions of disciples, is the simple theme of a "natural" rate of unemployment. This settles at "the level that would be ground out by the Walrasian system of general equilibrium equations," which allows for some "frictional" unemployment. Thus if the MA "tries to peg the 'market' rate of unemployment below the 'natural' rate" through enlarging the rate of monetary growth and thus "initially" lowering "interest rates . . . to stimulate spending," this will provoke "an excess demand for labor so real wages will tend to rise toward their initial level." Soon enough, "the rise in real wages will reverse the decline in unemployment, and . . . tend to return unemployment to its former level." Unemployment "can be kept below the 'natural' rate only by inflation."

To state the general conclusion still differently, the monetary authority controls nominal quantities—directly, the quantity of its own liabilities. In principle, it can use this control to peg a nominal quantity—an exchange rate, the price level, the nominal level of national income, the quantity of money by one or another definition—or to peg the rate of change in a nominal quantity—the rate of inflation or deflation, the rate of growth or decline in nominal national income, the rate of growth of the quantity of money. It cannot use its control over nominal quantities to peg a real quantity—the real rate of interest, the rate of unemployment, the level of real national income, the real quantity of money, the rate of growth of real national income, or the rate of growth of the real quantity of money.†

---

*   Monetarism has also inspired some economists to return to Keynes. See Paul Davidson, *Money and the Real World* and Hyman Minsky, *John Maynard Keynes*, and their respective articles in *Modern Economic Thought*. Previous writings by Kahn, Harrod, Kaldor, and, of course, Keynes himself, constitute the background literature. References appear in Davidson, and in my "Money Supplies and Price-Output Variations: The Friedman Puzzle," (with H. Habibagahi) in *KaM* Essay 5.

†   Friedman, "The Role of Monetary Policy, p. 11.

The dedication to "natural" law is inspiring—to Monetarists, at least. The economic outcome is irresistible, undaunted by behavioral convolutions despite routine Monetarist concessions to wavering and uncertain anticipations. Manifest is a heady commitment to "natural," mechanistic, Walrasian "real" equations establishing an ineluctable relative price pattern, undeviating in full employment, and affirming that the economic mosaic can only be sporadically interrupted by "nominal" inflation distortions. Redistributive shuffles and capital formation decisions under the price wave evoke no lasting consequences; anticipations are irrevocably entrenched to a deterministic "long run" regardless of the historical price course—or the Friedman $\Delta P - \Delta Q$ puzzle.

Hence the economic system is effectively dichotomized between real and nominal income sets: money doesn't *"really"* matter, allowing enough (unspecified) time, whatever the inflation ravages on individual and business lives. This is a "two-tier," compartmentalized economy, with nominal magnitudes capable of only transient disruption of the unshakable "real" tiger. Price history never modifies, maddens, nor mitigates real patterns, at least not for long.

The contention that the MA can "peg" the price level renders the whole scheme suspect. Several questions arise: (1) If the MA can do the trick, why has it failed so signally? Obtuseness in grasping the profound QTM? Or inability to exercise *direct* P-leverage—as the WCM would have it? (2) If the MA *did* control P, could this also not invite *real* Keynesian investment and neoclassical growth instabilities? Most of the Keynesian recession and Harrod "knife-edge" growth models *assumed* stable price levels. Fiscal instruments might still be imperative to "correct" fleeting or enduring chokes on effective demand—assuming too that the MA was proscribed from tampering with a "unique" M-magnitude. (3) If $P(t)$ cannot be flattened without reconciling the (w/A) terms, and if the alignment cannot be consummated by monetary manipulations, then there must be "real" costs attached to monetary policy. Real variables must wind a more crooked bend than the predestined Walrasian groove.

The failure to ponder unemployment prospects under a WCM domiciled P-determination dispels an unwavering faith to a sure and easy ride to the haven of Walrasian full employment. After all, if P is pegged by MA policy acting under Monetarist direction, nobody need act on any anticipation of inflation or any premise beyond a fixed $P(t)$. Yet Harrodian and Keynesian instabilities intrude in this Monetarist P-world to cloud the inflation success-story—unless we are persuaded by the need to raise our "natural" unemployment sights to whatever is needed to hold P stable.* Frightful unemployment, by quick verbal dexterity, would be painted as "natural," Walrasian, and a full-employment *magnum bonum*.

---

* Tales of rising "natural" rates of unemployment were being told more frequently in 1976 and 1977.

Perhaps the 1968 "natural" unemployment tale has been blotted out by the later recognition of the "hole-in-the-middle." Yet the same "natural" doctrines proliferate, too freely condemning as superfluous any attempt to reduce the oppressive post-1973 disorders by muffling Incomes Policy proposals before they are even uttered—or by stifling their publication.

The transmission mechanism

Vital to Monetarism is the "transmission" mechanism. Acknowledging it, some discussion is devoted to it and always in supplication of the need for more finality—duplicating unconsciously Cantillon's language of nearly 250 years back.

After observing that Keynesians regard ΔM as leading to $\Delta r < 0$, thereby affecting I and, through the multiplier, Q and N, David Fand writes:

Monetarists, following the Quantity Theory . . . suggest that an increase in money may directly affect expenditures, prices, and a wide variety of implicit yields (i.e., prices) on physical assets.

In a period of rising prices, inflationary expectations raise the cost of holding money and the public has an incentive to reduce the quantity of desired real balances by increasing expenditures. The link between money and prices is likely to be strengthened during an inflation.[*]

Thus the inflation process has a sturdy one-two punch: more M, a higher MV, and higher prices. Submerged are Friedman's ΔQ and ΔP "puzzles" as the OQTM rides again. Fand, however, by injecting anticipated price rises implies V-variability.

Friedman, in conjecturing on the MA striving to cut U below the "natural" rate, "which is consistent with equilibrium in the structure of *real* wage rates" sees unemployment as a fixture in the Walrasian "real" system, the Siamese twin that can be wrenched away only in the unending QTM inflation economy.[†] To Friedman, the Phillips curve represents mostly an optical illusion, confusing *nominal* and *real* wages: Phillips "wrote his article for a world in which everyone anticipated that nominal prices would be stable and in which that anticipation remained unshaken and immutable whatever happened to actual prices and wages."[‡]

Friedman explains, introducing a reference to Brazil for illumination, that after an initial ΔM increase, as "selling prices of products typically respond

---

[*]   Fand, reprinted in Gibson and Kaufman, p. 75.

[†]   "The Role of Monetary Policy," p. 8.

[‡]   There may be some controversy over this quick interpretation of history; Phillips curve data covered 1861–1957. Included was, at the start, the Civil War inflation. Then there was the mild upswing after 1900, to the big World War I jump and then the ramifications of the continental hyperinflation of the 1920s. Even in the depths of the Great Depression the howls of anguish of assorted New Deal critics predicted calamitous inflation. It is a loose perspective to generalize that "everyone" anticipated P-stability.

to an unanticipated rise in nominal demand faster than prices of factors of production," real wages *fall*. So "there is an excess demand for labor" and soon employees "demand higher nominal wages for the future"; thus, "real wages will tend to rise toward their initial level." Hence:

Even though the higher rate of monetary growth continues, the rise in real wages will reverse the decline in unemployment, and then lead to a rise, which will tend to return unemployment to its former level. In order to keep unemployment [below the "natural" rate] the monetary authority would have to raise monetary growth still more. As . . . in the interest rate case, [this can be accomplished] only by accelerating inflation.*

What this has to do with a world of growing productivity, of wages advancing faster than prices, and *any* feedback of nominal wages to prices is remarkably obscure. How labor can be in "excess" demand under widespread unemployment is peculiarly opaque.

Playing catch-up

At heart this is the "catch-up" theory, of $P(t)$ driving higher, through "too much money chasing too few goods," with labor a laggard in the chase, and then speeding on to close the gap. Professor Friedman could easily persuade unionists that they are always victimized, innocent of P-derangement by their catch-up tactics. The obtuse MA is the marauder rather than the human urge to secure a larger money income. Monetarism indicts the handful of central bankers, absolving everyone else in the "virtue must catch-up" scenario.

The myth has ample antecedents; earlier business cycle theorists also expounded that prices "lead" costs in the boom-bust cycles.† The Monetarists have freshened up the doctrine, fleshed it out with M^d (i.e., $\Delta V/V$ a constant) and proclaimed it an eternal verity.‡

The solitary stumbling block is its disregard for the facts in the temporal sequence. Suppose that to any date t_1 the $P(t)$ path has been rising. Invert the

---

*   Ibid., p. 10.

†   Cf. Wesley Mitchell, *Business Cycles and Their Causes* (Univ. of California, 1913, Part III, Reprint 1941), pp. 16, 31, 139–140.

‡   So far, without any attention to the analysis of Thomas F. Cargill, who concluded from data for England and the United States that "the wage-lag hypothesis has been accepted almost as an article of faith" yet "the results . . . indicate that . . . in the . . . short run . . . wages and prices appear to be coincident" and "when there is a time difference . . . there are many instances where no meaningful time differences exist, implying that wages and prices are coincident." "An Empirical Investigation of the Wage-Lag Hypothesis," *American Economic Review* (Dec. 1969), pp. 807, 811. For West Germany, over 1963–1970, another study concludes that on "the lagging of wages behind the price trend" the findings are that: "A conception of this nature finds no confirmation . . ." See Bernd Schips, "Lag Hypotheses in Macroeconomic Business Cycle Models," *The German Economic Review* (No. 2, 1974), p. 105.

WCM to read: $(A/k) = (w/P)$. Thus a real-wage drop—(w/P) falling—would signify $k(t_1) > k(t_0)$ or $\Delta A < 0$ until money wages "caught up."

Years of $\Delta A < 0$ have been infrequent in the last quarter century. Monetarists have yet to show sufficient flux in k to verify the garbled theory as a plausible surmise. The k-trend has been (slowly) falling while A has advanced.

Realistically, the appeal to declining "real" wages in the inflation process has slight relevance to the facts in the United States, Canada, United Kingdom, Germany, Japan, and, in general, all of the affluent countries over the last inflationary quarter century. Despite persistent inflation, real wages have *risen.** In the United States there have been only one or two recent years of (mild) real-wage decline. And this occurred in a period of *rising,* not falling unemployment, contrary to the Friedman doctrine.

Expectations of Inflation

It has become faddish to describe "expectations of inflation" as promoting the price upheaval.† Of course, expectations make the world go round, coloring all

---

* In a laudable effort to develop a "static" model of Monetarism, Robert H. Raasche finds that with an augmentation ΔM, "Real output, commodity prices, and money wages are all higher than their initial equilibrium values" although "the actual real-wage rate declines." This mixes the "diminishing returns" inflation, noted by Keynes and others, with changes in money wages. It has nothing to do with the money augmentation other than that more money is usually imperative to finance more output and more employment. When Raasche permits a "change in . . . the money-wage rate . . . less than proportional to the change in P," this is a "money-wage lag" hypothesis and rising k. One wonders what all this has to do with "*all* relative prices simultaneously ground out by Walrasian equations." See "A Comparative Static Analysis of Some Monetarist Propositions," *Monthly Review* (St. Louis Federal Reserve Bank, Dec. 1973), p. 19.

In defending Keynesianism against Monetarism, Ronald L. Teigen writes: "Modern Keynesian static analysis, based on the complete Keynesian system with flexible prices and inflexible money wages," and "Keynesianism implies sticky wages and money illusion in the labor market rather than rigid prices," concluding "there is very little if anything in Monetarist theory which is new and different."

Whatever the identification of Monetarism and Keynesianism, it has little to do with Keynes and the wage-unit as the inflation price-maker. See "A Critical Look at Monetarist Economics," Ibid. (Jan. 1972), pp. 21, 23.

Similarly, using *IS-LM* curves, there is the price level going toward infinite values while the money wage is constant. This remarkable feat demonstrates that it is possible to make anything happen in a textbook. See R. S. Holbrook, "The Interest Rate, the Price Level, and Aggregate Output," in *Readings in Money, National Income, and Stabilization Policy* (Homewood, Ill.: Irwin, 1974, 3rd ed.), W. L. Smith and R. L. Teigen, eds., p. 52.

† There is some tendency to regard the emphasis on "expectations" as peculiarly modern and novel. Yet Jevons, indeed practically all the theorists in the marginal utility "revolution," and Marshall, Lavington, Pigou on the business cycle (among others), Knight, Keynes, Robertson, Ohlin, Lindahl, Myrdal, etc., on money and

our actions, affecting all our decisions: we seek the pleasant outcome pictured in our anticipations of events. Yet disappointment, when culmination does not match prevision, is also a fact of life.

Disappointments are apt to inspire revised expectations. The "expectations" thesis must thus hinge on identifying the forces that have unleashed the unruly "expectations of inflation." And this query forces us to confront the continued surge in wages and salaries. For example, it hardly entails an astute knowledge of economic affairs to conclude that as construction workers gain substantial pay boosts the price of new houses will mount. Likewise, business executives experiencing successive rounds of pay hikes can readily "predict" higher prices.

Thus, so long as money incomes advance at the undue pace they have in the past, "expectations of inflation" will be aroused and will tend, as a self-fulfilling prophecy, to be confirmed by events. Only a more temperate money-income course can break the ongoing spiral in which the buoyant expectations literally feed on themselves, with the belief in inflation evoking soaring pay demands, etc. The unruly sequence can be broken by incomes restraints. Citing "expectations of inflation" without counseling remedial measures reflects an attitude of despair, waiting like Micawber for something to turn up, while individual pay claimants, acting in self-interest, strive to outrun other wage groups in a pell-mell rush.

To accede to the chant of "expectations of inflation" as a cause without a cure is to acquiesce in inflation. The self-generating seeds can be made dormant by measures to check the money-income path, compelling a revision of beliefs converging on an expectation of price-level constancy. As each group discerns that other groups are acquiring noninflationary income gains, the inflationary expectations will be dispelled and recede into memory. We can overcome the frantic pell-mell rush in which each group seeks money-wage insurance protection, only to be ravaged by the final price-level result which erodes the value of money and creates unemployment and financial instability by the application of conventional monetary policy responses.

---

investment, can be cited to form a long list. For our own generation, that penetrating and perceptive "majority of one," G. L. S. Shackle, has consistently championed the position and fashioned original tools. See, e.g., among his many writings, *Expectation in Economics* (Cambridge: 1949).

Friedman seems, to his credit, to have been especially early in injecting the concept of "expectations of inflation," as preceding quotes indicate. (The concept was very explicit in Keynes' "user-cost" where its importance is held in more modest, and proper, perspective.) The concept also has come to pervade Phelps' inflation writings. Most recently, to quell the unruly exuberance of wage expectations, William Fellner has suggested maintaining an above minimal "reserve-army" of unemployed—to use Marx's language for this new advocacy of Phillips curve doctrine, to be instituted by policy design. See *Towards a Reconstruction of Macroeconomics: Problems of Theory and Policy* (American Enterprise Institute, 1976).

The Demand for Money

Much of Monetarism constitutes an update of language surrounding the EOE and the OQTM: the NQT as such has hardly been an unmitigated success story. Lags add something to the empirical literature; there has been more measurement but there are some conceptual obstacles. The "steady-rule" is not new. Even though Friedman may have arranged the chords somewhat differently, or rediscovered what others were prone to cast off as outmoded, probably the most innovative contribution in the lode he tapped was the specification of the money-demand equation.

In the lead essay of a volume that ushered in the modern QTM revival (prior to the Monetarist christening), the older theory was described as misconstrued in being perceived as a theory of money *supply* rather than money *demand*.* The money-demand function (M^d) was offered as a legacy of the "oral tradition" of the Chicago School.† Thus:

$$\frac{M^d}{P} = f\left(y, R/W; r_m, r_b, r_e, \frac{1}{P}\frac{dP}{df}, u\right) \tag{9.3a}$$

$$\frac{M^d}{Y} = \frac{1}{v\left(y, R/W; r_m, r_b, r_e, \frac{1}{P}\frac{dP}{dt}, u\right)}, \tag{9.3b}$$

where $y = Y/P = Q$

R/W = relative income distribution

r_m = expected nominal rate of return on money (e.g., short-term interest rates)

r_b = expected bond interest rate

r_e = expected return on equities

$(1/P)(dP/dt)$ = expected price level change

u = utility preferences for liquidity.‡

---

* See "The Quantity Theory of Money-A Restatement," in *Studies in the Quantity Theory of Money* (University of Chicago, 1956). Considering the equilibrium equation of M^d and M^s, and the usual choice of equilibrium methods by Monetarists, some may see the elegance as overdrawn, especially in the final results of a "stable" money-demand function yielding $(\Delta V/V)$ = a constant other than zero. Selden credits Karl Brunner for coining "Monetarism" in "The Role of Money and Monetary Policy," *Monthly Review*, Federal Reserve Bank of St. Louis (July 1968).

† Readers of Keynes are jostled by the striking liquidity-preference chords. Cf. Don Patinkin, "Friedman On the Quantity Theory of Money and Keynesian Economics," Symposium, *Journal of Political Economy* (Sept./Oct., 1972), and Friedman's aggrieved reply. Also Patinkin, "The Chicago Tradition, The Quantity Theory, and Friedman," *Journal of Money, Credit, and Banking* (Feb. 1969).

‡ Equation (9.3a) follows the later statement in "A Monetary Framework," p. 13. The R/W ratio is used as an income-distribution variable in lieu of Friedman's "human" and "nonhuman" wealth ratio.

In Eq. (9.3a) the demand for "real-balances" of money deflated by the price level is stipulated. For a long-time this equation was assumed to be sufficient to determine the price level. The confusion was late to be rectified by reversion to an EOE equation for determining P; the omission becomes palpable when the real money demand is equated to the real money supply, or $(M^d/P) = (M^s/P)$, with P becoming redundant.

In Eq. (9.3b) the link to the NQT truism is stipulated. Given the determination of real income ($y \equiv Q$) through the Walrasian general equilibrium equations, and with other variables being either past (as R/W), or expectational (as r and dP/dt), or "given" (as u), then: (1) money income is determined, and (2) from invoking the implicit EOE in $Y = PQ$ (or Py), the OQT fallback, P, can be extracted.

In these equations V has become a function reposing on a string of variables, rather than a constant as $V = \overline{V}$ in the strict mechanistic OQT. Friedman assures us that the V function is stable; he has estimated the elasticity of money income to money supplies as 1.84 (using his definition of "permanent" income). Thus:

$$E_{ym} = (M\Delta Y/Y\Delta M) \approx 1.84.^* \tag{9.4a}$$

Invoking $(\Delta M/M) + (\Delta V/V) = (\Delta Y/Y)$, this signifies:

$$(\Delta V/V \approx 0.84 \text{ (for a "one-percent" run-up in } \Delta M/M). \tag{9.4b}$$

At the end of a long journey from the mechanistic OQT of $(\Delta V/V) = 0$, the spirited Monetarist revolution has led, for the United States, to a stable "permanent-income" velocity ratio of $(\Delta V/V) \approx 0.84$. Thus we can write the "money-income multiplier" as:

$$m(\Delta M/M) = (\Delta Y/Y), \tag{9.5}$$

with $m \approx 1.84$ instead of $m = 1$. Even this value follows with some "lag," for it embodies "permanent" income through some individualistic normalization of national income data. Vagueness still attaches to $(\Delta V/V)$ for GNP, GBP, or NI over any "short" period, say of one, two, or more years.

Friedman has, as in his E_{ym} computation, affirmed "the extraordinary empirical stability and regularity to such magnitudes as income velocity that cannot but impress anyone who works extensively with monetary data."†

---

* See *The Optimum Quantity of Money and Other Essays* (Chicago: Aldine, 1969), p. 227. The $(\Delta V/V)$ calculation, and in many remarks about monetary regularities Friedman avers high stability in the relative change in velocity. This premise is crucial to his "steady-rule" policy. Leonall C. Andersen, the leading resident Monetarist at the Federal Reserve Bank of St. Louis, finds a good deal of velocity variability only to conclude that this fact "taken alone" matters little for policy. Thus the regularity is a virtue for Friedman, and the instability not a vice for Andersen. See "Observed Income Velocity of Money: A Misunderstood Issue in Monetary Policy," *Monthly Review* (Federal Reserve Bank of St. Louis, Aug., 1975).

† "The Quantity Theory of Money," p. 21.

More recently, in referring to inflation as "everywhere a monetary phenomenon" he remarks that "a fully defensible statement would have to allow for autonomous changes in velocity . . . But I know of no case in which these qualifications are of critical importance."*

Velocity, for Friedman, after wrestling with the intricacies of a stable demand function, tracks a "constant" path analogous to k. Others are more dubious of relative-velocity constancy, at least over the near term, making the "law" more suspect as a strong, supporting pillar for economic stabilization.†

Notes on an alternative approach to money demand

Friedman's M^d function is thus concerned with the V (or m) determinants. Examining the variables, the demand for money depends on more than the need for it to serve as a medium of exchange to finance the current output flow—the transactions motive. In Chapter 4 the concern was solely with this aspect of money demand. Nonetheless, if Friedman's V-regularity were sustained empirically, monetary theory would be enormously simplified: other sources of money demand beyond transactions uses would be a fixed appendage of the PQ magnitude.

We consider here an alternative to the Friedman conception based on Keynes' liquidity-preference function where $L \equiv M^d$. As observed, there is a strong consanguinity between Friedman's formulation and Keynes' statement.

Keynes wrote (*General Theory*, p. 199):

$$M \equiv M_1 + M_2 = L_1(Y) + L_2(r) \equiv L. \tag{9.6}$$

In Eq. (9.5) $M =$ the money supply, segregated into M_1 serving the "transactions-demand" contained in the segment of the liquidity-preference function $L_1(Y)$. M_2 characterizes that portion of M drawn off to sate the "speculative-motive," the $L_2(r)$ portion of money demand being acutely responsive to interest rates. For Keynes, L_2 embodied the behavior of firms and individuals, especially money market "speculative" participants, who await opportune moments to buy a range of financial and also physical assets, not the least being government bonds. Without government bond price perturbations there would be no point in holding money, which is a noninterest-bearing

---

*   *Monetary Correction*, p. 10n.

†   Recently, Phillip Cagan has remarked, in a section on "What Went Wrong with the Money-Demand Equations?", that after mid-1974 through 1975: "The equations had gone haywire" and "the latest fiasco is another reminder to view the results of these equations with extreme caution." See "Monetary Problems and Policy Choices In Reducing Inflation and Unemployment," in *Contemporary Economic Problems*, William Fellner, ed., pp. 38–39, 41.

Curiously, Cagan notes (p. 49) the (w/A) influence on prices but fails utterly to see the pernicious influence of this recognition for a monetary theory of the price level.

government obligation (or hold minimum-yield checking or savings accounts),* when sure interest and principal repayment (in money) is obtainable on government bonds. The L_2 function is negatively responsive to interest rates, inasmuch as lower interest rates give more to fear than hope in view of growing prospects of higher interest rates while cutting the opportunity costs of holding cash.† At institutional interest-rate floors, where the general expectation is that the only future way out was up, there is the *cul de sac* of the liquidity-trap: more money by the MA would fail to depress interest rates further. At this institutional bottom, Keynes despaired of purely monetary maneuvers to lift I and restore the N_f track.

L_1 covers the business demands for money to finance the enormous volume of interfirm transactions in raw and semifinished materials, and of paying wages and other incomes to sustain the output scale. Likewise, for households the income flow Y would require "pocket" and checkbook money-demand to bridge the gap between paydays and purchase forays. Keynes' L_1 expression thus encompassed the medium of exchange function. Hicks has characterized the transactions or medium aspect as the demand for money as "a running-asset."‡ A long time ago, to inculcate the demand point, Dennis Robertson observed that money in circulation was always in somebody's possession, never "on the wing," but always money "sitting."§

As against Keynes' L_1 and L_2 expository compartmentalization, there is a tendency, already implicit in Robertson's "money-sitting," to generalize the "store of value" function as fundamental: comparisons are always being made on the importance of holding more money, at the margin, as against more consumer goods or financial assets. By detailing the wide spectrum of assets this comprises the essence of the "portfolio demand" theory of money: the array of alternatives is also implicit in Friedman's concept of money as "a temporary abode of purchasing power." The literally limitless variety of assets, consisting of the assortment of stocks and bonds, land, buildings, *objets d'art*, etc., comprise competing uses for money; all of them promise lucrative yields against the liquidity advantages of the nil interest or dividend asset, money.‖ As for a "capital gain," money can have this characteristic

---

* Checking accounts in the United States do not (1976) pay interest but have a "liquidity-yield." Clearly, Keynes' idealized $M_1, M_2, \ldots$, are not to be confused with Friedman's *measured* quantities.

† Clearly, L_2 could subsume the full range of assets as equities, land, etc. Confining the function to government bonds permits a direct exposition as only interest-rate risk is entailed, with default risk precluded.

‡ See Hicks, *Crisis*, p. 47, for an illuminating statement.

§ Robertson, pp. 37–38.

‖ For a portfolio-theory statement, see James Tobin, "A General Equilibrium Approach to Monetary Theory." The danger facing the general "portfolio-balance" approach is that in its focus on the chain of assets, the meticulous fascination with the attached uncertainties builds up a tendency to squeeze out the *sine qua non* of

only in an era of falling prices; otherwise it is a dwindling asset under inflation.

In any event, it becomes possible to write $L_2 = L(r_b, r_e, r_f, r_a)$, where the r's refer to returns on bonds, equities, other financial assets, and physical assets such as land. Presumably, these can be encapsulated into Keynes' condensed L_2 form where r is interpreted to mean the "full" structure of interest rates, or returns on alternative assets. Further, while money is held in lieu of other assets at the *prevailing* structure of returns, it is *future* prices of other assets that must be in mind in reaching a portfolio decision. Thus L_2 must carry some "expectational" variable, as $L_2(r, r^*)$, where r^* refers to the expected future yield structure, *including (implicitly) the dates at which they will be fulfilled:* in financial markets, the incontestable aphorism is that "timing is everything."

It can, of course, be argued that future expectations are already embodied in money demand at each r, or that expected future interest rates are already reflected in present rates. Nevertheless, if the demand for money is chained to interest rates currently existing, then each rate may, at different times, be tied to a different market consensus on the structure of expected yields, so that the $L_2(t_1)$ demand may diverge from $L_2(t_2)$: at the same Y the L-curve will shift. Keynes' words are still alive:

. . . *uncertainty as to the future course of the rate of interest is the sole intelligible explanation of the type of liquidity-preference L_2 which leads to the holding of cash M_2. (p. 201)*

. . . *what matters is not the* absolute *level of r but the degree of its divergence from what is considered a fairly* safe *level of r, having regard to those calculations of [subjective] probability which are being relied on. (p. 201)*

. . . *the rate of interest is a highly psychological phenomenon. (p. 202)*

It might be more accurate, perhaps, to say that the rate of interest is a highly conventional, rather than a highly psychological, phenomenon. For its actual value is largely governed by the prevailing view as to what its value is expected to be. Any level of interest which is accepted with sufficient conviction as likely to be durable will be durable. (p. 203)

Money supplies, and financial assets, are stock-variables capable of being disgorged now, or withheld till the future. P^* or r^* expected by transactors will be reflected in P and r, as is apparent in stock-market fluctuations. Unlike current output flows there are neither "normal" floors nor ceilings imposed by cost attributes in a time framework.

Amending the L-function, what seems required is a decomposition of $L_1(Y)$ into $L_1(P, Q)$, to make sources of money demand more explicit. Further, in extending the model there would need to be attached the WCM equation for P, and the multiplier equation of $Q = [I(r, \sigma)/s_w \omega + s_r \pi]$, where I is de-

---

money; in other words, to function as the medium of income payments and output purchase.

nominated in real terms, as in the *IS-LM* model: the term σ denotes an expectational variable affecting *I*-decisions.

Money demand-supply interdependence

The L_2 "store of value" functional statement is incomplete in neglecting the *wherewithal* to acquire financial assets. Just as money income is a determining variable of consumer-demand curves in microtheory, assets such as *money*, bonds, stocks, land, or the ability to create debt through promissory notes or bonds are *determinants* of the L_2 money demand. Given more *money*, or more shares of stock in individual portfolios, the demand for money balances will shift compared to a smaller (or larger) asset total. Thus if X denotes the asset *total*, we would have: $X = M$ + Bonds + Shares of Stock + Other Financial Assets + Land + Jewelry + . . . + Borrowing Power.

L_2 thus becomes a slippery concept: the demand for money depends on "all" available assets, *including the money supply*. There is a curious kind of interdependence here, for once the Fed (MA) engages in open-market purchases of bonds it, in effect, endows market individuals with more money while divesting them of bonds. Consequently, they become more insulated against increases in interest rates: this must color their L_2-demand. Likewise, when the Fed acts to reverse the open-market process, a kind of "irreversibility" arises insofar as bond purchases and sales are not consummated over time at identical prices.*

Too, the demand for L_2 balances is fairly open-ended, depending on the ability and willingness of borrowers to create, and lenders to absorb, newly created bond and stock issues, or promissory notes generally. Over time, the same r and an equivalent expectational r^* can signify a different L_2 demand.

A stronger L and M interaction involving psychological shifts can occur through the influence of ΔM_s on L_2 through r^*: for every time the MA enters money markets to engage in open-market operations, market transactors sense a directional and amplitude clue to future interest rates. Thus whereas it is usual to write $(\Delta L_2/\Delta r) < 0$, the sign can often be reversed: once the MA increases ΔM, it is possible to have $(\Delta L_2/\Delta r)(\Delta r/\Delta M) > 0$. That is, a fall (rise) in interest rates through an increase (decrease) in money supplies may evoke a belief that the flurry is a false harbinger of things to come, that the MA will in the future backtrack and tighten (relax) its policy so that the upshot will be not a decreased (increased) but an *increased* (decreased) L_2, or higher current interest rates. It may take a lot of MA open-market stamina to counter the prevailing wisdom.

---

*   On this see my *Approach*, Chapter 8, and the comments by George Horwich and by Richard M. Davis, "A Re-Examination of the Speculative Demand for Money," *Quarterly Journal of Economics* (May, Nov. 1959).

The interdependence of M and L can impart ratchet effects on the *LM* curves in conventional *IS-LM* analysis. The point has been widely ignored.

Sometimes, therefore, the mere stirring of an opinion on MA intentions may permit it to execute its designs while firing just a small amount of open-market ammunition. At other times it may be locked in stalemate with the market scoffing at the seriousness, or intent, or ability of the MA.

There is a good deal of interdependence between the L and M functions that has escaped monetary models of stable functions.

Other *L*-determinants

These views lead, at a minimum, to:

$$M_1 + M_2 = L_1 (P, Q, P^*, Q^*, \sigma) + L_2 (r, r^*, X, M), \qquad (9.7)$$

where $X =$ the spectrum of existing or *potential* financial claims that transactors may create, $M = M_1 + M_2$, and * marking expectational variables, with σ referring more specifically to I-decisions.

Minsky has recently proposed writing the function as:

$$M = M_1 + M_2 + M_3 - M_4 = L_1(Y) + L_2(r, P_k) + L_3(F) - L_4(NM)† \qquad (9.8)$$

where $P_k =$ prices of capital goods, or P_i, $F =$ precautionary demand to cover outstanding maturing financial claims, and $NM =$ the assortment of near-monies, as Treasury bills, time deposits, etc.

With respect to L_1 and L_2 Minsky's function could be amended as in Eq. (9.7).‡ Whether P_k (or P_i) should be introduced separately is moot: including P in L_1 could cover it though the more explicit statement has merit.

L_4 is a valuable supplement on what we mean by money, of where we draw the line. Minsky thus places the Friedman version of M_1, M_2, M_3, ... in perspective, for treatment depends on the ends to be served in any particular analysis.

It is in L_3 that Minsky, along with Kahn, Harrod, and Davidson, spotted a raw nerve untended in much of the Keynesian tradition; for Keynes, a parallel concept of the "finance motive" was hailed as the "coping stone" of

---

† Minsky, *Keynes*, pp. 75–76.

‡ As indicated, Keynes', or Minsky's (or my own) M_1, M_2, M_3 ... has only tenuous connection to Friedman's measurement of different definitions of money supply. The Keynes M_1, M_2 symbols "compartmentalize" those parts of the money supply held to satisfy different "motives" for demanding money, not that Keynes regarded this as anything but an expository tool. D. Laidler has derided this demand compartmentalization, observing that the "ice cube" and "cold milk" demand for refrigerators is not isolated. See his *The Demand for Money*, p. 57. Yet it is exactly this compartmentalization of demand *attributes* that comprises the foundations of the fascinating approach to demand theory of K. Lancaster, "A New Approach to Consumer Theory," *Journal of Political Economy* (1966) and "Change and Innovation in the Technology of Consumption," *American Economic Review* (1966). Despite the moment's fun, Laidler also "compartmentalizes," albeit implicitly, with overlaps, in combining all variables in a general function: the issue is basically one of "additivity."

his theory when, under assault by Robertson, he agreed that an increase in I would tend to lift interest rates unless the banking system provided the extra financial wherewithal to energize the multiplier-process and generate the off-setting S-flows.* Subsequently, the aforementioned authors have tended to promote Keynes' "precautionary motive" from some casual mention after the speculation-motive emphasis, as a subordinate afterthought, to practical dominance in L-*volatility*. Harrod has stressed the need for precautionary balances against escalating international payments faced by the large firms, and banks, engaged in world trade. Kahn has generalized the precautionary motive as swallowing the speculative demand. Minsky has been especially perceptive and persistent in pressing the redoubtable feedbacks between financial sector eruptions ensuing from the tenuous and overextended layering of claims, and the precarious institutional menace to job markets and production. This can reach crisis proportions affecting Q and N in periods of "credit-crunch" where firms must borrow to "roll-over" maturing financial obligations at the very moment when the MA is adamant in tightening credit. Bankruptcy, when big firms are involved, can exert a domino effect on a number of otherwise viable firms. The latent fragility of the financial structure has ramifications with ominous overtones for real phenomena.†

Money supply endogeneity

Some case can be made for the endogenous aspects of the money supply. The MA is not immune to Q, N, and r events; it too has its political ear to the ground—with lags and with some aberrant performance.‡ The MA is cog-

---

* Keynes, "The 'Ex-Ante' Theory of Interest," *Economic Journal* (Dec. 1937), pp. 663–669.

† While Minsky has stressed these aspects in a series of valuable papers covering neglected phenomena, for earlier work, in a less concrete and more general setting, see R. F. Kahn, "Some Notes On Liquidity Preference," *The Manchester School* (1954). For an important application in the import-export sector, see Sir Roy Harrod, *Money* (London: Macmillan, 1969), pp. 168–173. For articulation in a theory originating in Keynes' *Treatise*, see the exemplary account in Paul Davidson, *Money In the Real World*, Chapters 6–9. Davidson also has frequently stressed the "Finance Motive."

To buttress the Minsky theme of macroeconomic fragility through financial market linkages, Douglas Vickers has cast strong doubts on the Walrasian *assumption* of equilibrating tatonnement processes in financial markets. His "Finance and False Trading in Non-Tatonnement Markets," *Australian Economic Papers* (Dec. 1975) deserves a wider audience.

‡ Cf. (Lord) Nicholas Kaldor, "The New Monetarism," *Lloyds Bank Review* (July 1970). Kaldor also provides the useful reminder that purchases are in large measure —for expensive items, anyway—made at agreed prices, and with delivery in *advance* of payment: money outlays *follow* purchases, so that *MV* lags *PQ*. Wesley Mitchell (*Business Cycles*) noted this years ago; the point has apparently been lost on Monetarists. For a reply to Kaldor, and then a rejoinder, see Friedman and then the solemn note of K. Brunner, "The Monetarist View of Keynesian Ideas," Ibid. (Oct. 1974).

nizant of the facts of economic life and the political explosiveness of un-employment even as it may not be uncomfortable with its economic costs. Thus M_s-endogeneity may not be complete; it has been erratic and only intermittently predictable. Nevertheless, it exists, though the relationship is not readily captured in a tidy analytic model: it involves predicting the forces motivating a small group of individuals and their responses to pressures. It might require a psychological profile of MA personalities and staff to extract predictive material. Small wonder then about the refuge into exogeneity, or to tendering alternative econometric forecasts of A, B, C, . . . with each predicated on different monetary assumptions for the projected period.

CHAPTER TEN

Keynes and the Keynesian Detours

In an eloquent passage, Keynes wrote that "Ricardo conquered England as completely as the Holy Inquisition conquered Spain."* Had Keynes lived to chronicle the 1950–1970 period he might have been bewildered at his own acclaim, especially as the doctrines that masqueraded in his name were telescoped into a set of fiscal policy precepts for full employment, bereft of a price level and, so, hapless in the face of secular inflation. Phillips curve inferences of complacent resignation under the inflation and unemployment syndrome would have dismayed him. Too, in some hoax on Keynes, the dominant message of the Keynesian missionaries was *Hicksianism*, for Hicks' version suffused the literature. Recently, Hicks has amended his account; after a lagged and muted learning-diffusion process his recantation should filter down to the textbook mill.†

---

* J. M. Keynes, *The General Theory*, p. 32. Some parts of this chapter are taken from "Hicksian Keynesianism: Dominance and Decline," in my edited volume on *Modern Economic Thought*, and "Beyond Keynesianism and Monetarism: Some Theoretical Revision," in *Pioneering Economics: International Tribute to Giovanni Demaria* (Rome, 1977). Also, "The Keynesian Light that Failed," *Nebraska Journal of Economics and Business* (Autumn 1975).

† The influential article was J. R. Hicks, "Mr. Keynes and the Classics," *Econometrica* (1937). The altered view appears in his *The Crisis in Keynesian Economics* (New York: Basic Books, Inc. 1974). See my "Some Revision and Recantation in Hicksian Economics," *Journal of Economic Issues* (Sept. 1976). A recent article giving a more precise interpretation of Keynes can be recommended: Ivan C. Johnson, "A Revised Perspective of Keynes' *General Theory*," *Journal of Economic Issues* (1978). A broadside attack is contained in John H. Hotson, *Stagflation and the Bastard Keynesians* (University of Waterloo, 1976).

Keynesianism fumbled the inflation issue and now stands in disarray. Ignored was Keynes' injunction to work in wage-units so that the price-level implications eluded Keynesian analysis.* Actually, Keynes was driven to write the *General Theory* because of the prevailing belief that unemployment could be eradicated by cutting money wages: it was this idea that had to be dispelled. If it were valid (without compelling bankruptcies drying up invest- ment and nourishing the social strains attached to the real-balance effect discovered later) his more complex analysis of the routes to full employment would be superfluous.† His path-breaking theme linked money wages to the price level—his *P*-theory—with a monetary policy strategy in conflict with Quantity Theory doctrines.‡ His *P*-theory has been poorly attended to in comparison with his *N*- or *Q*-theory (of employment or output).§

The Keynesian detours will be sketched after a brief scan of Keynes' *P*-theory views. Largely, his ideas coalesce with the WCM determinants despite the mental block of too many Keynesians in making the association.

Keynes and Keynesians

Theoretical Keynesianism is generally identified by its technical baggage, with stickers labeling the consumption, investment, and liquidity preference func- tions, and the multiplier: these were Keynes' innovations. Keynesians advocate full employment, mainly through fiscal policy, involving government outlays and taxes as the promotional levers.‖ To many, the policy precepts spring remorselessly from the theory. Others shun the theoretical pastime, eschewing the technical symbols while targeting employment objectives as if the welfare state connoted the Keynesian credo. Both wings wave the Keynesian flag, with both intellectually comfortable in decrying unemployment and chiding official-

---

*   Cf. *General Theory*, Chapters 4, 21.

†   The "real-balance," or Pigou, or Patinkin, or "net-wealth" effect covers the change in the real value of nonbank ("outside") money balances as the price level varies, or thus changes in M/P with effects on consumption and investment behavior. Cf. Don Patinkin, *Money, Interest, and Prices* (Harper & Row, 1965, 2d ed.), Chap- ter VIII.

‡   Cf. the title essay in *KaM*.

§   Long ago I criticized this egregious Keynesian oversight, calling the result "Classical Keynesianism." See my *Classical Keynesianism, Monetary Theory, and the Price Level*. Joan Robinson castigated related doctrines as *Bastard*-Keynesianism. Axel Leijonhufvud, in his influential volume *On Keynesian Economics and the Eco- nomics of Keynes* (New York: Oxford, 1968), succeeded in promoting general aware- ness of the contrasting ideas though, in my view, his work does not come down strongly enough in affirming the pivotal money-wage variable.

‖   Faith in the efficacy of fiscal policy as *the* instrument for fairly quick banishment of economic woes was termed "fine tuning." For a persuasive expression of the fiscal mechanics, see Walter W. Heller, *New Dimensions of Political Economy* (Cambridge: Harvard University Press, 1966).

dom; in economic recessions both exude reborn confidence in their separate orientation.

Curiously, in the nearly successful assault on the full-employment salient in the United States in 1968 the more theoretical Keynesians advised an income surtax to quell fears of "overheating" the economy into inflation. In sight of the Promised Land to full employment, they beckoned the trumpets to sound the retreat, to stall the march into the blissful gates, and instead to induce unemployment—thereafter they could admonish the government for unemployment apathy! The premises of the WCM inflation roots were spurned; instead, there was a conviction that by reducing "excess real demand," via taxes, the price outbreak would be nipped.

Unfortunately, wage earners were not avid readers of Keynesian textbooks, so as their pay envelopes thinned, the clamor for pay hikes to allay the tax bite touched off an enduring wage-price spiral.

Keynes wrote a cogent message on w and P. In his Chapter 2, in disputing the advocacy prevalent in the 1930s of money-wage cuts to beat down real wages and restore employment, Keynes wrote:

Now the assumption that the general level of real wages depends on the money-wage bargains between the employers and the workers is not obviously true.... For it is far from being consistent with the general tenor of the classical theory, which has taught us to believe that prices are governed by marginal prime cost in terms of money and that money-wages largely govern marginal prime cost. Thus if money-wages change, one would have expected the classical school to argue that prices would change in almost the same proportion, leaving the real wage and the level of unemployment practically the same as before....

There may exist no expedient by which labour as a whole can reduce its real *wage to a given figure by making revised* money *bargains with the entrepreneurs. This will be our contention.**

In Chapter 4, Keynes spoke of "the three perplexities which most impeded my progress in writing this book," including "firstly, the choice of the units of quantity appropriate to the problems of the economic system as a whole" (p. 37). Thus:

In dealing with the theory of employment I propose, therefore, to make use of only two fundamental units of quantity, namely, quantities of money-value and quantities of employment. The first of these is strictly homogeneous, and the second can be made so. For, insofar as different grades and kinds of labour and salaried assistance enjoy a more or less fixed relative remuneration, the quantity of employment can be sufficiently defined for our purpose by taking an hour's employment of ordinary labour as our unit and weighting an hour's employment of special labour in proportion to its remuneration; i.e., an hour of special labour remunerated at double ordinary rates will count as two units. We shall call the unit in which the quantity of employment is measured

---

*   *General Theory*, p. 12, 13.

the labour-unit; and the money-wage of a labour unit we shall call the wage-unit. Thus, if E is the wages (and salaries) bill, W the wage unit, and N the quantity of employment, E = N.W.*

The choice of units

For many Keynesians this emphasis on the "wage-unit" constituted some quaint eccentricity; on whether to deflate money output sums by price or wage units, Hansen wrote "fundamentally the matter is of no great consequence."† Yet it has made a devastating difference, particularly in the maladroit Keynesian inflation parable. By correcting money-income sums by the price level, and thereby eliciting *real*-income, Keynesians were prone to seize on excess demand and become immune to WCM aspects. For Keynes, inflation was born on the money-wage scale.

Keynes' wage-unit, despite the artful Keynesian dodge, had sturdy classical forebears.‡ The assumption of a "given" wage-unit implicitly assumed a constant wage structure, or "relativities," as Australian usage puts it. A doubling of the wage-unit would mean that everybody formerly earning $1 per hour would get $2, those earning $2 would get $4, etc. Thus a *proportional* money-wage dislodgement would be analyzed first, and thereafter qualified for adjustments in "relativities."§

The *P-N* theories and post-Keynesian interpretation

Keynes conducted his N-theory on the simplifying hypothesis of a *given* money-wage unit, signifying that w was constant. After the N-theory was worked out, the P-theory was elaborated by allowing for changes in w.‖ Keynes' thinking, and its consonance with the WCM, appears in Chapter 21 (titled *The Theory of Prices*):

In a single industry its particular price-level depends partly on the rate of remuneration of the factors of production which enter into its marginal cost,

---

*   Ibid., p. 41. His footnote reads: "If X stands for any quantity measured in terms of money, it will often be convenient to write X_w for the same quantity measured in terms of the wage-unit."

†   Alvin Hansen, *A Guide to Keynes* (New York: McGraw-Hill, 1953), p. 34. Actually, Hansen saw the potential of money-wage inflation, in some digression from his fundamental model, in his lucid book on *Monetary Theory and Fiscal Policy* (New York: McGraw-Hill, 1949).

‡   In recourse to labor as the "measure" of value, and in the search for a unit of standard labor, Keynes' wage unit follows classical tradition. Cf., e.g., Adam Smith, *The Wealth of Nations* (Modern Library edition), Book I, Chapter V, opening paragraph; David Ricardo, *On the Principles of Political Economy and Taxation* (Cambridge, Vol. 1, Sraffa edition), p. 20; Karl Marx, *Capital* (Modern Library), p. 46.

§   Cf. my *Approach to the Theory of Income Distribution* (Philadelphia: Chilton, 1958). Chapter 7 deals with the theoretical structural problems on recognition of heterogeneous labor.

‖   I have laid stress on the P- and the N- (or Q-) theory, as the *two* separate strands in Keynes, in *KaM*, title essay.

*and partly on the scale of output. There is no reason to modify this conclusion
when we pass to industry as a whole. (p. 294)*

The reference to "scale of output" entails, of course, the implicit "laws of
return," and diminishing returns (and so A) under market competition. In
referring to the Quantity theory, he observed:

*For the purposes of the real world it is a great fault in the Quantity theory
that it does not distinguish between changes in prices which are a function of
changes in output, and those which are a function of changes in the wage-
unit. (p. 209)*

This endows the wage-unit with ultimate price-level significance except in
conditions of high supply *in*elasticity. Both the wage-unit and productivity
phenomena under output changes are captured, as in the w/A ratio, in an
important passage:

*If we allow ourselves the simplification of assuming that the rates of remuner-
ation of the different factors of production which enter into marginal cost all
change in the same proportion . . . as the wage-unit, it follows that the general
price level (taking equipment and technique as given) depends partly on the
wage-unit and partly on the volume of employment. (p. 295)*

*Perhaps the most important element in marginal cost which is likely to change
in a different proportion from the wage-unit, and also to fluctuate within much
wider limits, is marginal user cost. (p. 302)*

User costs refer to estimated *future* profits foregone by the wear and tear
of using equipment today: user costs thus embed implicit *expectations* of
future prices and profits. The ideas are essentially absorbed in k in the WCM
equation; also, for realistic measurement, and in recognition of monopoly
instances, the A-term would replace the elusive marginal product.* Keynes'
P-theory thus coheres with the WCM components.†

For the consumption function, Keynes wrote:

$$C_w = \chi(Y_w) \text{ or } C = w \cdot \chi(Y_w).‡ \qquad (10.1)$$

The w-subscript denotes the wage-unit. Keynes thus asserted that C-out-
lays depended on money income, *where both were deflated by the average
money wage.* In a deep sense he conjectured (as did Adam Smith) that in
consumption we were absorbing the product of a definite amount of labor:
our income provided access to command a certain amount of labor. If we

---

* Cf. the expectational target k_c for the consumer price level.

† Keynes' "generalized statement" of the Quantity Theory of Money converges
on the w, A, k terms. See Keynes, p. 305 and my "Keynes and the Quantity Theory
Elasticities," in *KaM*, Essay 2 (with Hamid Habibagahi).

‡ *General Theory*, p. 90.

spend $15,000, with the average money wage $7,500, we are gobbling a basket of goods equivalent to the services of two workers.*

Investment, for Keynes, depended on the marginal efficiency of capital (MEC), or estimates of future earnings on plant and equipment compared to the present capital goods cost (or supply prices).† The earnings stream belonged to the future, obscured by uncertainty, and unknown at present.

The outstanding fact is the extreme precariousness of the basis of knowledge on which our estimates of prospective yield have to be made. Our knowledge of the factors which will govern the yield of an investment some years hence is usually very slight and often negligible. (p. 149)

Even apart from the instability due to speculation, there is the instability due to the characteristic of human nature that a large proportion of our positive activities depend on spontaneous optimism rather than on a mathematical expectation, whether moral or hedonistic or economic. Most, probably, of our decisions to do something positive, the full consequences of which will be drawn out over many days to come, can only be taken as a result of animal spirits—of a spontaneous urge to action rather than inaction, and not as the outcome of a weighted average of quantitative benefits multiplied by quantitative probabilities. Enterprise only pretends to itself to be mainly actuated by the statements in its own prospectus, however candid and sincere. Only a little more than an expedition to the South Pole [circa 1930], is it based on an exact calculation of benefits to come. Thus if the animal spirits are dimmed and the spontaneous optimism falters, leaving us to depend on nothing but a mathematical expectation, enterprise will fade and die;—though fears of loss may have a basis no more reasonable than hopes of profit had before. (pp. 162–163)

"Animal spirits" thereby drove Keynes' enterprise chariot, by determining the investment (I) volume; the investment "multiplier" determined the associated consumption and, thus, Y and N. "Animal spirits" permeate the Post-Keynesian revival to temper the mechanistic "classical" or "bastard" Keynesian models.‡ Considering the volatile urges animating I, Lord Kaldor distilled the character of the Keynesian Revolution in the premise that "I determined S," and thus (via the multiplier) I was the "prime mover" of activity and the growth path.§ Neoclassical growth models, in contrast, usu-

---

* Thus correcting money sums by the price level, or the wage-unit, would not matter *if* both series moved (over time) in the same ratio.

† Ibid., p. 135.

‡ Cf. Jan A. Kregel, *The Reconstruction of Political Economy: An Introduction to Post-Keynesian Economics* (New York: Wiley, 1973). Also, almost all of the recent writings of Joan Robinson, e.g., *Economic Heresies* (New York: Basic Books, 1971), and her textbook, *An Introduction to Modern Economics* (New York: McGraw-Hill, 1973), in collaboration with John Eatwell.

§ Nicholas Kaldor, "Economic Growth and the Problem of Inflation," *Economica* (1959), reprinted in *Essays on Economic Policy* (London: Duckworth, 1964), Vol. I, pp. 168–169. Also, "A Model of Economic Growth," *Economic Journal* (1957), really postulate that *savings* govern the investment volume and, thus, the growth path: this slight transformation, innocuous to the unwary, entails a reversion to the neoclassical view.*

Keynes, on the business cycle, had written that this "is best regarded . . . as being occasioned by a cyclical change in the marginal efficiency of capital" (p. 313) and: "A boom is a situation in which over-optimism triumphs over a rate of interest which, in a cooler light, would be seen to be excessive" (p. 322). Thus, while it is common to find the investment function written as $I(r)$, Keynes would have it as $I(r,\sigma)$ where σ denotes the expectational backdrop which contains all the amorphous, flighty, psychological vagaries of "confidence" affecting business decisions.

The volatility of σ must impart fuzziness to any tidy econometric formulation of investment which rests mainly on the acceleration principle, as:

$$I_1 = \beta(Y_{-2} - Y_{-1}), \text{ or } I = \beta\Delta Y, \tag{10.2}$$

where $\beta =$ the accelerator-coefficient.

In Eq. (10.2) the subscripts refer to "periods," or "years," with investment "this" year tied indissolubly to the *past* output growth. Alternatively, $I = \beta(Y^*_2 - Y_1)$ would build in an *expected* output growth. Yet any election of a "stable" β invokes a more mechanistic linkage than Keynes envisaged.†

Keynesian 45-Degree Models

Keynesianism lured its eager disciples largely through the Hansen-Samuelson 45-degree graphics and Hicks' elegant *IS-LM* compression. Considering the contemporary focus on the stagflation doldrums these techniques plotted some wasteland tours off Keynes' map.‡ Later, the Phillips curve detours of the 1960s will be surveyed.

---

printed in *Essays on Economic Stability and Growth* (London: Duckworth, 1960), pp. 263, 270.

* For illuminating studies of the contesting growth theories, see Karl Shell, "The Neoclassical Growth Model," and A. Asimakopulos, "Post-Keynesian Growth Theory," in *Modern Economic Thought*. See also Alfred S. Eichner and J. A. Kregel, "An Essay on Post-Keynesian Theory: A New Paradigm in Economics," *Journal of Economic Literature* (Dec. 1975).

† So far as liquidity preference and the rate of interest were concerned, for the time at which he wrote Keynes observed the low rates of interest then prevailing, and the obstacles in the way of driving them lower. Thus he remarked: "I am now somewhat sceptical of the success of a merely monetary policy directed towards influencing the rate of interest" (p. 164). For our purposes, the interest-rate dialogue is of less immediate significance compared to Keynesian confusion on inflation. See, however, Chapter 9, especially the discussion of monetary policy under full employment.

‡ Combining wit and wisdom in generous proportions, J. K. Galbraith concluded that: "Keynes had long been suspect among his colleagues for the clarity of his writing and thought, the two often going together. In *The General Theory* he re-

The 45-degree Keynesian cross

The famous equilibrium "cross" of the $C + I$ function and the 45-degree line expounded in Paul Samuelson's *Economics* textbook was pronounced as a symbolic crown for macroeconomics, as bedazzling as Marshall's microeconomic supply-demand scissors intersection.* As the 45-degree model is the mother's milk of textbook economics, propounded by the legion of product imitators differentiated by book weight and color charts, only the essential equations need be reproduced here.

First, the consumption function:

$$C = C(Y, r), \qquad (10.3)$$

where $Y = real$ output (Q) or *real* income $(Y = PQ$, with $P = \bar{P})$, $r =$ the interest-rate structure and level.

Next, the investment (I) relation:

$$I = I(r), \qquad (10.4)$$

where $I = real$ investment. Real C-outlay would increase with more real-income, subject to the "law of the marginal propensity to consume" that $1 > (\Delta C/\Delta Y) > 0$. Real-investment outlay would expand at lower interest rates: $(\Delta I/\Delta r) < 0$.

The liquidity-preference or money-demand function (L) was written:

$$L = L(Y, r). \qquad (10.5)$$

Higher real income would elevate the demand for money to finance the larger volume of transactions. Further, through Keynes' "speculative-motive," lower rates of interest would enlarge money demand inasmuch as: (1) the interest sacrifice in holding money rather than government bonds would be reduced and (2) at lower interest rates the fear of a subsequent rise would grow more acute: the higher interest rates would cut the market price of bond holdings. At very low interest rates, at institutional minimum floors for bank lending, liquidity-preference would turn absolute: the L-function would turn flat and perfectly elastic as the demand for money in lieu of bonds became a speculative universal obsession. The flat-land was christened (by Dennis Robertson) as the "liquidity-trap."

---

deemed his academic reputation. It is a work of profound obscurity, badly written and prematurely published. All economists claim to have read it. Only a few have. The rest feel a secret guilt that they never will." *Money: Whence It Came, Where It Went*, pp. 217–218.

It is possible to disagree with Galbraith on the "profound obscurity" of the *General Theory*. It is as luminous, in the same sense as Ricardo, for those who stay the course. But it is not a once-over light reading treat.

*   See his article on "The Simple Mathematics of Income Distribution," in *Income, Employment and Public Policy: Essays in Honor of Alvin H. Hansen* (New York: Norton & Co., 1948), p. 135. Early editions of the popular teaching opus embossed the diagram on the cover, an attachment reminiscent of von Thünen (in another age) for his formula on the "natural wage."

The money supply, interpreted as an exogenous creation of the central bank, and generally defined as comprising currency and demand deposits, was held constant:

$$M = \overline{M}. \tag{10.6}$$

Finally, the Keynesian system was boxed with the definitional equation to denote the equilibrium balance (the 45-degree "cross"):

$$C + I = Y. \tag{10.7}$$

Substituting Eq. (10.3) and Eq. (10.4) into Eq. (10.7) yields one equation and two unknowns. Equating $M = L(Y,r)$ establishes a second equation in the same unknowns. Thus (with proper restrictions on the form of the equations) the model was determinate. To include government purchases (G) of current output, Eq. (10.7) would be written as $C + I + G = Y$, where $G = \overline{G}$. Government outlay would also be specified as exogenous with immediate real-income effects comparable to commensurate I-outlays.

Geometry of the 45-degree model

The model was amenable to a neat geometric portrait. Figure 10.1 contains the ubiquitous 45-degree line; each point along its course joined $C + I = Y$ so that the final equilibrium had to settle on the bisecting 45-degree track.

A C-function of conventional form is graphed and supplemented by the real I-outlays. The intersection of the combined $C + I$ function with the 45-degree line establishes the equilibrium real income-output position (Y^*), and the C and I equilibrium real outlays. From an appended production function binding employment to real output, where $N = N(Y)$, employment was implicitly determined.

Figure 10.2 traces an I-function, with investment negatively responsive to lower interest rates. At r_1, investment I_1 would be forthcoming. The I_1 magnitude, say, was superimposed on the C-function in the diagram. As the ensuing equilibrium ΔY increment surpassed the I-magnitude, the Kahn-Keynes "multiplier" reaction was implicit: investment outlay would yield an income growth of $(\Delta Y/\Delta I) > 1$.

Inflationary and deflationary gaps

Equilibrium prevails at Y^* in Fig. 10.1. If Y_f denotes the full-employment output volume then the short-fall ($Y_f - Y^*$) measures the "deflationary gap." Steps to raise C, say, through cutting personal income taxes, or to lift I through business tax incentives, or through monetary policy to lower r, were in order. Higher government expenditures could buttress I to provide an analogous multiplier punch.

If (somehow) the $C + I$ intersection occurred rightward of Y_f there would be an "inflationary gap." Fiscal policy would aim to repress C, I, and G. Inflation and deflation (unemployment) were visually symmetrical even though deflation would mean lost output and jobs while excess demand would mean

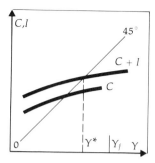

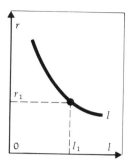

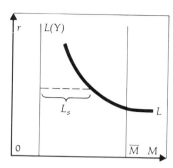

Figure 10.1 **Figure 10.2** **Figure 10.3**

ascending prices—an odd coupling. One or the other could prevail so that wise economic steering would turn the fiscal tap to run either hot or cold until the mixture was just right for the full-employment equilibrium (Y_f).*

The liquidity function

Figure 10.3 portrays the determination of "the" interest rate. The demand for money was inscribed as an amalgam of $L(Y) + L(r)$, where $L(Y) =$ the "transactions-demand" of Keynes, with more output and employment requiring more money financing; this part of demand was (largely) interest inelastic. $L(r)$ denoted the "speculative-motive," associating interest rates and money demand: the "speculative" interest-elastic portion of L is measured by $L - L(Y) = L_s$. A "precautionary-demand" could be tied to Y or r, to include contingency demand for money as a reserve for unexpected bills or opportune purchases or, generally, as provision for unforeseen outlays in an uncertain economy moving out in time.

The supply of money is captured by the perfectly inelastic line $\overline{M}$, at a magnitude decided by the central bank. Outside the liquidity-trap, where the L-function turns flat, changes in M would affect interest rates. Inside the trap segment, ΔM would not shake the interest rate.

Misgivings over the 45-degree model

Misgivings over the 45-degree model fell on deaf ears during its heyday.†

1 Most mischievous was the cultivated myth that the unstable economy

---

* One account of the symmetry, and referring to Samuelson's work, reads: "Depression and inflation are essentially opposites, the one a consequence of too little effective demand, and the other a consequence of too much." See Robert L. Bishop, "Alternative Expansionist Fiscal Policy," *Essays in Honor of Alvin H. Hansen*, p. 318. James Tobin had such models in mind in remarking that "much discussion of current policy is based on an overly simple model which my generation of economists learned and taught. . . ." in "Unemployment and Inflation: The Cruel Dilemma," *Prices: Issues in Theory, Practice and Public Policy* (Philadelphia: Univ. of Pennsylvania Press, 1967), A. Phillips and O. Williamson, eds., p. 101.

† This proposition reflects some personal experience. Cf. *Classical Keynesianism.*

could not experience double trouble; *either* unemployment *or* inflation was an unpalatable alternative, with each amenable to subjugation by deft monetary or fiscal strokes. The symmetry doctrine flourished despite Keynes' warnings that the afflictions were not simple diametrics.

Even as the Keynesian textbooks conquered the world many countries, especially underdeveloped lands, were experiencing *simultaneous* inflation and unemployment. Yet the Keynesian wisdom advised raising C and I under unemployment, and cutting the C and I magnitudes under inflation!* Skepticism at the tenuous contact of the theory with reality had to await stagflation in the affluent countries before the Keynesian blinders could be lifted.

Some prominent Keynesians tenaciously ascribed all inflation to "excess-demand"; to this day, they blithely skip over wage excesses as the inflation bomb.†

2 Examining the equations and the diagrams, *all quantities are expressed in real terms;* a price level is wholly suppressed. This is the appalling incongruity: inflation was discussed in a model lacking a price level! To be sure, inflation was sighted in the far reaches of the diagram, beyond the full-employment block.

Keynes, as noted, dwelt at length on the "wage unit," and its P aspects. Vintage Keynesianism disdained w as the P and M catalyst in their macro-models of the economy. This blind spot hid the rock that toppled the Keynesian reign.

3 Keynes had taught that I was motivated by "animal spirits" which hurdled uncertainties: the will to act, rather than neat and mechanistic calculations, spurred capital-formation decisions; for Keynes $I = I(r, \sigma)$. Keynesians are prone to render investment a tidy function of r, or invoke tight accelerator ties which make capital outlays a prisoner of past events. The search for "the" I-function fills many writings.

Too, the model *assumed* that investment decisions are rendered in *real* terms, and that inflation will have no real effect on the I-function. Yet *some* government programs stipulate a fixed sum of, say, $1 million for a school, or local improvement project. If prices rise between the protracted interval in floating a bond issue and commencing construction, some parts of the project will be stripped to fit the $1 million jacket. The same applies to some outlays at the federal government level, or universities, and, undoubtedly, in private business. For the latter, often dependent on amortization funds whose value depreciates under inflation, there will be trimming of real investment sails

---

* Keynesian textbooks were commonly imported into underdeveloped countries for college courses despite their utter irrelevance to the inflation-unemployment problems.

† Pernicious "excess real-demand" models as *the* inflation-maker still prevail in pseudo "general equilibrium" models.

with price gusts between project conception and implementation. Thus a descriptive investment function would have to include a P variable, as $I = I(r, \sigma, \Delta P)$ where ΔP refers to the price breaks over the course of construction.*

4 Keynes never taught that as Y and N advanced M would remain constant. Yet stacked Keynesian decks of $M = \overline{M}$ proliferated for conveying his ideas; some analytics and diagrammatics keep $\overline{M} = M$ while income advances from zero to trillions of dollars! This is a caricature of Keynes. Keynes would have posited *some* endogeneity of $M_s = M(N, r, p,* \ldots)$.

5 Income-distribution aspects were virtually ignored; Keynes can be faulted for this omission; Joan Robinson and Kaldor (and the present author) have tried to rectify it.†

6 Macrotheory became unnaturally estranged from microtheory: specialists have come to live in the one world or the other. Yet it is possible to wed the theory of the economy to happenings in industries and firms. (See the Aggregate Demand and Aggregate Supply analysis below.)

The *IS-LM* Model

The 45-degree approach succumbed to Hicks' *IS-LM* version because of an internal inconsistency. The circularity can be put tersely.

The *IS-LM* model

In the $C + I$ diagram the I-volume is superimposed on the C-function. Thereupon Y is set at the "cross." But to determine I, r must first be known. But r depends on $L(Y, r) = \overline{M}$. Thus to determine r it is necessary to know the transaction demand Y, while to know Y it is necessary to know r. The *IS-LM* apparatus averted the logical dilemma.‡

From $Y = C + S$, where $S =$ savings, given the consumption function $C(Y)$, the savings function $S = S(Y, r)$ was derived. From the Keynesian identity of $I = S$ (for $Y = C + I$ and $Y = C + S$), the *IS* equation quickly evolved. Thus:

$$S(Y, r) = I(r). \tag{10.8}$$

Equating the L-function to the money supply:

$$L(Y, r) = \overline{M}. \tag{10.9}$$

---

* See my *Approach to the Theory of Income Distribution*, pp. 37–38, and *Employment Growth and Income Distribution* (Philadelphia: Chilton, 1966), p. 18. Also, Ivan Johnson, "A Revised Perspective."

† Cf. my "Macrodistribution and Marginal Productivity Theory," in *KaM*.

‡ J. R. Hicks, "Mr. Keynes and the 'Classics'."

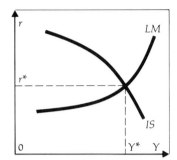

Figure 10.4

With two equations in two unknowns the system is, in principle, solvable. In Eq. (10.8) r is inserted as a parameter to derive the IS function; in Eq. (10.9), using Y as a parameter the LM curve emerges. The intersection of the two functions constitutes a mutually compatible equilibrium solution.

The functions are drawn in Fig. 10.4. A shift in the I, S, or L function, or an altered M, would dislodge the curves; full employment would require a shift in one or both functions to intersect above Y_f. Intersections to the left spelled unemployment, while to the right there were some dangling utterances over "excess-demand" inflation. Symmetry reigned.

Ordinarily, the IS-LM version of Hicksian-Keynesianism was reserved for "advanced" students, as too sophisticated for introductory classes.

A critique

Hicksianism shares the 45-degree vulnerability for its lack of a price level and its suppression of money wages.* Stagflation or slumpflation prospects remained exiled to a somewhere else never-never land.

Distribution forces could easily have been entered into the theory in the derivation of the IS function from $I = S$:

$$Y = I\,(r)/s, \qquad (10.10)$$

where $s = S/Y$, the average propensity to save. Relation (10.10) defines the "average" multiplier which sets the IS path thereafter as:

$$s = s_w\,W/Y + s_r\,R/Y, \qquad (10.11)$$

where W = the wage bill (wN), R = gross "profits" (or total *nonwage* in-

---

*   Most recently Hicks has urged recognition of Keynes' "wage theorem":

When there is a general (proportional) rise in money wages . . . the normal effect is that all prices rise in the same proportion—provided that the money supply is increased in the same proportion (whence the rate of interest will be unchanged).

Crisis, pp. 59–60. The WCM formula suggests the need to consider k and A, or at least A; the reference to money supplies confuses the issue by comforting Monetarists in their singular evasion that it is money supplies that "ratify" the price-level increase.

come). Writing $\omega = W/Y$ (the wage share) and $\pi = R/Y$ (the nonwage share):

$$Y = I\,(r)/s_w\omega + s_r\pi. \tag{10.12}$$

In Eq. (10.12) the income division between wages and profits is shown to *determine* income so long as $s_w \neq s_r$, with $s_r > s_w$ historically. Where "wage earners spend all and capitalists save all," then $s_w = 0$ and $s_r = 1$: income then depends on investment and the size of the profit share. (Intra-wage or intra-nonwage income shifts can affect the multiplier so long as individual savings propensities differ.)

Phillips Curve Keynesianism

IS-LM debate was usually preoccupied with conjectures on the form of the functions. But this was an immersion in detail considering the theoretical straitjacket of the missing *P*-equation.

A remarkable paper by A. W. Phillips held promise of a Keynesian rescue. From United Kingdom data covering 1861 to 1957, Phillips correlated unemployment rates with money-wage changes, fitting a curve running S.E. in a diagram which plotted $\Delta w/w$ against U', where $\Delta w/w$ denoted the average annual rate of money-wage change and U' denoted the unemployment rate.* The scatter of points was formalized in a curve resembling an ordinary convex down-to-the-right demand curve (or the *L*-function in Fig. 10.3, with some tendency to cut the U' axis at "high" rates of unemployment).

Armed with the Phillips curve, of $(\Delta w/w) = w(U')$ with $[\Delta(\Delta w/w)/\Delta U']$ < 0, Keynesianism acquired a *plausible* theory of inflation. The Hicksian model yielded real output and, from $N = N(Q)$ where $Q \equiv$ real Y, employment was extracted. Then, by calculating unemployment and by recourse to the Phillips curve, the "normal" $(\Delta w/w)$ would be revealed. With an equation (such as WCM) linking Δw to ΔP, the predictable degree of inflation could be attached to each Q, N, U combination.†

Phillips curves and Keynesian trade-off complacency

Ironically, while grafting a plausible *P*-theory on Keynesianism, Phillips curves also rationalized some complacency in the face of unemployment; Keynesians now gave currency to the doctrine that the economy had to endure *both* inflation and unemployment: it could suppress some of one only by

---

* A. W. Phillips, "The Relation Between Unemployment and the Rate of Change of Money Wage Rates in the United Kingdom, 1861–1957," *Economica* (1958). An early effort to apply the idea to U.S. data appeared in Paul A. Samuelson and Robert M. Solow, "Analytical Aspects of Anti-Inflation Policy," *American Economic Review* (May 1960).

† Phillips curve connections to the WCM, with minor subtleties, appear in several econometric forecasting models.

ushering in more of the other. Learned talk of "trade-offs," of more unemployment and less inflation, or vice versa, was rife. The unpalatable alternatives were endowed with the status of immutable natural law; we had to tolerate one or the other, or suffer from both. Keynes' optimistic vision became dashed under the spell of a "natural" choice among evils.

Tossed between the devil and the deep sea, many "Keynesians" abandoned the commitment to full employment. Where Keynes acted on the credo that human intelligence must be mobilized to ease and erase economic ills, many Hicksian-oriented Phillips-curve-Keynesians deferred to Keynes mainly in deploying the C, I, or L jargon, rather than abiding the full-employment objective: jobs for all was no longer the moral—and economic—imperative that Keynes had discerned, of an end to be pursued sedulously without violating the tenets of freedom. Keynesianism became impaled on the unemployment and inflation pike: the theory of the stagflation economy ascended to a modern Physiocratic "natural order" dogma.[*]

As another anomaly, those more alarmed at the inflation outburst became erstwhile Keynesians, allied with Monetarists in advocating tighter money and more unemployment as an inflation suppressant. Monetarist unconcern with jobs for all emerged as an eclectic Keynesian ideological stereotype.

Shifting Phillips curves

Controversy arose over the Phillips curve data and over the admissible variables, e.g., whether money wages were not more crucially linked to profits inasmuch as U' was low during prosperity phases when R was high.[†] Others specified a dependence on productivity improvements, others on trade union militancy.[‡] Undoubtedly, if the Phillips curve data continued to traverse the envisioned S.E. path, with only occasional departures, there would, by now, be a ponderous function relating money wages to a house-full of variables.

Much of the esoteric controversy was shattered by events. After about 1968, in the United States, United Kingdom, Canada, Australia, and elsewhere, money-wage moves ran contrary to Phillips curve pronouncements: higher money wages were correlated with *higher* unemployment. Phillips curve points flew N.E. rather than diving S.E. Hence an instant "theory" of *shifting* Phillips curves was devised.[§]

---

[*]   On this thesis search-cost unemployment ideas found ready Keynesian allies: the automatic-full-employment models were once more in the saddle with unemployment translated as "natural." Cf. Phelps, *Inflation Policy*.

[†]   Cf. Nicholas Kaldor, "Economic Growth and the Problem of Inflation," Part II, *Economica* (November 1959).

[‡]   Cf. Edwin Kuh, "A Productivity Theory of Wage Levels—An Alternative to the Phillips Curve," *Review of Economic Studies* (October 1967). A. G. Hines, "Trade Unionism and Wage Inflation in the United Kingdom," Ibid., 1964.

[§]   An influential article was that by E. S. Phelps, "Phillips Curves, Expectations of Inflation and Optimal Unemployment Over Time," *Economica* (1967).

If higher money wages accompanied higher unemployment, then "the Phillips curve must have shifted." After being originally hailed as a significant empirical "law," the Phillips curve entered a humbling phase as it became quickly transformed into an ad hoc, ex post rationalization. Phillips curves now generated postmortems, not predictions.

Theoretical genius for improvisation ventured forth with the conjecture that the curves shifted because in embarking on their wage deliberations workers (or their union leaders) were prompted by "expectations of inflation." Expectations prompted higher money-wage demands so that, despite job losses, Δw mounted. Rather than deducing from the amorphous expectational doctrine the imperative of policies for money-wage restraint, i.e., Incomes Policy, the bland counsel was to be patient in waiting for "expectations" to collapse or, in a supreme "Keynesian" reversal, to advocate unemployment through monetary policy to disrupt the expectational tide and ultimately depress the pace of Δw.*

The whole thought scheme was curious: "expectations" alone can hardly lift prices by 75 percent in under a decade without concomitant wage boosts which drive up business costs and enhance consumer demand. Otherwise, a significant rise in profit margins, in k, would have to be revealed. No such showing was reported.

Phillips curves writings have subsided as the mid-1960s fad was buried under the avalanche of untidy history.

Ignore inflation and indexation Keynesians

Deprived of the Phillips curve security blanket, and lacking any policy to contain inflation, many prominent Keynesians urged four-square that we ignore inflation and drive ahead for the full-employment objective.† Apparently, a stable P was a less laudable goal. Advice was plentiful to "correct" for the inequities of inflation by padding Social Security payments, by issuing a fixed purchasing power government bond, by encouraging business firms to do likewise, etc. Long on generalities and short on specifics, "Ignore-inflation" Keynesianism merged naturally with "Indexation Keynesianism,"

---

* So far as I can see, wage and price anticipations create inflation, and monetary and fiscal policy for demand management can abort it, in Phelps, *Inflation Policy*. Generally it is the reader's intuition, under a legacy of QTM thinking, that is relied on to sustain the theory; explicit statements, despite the size of the volume, are few and sparse.

† Cf. Walter Heller's 1975 advocacy of full employment, belittling inflation fears because of unemployment and excess production capacity. Op. Ed., *New York Times* (June 30, 1975). Apparently, stagflation lessons since 1968 were quickly unlearned.

Standing aside from the Keynesian mainstream, J. K. Galbraith refused to dismiss inflation in the superficial Keynesian way; he continued to recommend price-wage controls at President Ford's economic summit in September 1974—and at every one of the many opportunities which he is so gifted at creating.

with "corrections" linked, as a rule, to movements in P_c. Interestingly, indexation was also recommended by the most prominent Monetarist, so that the *entente cordiale* of Keynesians and Monetarists spanned the formidable ideological chasm.*

Six brands of Keynesianism thus appeared in the space of about fifteen years. Keynes' *General Theory*, however, would have been sufficient to comprehend the phenomenon.

Fiscalism: Functional Finance

To many the formal apparatus of Keynesianism provided a respectable prop for an activist fiscal policy of government programs to shoal up the market economy. Fiscalism comported comfortably with Keynesianism either as a stabilization instrument and market-economy adjunct or as a tool for extended government intervention or participation—depending on ideological tastes.

Early Keynesianism was colored by the apparent insensitivity of investment to interest-rate reductions in the 1930s. As the rate on long-term government bonds, as late as 1940, was 2.4 percent, with short-term rates at 0.014 percent, little scope existed for interest-rate declines compared, say, to 1975 where the corresponding entries were 8 and 7 percent. Government expenditure in the earlier Keynesian days promised to be a stouter multiplier stimulant than further monetary ease. Likewise, at the earlier 1930s levels of income tax collections, tax cuts offered meager play for augmenting consumption. By the 1960s, in the Kennedy years, at the higher income tax bill prevailing, a major tax revision was engineered.

Favoring G-outlays in the postwar period was the pithy observation of Galbraith that the world of affluence was marred by "private plenty amid public squalor"; the public domain was "starved" by lack of ample outlay with communal urban shabbiness outside the house portals distorting the interior household esthetics; government outlays transcended tax cuts favoring frivolous private consumption.†

The detailed precepts of fiscalism need not detain us in this overview of Keynesianism, for the doctrines are implanted by textbook reiteration. What is best in fiscal Keynesianism is neatly encapsulated by Lerner in *Functional Finance*. Lerner conjectured that everything that government could do about employment could be collapsed into three terse statements: (1) it could buy or sell, (2) lend or borrow, (3) pay subsidies or tax. Acting on the first item

---

*   Cf. Milton Friedman, *Monetary Correction.*

†   J. K. Galbraith, *The Affluent Society* (Boston: Houghton Mifflin, 1958), Chapter XVIII–XXII. Galbraith, never one to shirk an unpopular stand adduced by his logic, also urged higher sales taxes if these were the only means to finance overdue communal projects.

of each pair would enhance Q and N, while the opposite acts would restrain production.

There was also an early 45-degree line belief that inflation would cease as output contracted; Professor Lerner, whose logic has always triumphed over shibboleths of dogma, has become most explicit that the price level can only be stabilized by Incomes Policy, in conspicuous contrast to the immutable fiscal Keynesians.*

Fiscalism, leaning more to outlays and less to tax variations, or vice versa, depending on judgment and ideological vicissitudes, remains an indispensable stabilization instrument. Impacts, however, are on Q and N, with only indirect transmission to wages; it cannot fulfill the Keynesian dream of serving as a P stabilizer as well. Fiscalism shares with monetary policy a fairly direct potency on jobs; whether it is a "stronger" or "weaker" employment vehicle is a question which can be deferred. Sometimes the call will be for more of one and less of the other; in other circumstances both may be mustered toward restoring N.

The Keynesian Inflation Irrelevance

Keynesianism, to be sure, has magnified awareness of demand management in forging national income, output, and employment. If it had built sedulously on Keynes it would have had the wage-unit as a building block in the structure from the start, cemented the distributional forces in the C-function, closeted prices in the L-function, and inflation and expectational underpinnings in I. The entire theory would have become a relevant edifice, alerting policy on the stagflation ordeal and impelling a focus on the design of Incomes Policy to protect the price level.

Instead, early Keynesianism maneuvered itself into an identification with full-employment objectives engineered through fiscal expedients. Later, Phillips curve Keynesianism detoured itself into some complacency, and atrophy, in renouncing the full-employment ideal and accepting one or both instabilities in "natural" oscillations. Keynesianism has thus been riven into separate camps, with some of the old faithful gamboling with Monetarist prescriptions, despite the unemployment distress; while others shout full em-

---

* Cf. A. P. Lerner, *The Economics of Employment* (New York: McGraw-Hill, 1951), p. 127. Also, the enlightening, insightful, and entertaining compendium on *Flation* (New York: Penguin Books, 1973) and "Keynesianism: An Exaggerated Demise and A Premature Funeral," *Conference on the Relevance of the New Deal to the Present Situation* (City University of New York, June 23–25, 1975), mimeo. On the price level, see his Richard Ely lecture "Employment Theory and Employment Policy," *American Economic Review* (May 1967) and "From the *Treatise on Money* to *The General Theory*," *Journal of Economic Literature* (March 1974).

ployment—and damn the inflation: the price inequities can be patched up, in imagination if not in execution.

Keynesianism, as distinct from Keynes, has thus come to a dead end on the macrocrisis of our day. Despite being ill served by his interpreters, Keynes comes off unscathed by the eerie Keynesian twists into model irrelevance; for Keynes contemplated a policy of money incomes matching productivity advances though, to be sure, he stopped short of plans for implementation. Keynesians have yet to match his studied progress; many have not even recognized the P-theory strand in his thought which led Lerner to say "Keynes was often ahead even of himself."*

This is to close on an adverse evaluation of Keynesian *inflation* theory and policy. The 1950–1965 optimism of a historic phase of full employment has been routed; the school is in disarray, its laurels tarnished as some cavort with Monetarism. To many there is a lingering nostalgia over past triumphs while the future slips away. President Nixon would characteristically denounce skeptics for "downgrading" America, to stifle any constructive reforms. Prominent Keynesians too often close ranks as a sect against charges of theoretical inadequacy and policy ineptness.†

So far as unemployment goes, compared to the pre-1940 world, the Keynesian feats cannot be denigrated; while short of miracles, the 1961–1968 employment path was exemplary until the post-1968 debacle. Fiscal Keynesianism, once the inflation trauma passes, contains viable principles for opening job opportunities for all who want work. But fiscalism covers only part of the full stabilization package.

A Note On Aggregate Demand and Aggregate Supply

An alternative version of Keynesianism, more attuned to Keynes' money-wage and price-level ideas, invokes the concepts of Aggregate Demand and Aggregate Supply. Although the approach is free of the shortcomings of Hicksian Keynesianism, it has had far less attention.‡

---

* Cf. the closing section of the *General Theory,* Chapter 19, pp. 269–271; also, Lerner "From the *Treatise,* etc.," p. 42.

† For a more favorable assessment of Keynesian triumphs (while noting the inflation failures) see the American Economic Association presidential address of Walter W. Heller, "What's Right With Economics," *American Economic Review* (March 1975).

‡ For some statement of the postulational basis of the theory, see my *Approach to the Theory of Income Distribution* (Philadelphia: Chilton, 1958), Chapter 2. For a textbook, see Paul Davidson and Eugene Smolensky, *Aggregate Supply and Demand Analysis* (New York: Harper & Row, 1964). Also (with some modification in output units) Miles Fleming, *Introduction to Economic Analyses* (London: Allen & Unwin, 1969), Part III. Also, Paul Wells, "Keynesian Disequilibrium Theory," in *Modern Economic Thought.* The theory has been extended to growth analysis in my *Employ-*

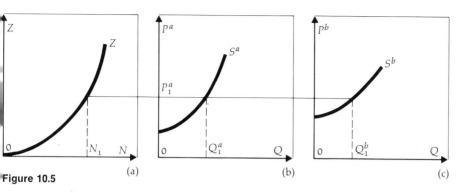

Figure 10.5

(a)　　　　　　(b)　　　　　　(c)

In Fig. 10.5 (b, c) a (Marshallian) supply curve is drawn for industry A and industry B, each viewed as "representative" of typical industries. At a price of P_1 there are the respective Q_1 outputs in A and B. Multiplying each PQ we can arrive at $\Sigma PQ = P_1^a Q_1^a + P_1^b Q_1^b + \ldots$, with $\Sigma P_1 Q_1$ thereby representing the aggregate of industry proceeds *expected* at supply prices P_1. The employment total implicit at each industry Q_1 can be extracted from the industry production functions of $N = N(Q)$. In Fig. 10.5(a), the employment level attached to each aggregate *expected* proceeds level ΣPQ is explicitly entered.

At each aggregate proceeds total (written as $Z \equiv PQ$) we can thus reach down to industry supply curves and ascertain the output and employment levels. One restrictive hypothesis is involved, namely, that any aggregate proceeds sum (PQ) is uniquely allocated among industries. Hicksian, and Hansen-Samuelson, analyses use an even more restrictive hypothesis by supposing that the output *composite* is unchanged: all outputs are assumed to vary proportionately whenever Y changes.*

For the Aggregate Demand curve we can ask: How much output will be *demanded* when each industry produces $Q_1, Q_2, \ldots$ etc., along the course of each industry supply curve? Thereby, the intended demand-volume of outlays at each supply price can be ascertained, forming a "D-0" demand outlay curve in each industry, as in Fig. 10.6. This is a cross-cut of the ordinary demand curves of price theory where each demand is drawn on the assumption of "given" Y or "given" N. For example, in Figure 10.6 a quantity Q_1^{ad} is wanted, at an outlay of $P_1^a Q_1^{ad}$, at an accompanying supply price P_1^a and

---

ment Growth and Income Distribution, and Paul Davidson, *Money in the Real World.*

* Thus for the horizontal axis $0Y$, magnitudes of Y are multiples of a unique commodity, with \$500 billion of real income Y containing five times the composite in \$100 billion. Without this proviso there would be no plausible reason for the consumption function to run north-east. If \$100 billion of Y contained an assortment of goods and \$500 billion only fish worms the C-outlay would surely turn down.

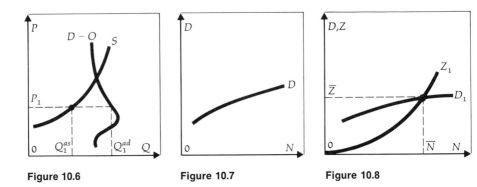

Figure 10.6   Figure 10.7   Figure 10.8

output Q_1^{as}. By aggregating the *intended* purchase outlays over the full economy, an Aggregate Demand curve is built, as in Fig. 10.7. At each N-level exactly the same prices are embedded in Aggregate Demand (D) as in Aggregate Supply (Z).

D and Z are joined in Fig. 10.8. The intersection yields the equilibrium balance of N and Y ($\equiv$ Gross Business Product).

Ordinary industry supply curves are erected on two major hypotheses: (1) given factor prices, and (2) given factor productivity, meaning a specific production function. The dual hypotheses yield the supply curve for the industry, which also presupposes competitive markets. In (2), for short-period macrotheory, labor is the variable factor.*

Thus every time w alters, the industry supply curves will shift: likewise, as the money-wage alterations change money incomes, w will be a shift-parameter for both the Z and D functions. This is illustrated in Fig. 10.8 where D_1 and Z_1 are contingent on the money wage w_1, and D_2 and Z_2 on w_2, where $w_2 > w_1$. Thus a family of D and Z functions can be drawn. If the higher money wage acts to diminish the equilibrium employment the results are as in the orthodox pre-Keynes theory; the conclusion follows, however, only under some restrictive monetary hypotheses.†

Parametric boosts in w can yield a demand curve for labor, forging a chain between *money*—not real—wages and employment. The same apparatus could be extended to the theory of growth, and to illuminate the part played by money supplies and income distribution.‡

---

* User cost, which in the integrated model refers to the expected loss in *future* proceeds, comprises the other main component.

† Although the conclusion is pre-*General Theory*, many economists still write as if the descending neoclassical labor-demand curve is an unassailable principle. Cf. *Approach,* Chapter 6; also Chapter 5 above.

‡ Cf. my *Employment Growth and Income Distribution* and Paul Davidson, *Money and the Real World.* See also the "borrowing" (without acknowledgment) of M. Chatterjee, "Cost Inflation and the State of Economic Theory: A Comment," *Economic Journal* (March 1975), pp. 151–153. Interestingly, Chatterjee speaks of

The apparatus builds in a price level from the start.* With the collapse of the *IS-LM* apparatus this alternative version of Keynes' theory might be reviewed as a teaching vehicle. It can assimilate micro-macro theories, for a unified "one-world" economic theory.

this as an "orthodox" Keynesian model—which presumably consigns Hicks, Hansen, and Samuelson to some "heterodox" status. See my comment, Ibid. (June 1976).

* Along given D and Z functions, $w = \overline{w}$ with $A = A(Q)$. Thus the (w/A) relation of the WCM theory is embodied in the functions; with $(kw/A) = (w/M)$, or $M = A/k$ where $M =$ the marginal product of labor, the functions are applicable to the competitive case and under monopoly where $k > 1$ the WCM captures the monopoly price-markup in Z. The D-function in the consumer sector also embeds w, as in $D_c = \alpha w N$.

CHAPTER ELEVEN

Monopoly Malevolence

In the court of public opinion big business, big unions, and big government are blanketed and blamed for inflation. Unions and their money-wage exactions are already implicit in the WCM theory; monopoly and government budgets merit separate assessment.

Allegations, it will be concluded, are overdrawn. Monopoly, for example, may deserve censure for "high" prices through an oversized k. Yet on the cumulative march of *rising* prices that constitutes the inflation disorder, an enlargement of monopoly power would have to be shown *in consecutive periods*, not the fact of its mere existence.*

Distortion abounds in flailing government outlays as the inflation beast. Our imperfect democracy is spotted with shortcomings galore, with sins of omission and commission. But chronic inflation is not to be cornered in flaps over the leviathan's prodigious outlay wings; the pertinent censure would cite its groping irresoluteness on initiatives to check the extravagant money-income adventures.

Ventilating these inflation ideas enlarges the laundry list of explanations. An open-minded attitude that "everything plays a part" mixes the air of tolerance with the aroma of banality. An "n-factor" theory shrinks from even

---

* Protests over monopoly breeding inflation are not exactly original; Jean Bodin, the herald of the OQTM, mulled over it before casting it aside as a lesser cause. Aristotle, fleetingly, uttered a denunciation of *higher* monopoly prices. It was a fairly common doctrine during the Great Depression and baited, before the *General Theory*, an eager audience for the theories of monopolistic competition with their excess capacity implications. Yet it was also true that it was during the long wave of *falling* prices, in the late 19th century, that the antitrust movement gathered momentum.

the attempt to penetrate the inflation shell: the analytic probe must ferret out a *general* theory capable of absorbing, without abandoning its character, the whole spectrum of potential P-agents.

The Monopoly Inflation Shadow

Unless the word monopoly is to be corrupted as a synonym for bigness, it must be reserved to describe prices surpassing competitive norms. Giant firms of 10, 20, 30 years ago resemble two-seater biplanes interspersed among jumbo jets; a future quantum leap seems destined. The thrust of the monopoly denunciation must be a *relatively* high product price, compared to the competitive outcome, unless bigness itself is the target, rather than inflation. Fundamentally, the allegations must substantiate that at any (w/A), k-mon $>$ k-com. The inquiry thus graduates into a comparison of associated mark-ups unless it can be established that $(\Delta A/A)$ deteriorates under a monopoly-oligopoly structure or that $(\Delta w/w)$ accelerates sharply. Of course, if the relative pricing structure was altered the development path of income distribution, output composition, growth rates, and the nature of government market intervention would look different. The shape of things must remain obscure without a detailed account of which industrial price and output practices are revised. The contact of monopoly to inflation, in the structure we know, centers on the k magnitude.*

Courage in denouncing monopoly parallels eloquent trumpeting of motherhood and the Boy Scout movement; capitalist cynics and ideological admirers can unite for a common cause.† Ranks break over the substance of reform and the time frame for implementation, running from an impatient fervor for socialism to anemic gestures for publicity, with most centrist camps pleading for more study—to evoke later proposals for more study. Galbraith has acutely observed that the giant corporations most regularly ticketed for antitrust violations are also most frequently tapped for a place of honor on the itinerary of foreign VIP's anxious to gaze at the marvels of American technology.‡ Almost 75 years have elapsed since the Republican Teddy Roose-

---

* Those who prefer a profit-maximizing monopoly-competitive contrast would use price = marginal cost (MC) against $P > MC$ = marginal revenue. But $P = MC$, for the one variable factor case, would entail $MC = w/MP$, where MP = marginal product of labor. So the conflict boils down to $(k/A) = (1/MP)$. Clearly, user cost must also enter into marginal cost so that $MC > w/MP$. Using k/A permits far easier measurement than the MP formulation.

† Thus Henry Simons, the wise and respected intellectual parent of the modern Chicago school, saw the elimination of monopoly as indispensable to an efficient and more equitable capitalist society. See *Economic Policy for a Free Society* (Chicago: University of Chicago, 1948).

‡ J. K. Galbraith, *American Capitalism: The Concept of Countervailing Power* (Boston: Houghton Mifflin, 1952). Galbraith has been one of the conspicuously

velt waved the big stick at what passed for monopoly bigness then. Predictably, our concentrated industrial structure is unlikely to be fragmented dramatically in the foreseeable future for there is neither political nor public ardor for the campaign. Public attitudes, buttressed by TV options for the large firms, list the other way. Not least, the blighted English experience with nationalization, and the diffusion of ideological issues in the cold war confrontation with the Soviet bloc which has been guilty of compromising human rights in compounding human miseries, has raised a more impenetrable protective shield over otherwise assailable big business redoubts.

Some monopoly implications

The economist's displeasure over monopoly resides in its resource inefficiency through higher relative prices, implying an output deviation from the Pareto optimum; the extended proof shows that a competitive-type price would enhance real income all around.* The conclusion follows whether the monopoly is concentrated in a single firm or manifested by an organized cartel group as exemplified by the OPEC oil cartel, or through oligopoly cohorts abiding some informal rule of their own market reason. Criticism of their pricing tactics invariably emanates from static models of demand, cost, and product varieties. Nonoptimality is rigorously deduced in *stationary* conditions.

Yet monopolists, or oligopolists, may exercise price restraint on assessing the threat of *potential* competition, and from giant firms sensing new profit opportunities: the product turf is rarely shut to invasion. Too, predatory price gouging can be meliorated by the latent power of government antitrust or by public opinion crystallized by howls in legislative chambers. Available substitutes in world markets furnish another limitation, as domestic steel, auto, and electronic firms can testify.

Dynamically, how a "purely" competitive world would operate is obscure; textbook apostles have not provided light in their immersion with models cloistered in specifying a given array of "*m*-products." In the innovative society the commodity spectrum is assuredly *not* "given," for "*m*" is a number capable of quick fluctuation. How new products would enter without patent and trademark protection, and what incentive there would be for innovation where successes are subject to immediate emulation and failures to suffer losses as an orphan, is conspicuously obscure: trademarks and

---

few, and the most articulate and persuasive among economists, to advocate more nationalization in recent years. Even with his wit and wisdom there appear to be few converts and followers. See his *Economics and the Public Purpose* (Boston: Houghton Mifflin, 1973). The new Radical Economics group still constitutes a small professional minority striving for a receptive audience.

* Perfect competition is only *one* means of accomplishing the optimal price result. In principle, nationalized firms acting under the *MC* rule could accomplish the same result, as could regulated firms. See my *Price Theory*, Chapter 6.

patents are themselves a contradiction to the pure competition model. Older economists deferred the study of such dynamic questions to a future Volume II which old age then placed beyond their scrutiny. Less excusably, modern economists have bypassed the intriguing complex analysis, being content to reiterate that in a medieval static economy, competition would confer unalloyed gains.*

Manifestly, monopoly prices and practices are profitable to the practitioners: there is income benefit to monopolists. Further, the output configuration will reflect the monopoly pricing facts, compared to the $P = MC$ norm. Yet higher prices, as Chamberlin demonstrated, encouraged monopolistic competitors brandishing differentiated products.† Progress has been, in part, associated with new products, so that the debate runs to the fascinating dilemmas of product standardization versus commodity diversification; variety contributes to the coloration of society and some of its enrichment; also, as Mrs. Robinson noted, differentiation gratifies the needs of personality individualists and eccentrics, while uniformity appeases the conformist types.‡

Administered prices

Some rail against monopoly and, in almost the same breath, advocate higher wages to counteract the price exactions. This adds a bit of whimsy and counterproductive illogic. Of course, there are always some who stand foursquare for a price rise to suppress inflation!

Themes of administered prices as the inflation-maker still lie about, as a remnant from the Great Depression when price discretion was considered instrumental in the job and output collapse and indicted for impeding a *drop* in prices. Where once price inflexibility was the rub, it is now the easy price escalation that attracts opprobrium. Logic is retained only insofar as "administered prices" are identified with monopoly, and involving a consistent theme of prices "too high" in the Great Depression and "too high" during stagflation.§

---

* Cf. Ibid., pp. 230–233. Despite the passage of years the study of the problem has been honored in the breach. Joseph Schumpeter considered the range of issues, to colossal subsequent neglect in mathematized general-equilibrium models. See *Capitalism, Socialism and Democracy* (New York: Harper & Row, 1942).

† E. H. Chamberlin, *Economics of Monopolistic Competition* (Cambridge: Harvard, 1933).

‡ Joan Robinson, *Accumulation of Capital* (Homewood, Ill.: Irwin, 1956).

§ An original exponent of the administered price thesis, Gardiner C. Means, has revived the argument for the present circumstances. See "The Administered Price Thesis Reconfirmed," *American Economic Review* (June 1972). The ideas dominated the *Temporary National Economic Committee* (TNEC) hearings in the late 1930s which developed a mass of valuable materials deserving of a better fate than library fossil status.

J. K. Galbraith, while adhering to some tenets of the administered price doctrine, has never been confused on the primacy of the money wage and price nexus. See *The New Industrial State* (Boston: Houghton Mifflin, 1967), Chapter XXII.

The income conflict

The monopoly inflation imbroglio boils over into a bout over the k-magnitude. As debate over the size of profits entails conflict over economic power, income division, and amenities of economic well-being, resolution will never be easy, as Marx long also discerned. Political muscle, diversionary tactics, and inflammatory rhetoric are bound to accompany any concerted move to slice profits, with financial markets and jobs under siege as investment falters. How the drama would end must be left to the future historian cognizant of the means, the actors, the emotions, and the contrived images. Quarrels over income are never wholly admirable, whoever wins; participants on all sides are animated by the same protective forces to defend income shares already possessed, with each avid for aggressive inroads into the parts staked out by others. The ancient Greek philosophers, enjoying the comforts and rationalizing slavery, were doubly blessed; they could stand serenely above the fray and belittle material wealth from the comfort of their own position.

In a market economy, the indispensable prerequisite is to get the system to function, to produce current goods, and to offer a fairly sure promise of higher future real-income opportunities for all—more jam all-around, tomorrow, despite misgivings over the marmalade allotments today. What share will induce capitalists to mobilize their best efforts? Can the acceptable rate of return be sliced over time? Or is convention so ingrained that future rates of return will have to approximate past profit margins? Are there humanistic alternatives for accomplishing parallel resource organization results? These are vast subjects transcending the inflation crisis.

An effective democracy requires some communal consensus over *functional* rates of return, while eliminating, with deliberate speed, the disfiguring obscenities in income distribution.* An acceptable erosion of rates of return must be a plant of slower atrophy, unless there is some untapped reservoir of sacrificial goodwill. Obviously, the obstacles to change entrench the status quo; there remains the hard nut of the irreconcilables of resistance versus the productive need for harmony in complex societies: the alternatives of bureaucracy and totalitarianism have richly earned a bad name in the democratic West.

The absolute and relative size of *k*-components

It may be that the gravity of the discussion is misspent—in the inflation context. Better, some may conclude, to hold out the glitter of the lottery prize of big gains than a quarrel over the transfer of piddling sums when widely

---

* For some statement of the problems, from all shades of opinion, see the collection of essays in *Income Inequality* (Annals of the American Academy of Political Science, September 1973), edited by the present author.

disbursed. This is one interpretation of the profit data.* Undoubtedly, the worst immediate troubles lie elsewhere, in unemployment, inflation, ecological unconcern, oversell of dubious product items, and the imperfect sifting of abilities for executive advancement in organizational-centered leadership screening. Also, there are idealistic misgivings over the obsession with material accumulation as a malaise of the human spirit. Income disparities may be more amenable for cures than the psychological motivations.

Examining the data, if profits of big firms are the architect of stagflation, then it should be possible to show large unruly upcreeps in their proportions. This has not happened. Likewise, $P(t)$ behaved reasonably well after 1950 compared to the virulent outbreak since 1968. Yet roughly the same roster of firms comprised the industrial list of "who's who," so that it stretches plausibility to perceive the "monopolists" suddenly behaving more irresponsibly.

The data refer to the nonfinancial corporate sector, embracing the usual conception of the monopoly arena, contributing 55 to 60 percent of the GNP. Omitted are the financial sector, much of agriculture, and most small business. Monopoly invectives might be hurled at the financial sector, too, but the farm and retail sectors are usually relieved of the more acerbic charge.

The wage-salary bill, according to Table 11.1, hovered at about 65 percent

Table 11.1

Gross Product and Components of Nonfinancial Corporations,
in billions of dollars

Item	Dollar amounts				Percent of total			
	1950	1960	1970	1975	1950	1960	1970	1975
Corporate Gross Product	151.9	277.3	560.6	870.4	100.0	100.0	100.0	100.0
Depreciation*	12.6	27.0	53.1	96.6	8.3	9.7	9.5	12.0
Indirect Business Taxes	14.1	28.3	61.8	93.4	9.3	10.2	11.0	10.7
Employee Compensation	94.7	181.1	377.1	577.1	62.3	65.3	67.3	68.6
Pretax Profits	38.5	39.5	55.1	95.5	25.3	14.2	9.8	10.9
Posttax Profits	21.6	20.3	27.9	55.8	14.2	7.3	5.0	6.6
Dividends	7.9	11.5	19.9	29.0	5.2	4.1	3.5	3.3
Net Interest	0.9	3.5	17.0	30.8	0.6	0.1	3.0	3.5

Source: *Economic Report*, Council of Economic Advisers (January 1977).
*   Officially titled "Capital Consumption Allowances."

---

*   Lest these remarks be misconstrued, the reference here is to profits, rather than to egregious salary and wage discrepancies, or posttax rental and interest shares, per rentier.

of the total.* Profits, before taxes, were generally about 10 to 14 percent of the total, though in 1950 they swelled to 25 percent. After taxes, the figures deflate to about 7 percent, though the 1950 figure sticks out at 14 percent. Interest payments at 4 percent, from under 1 percent, reflect the tight money policies of the Fed's Pavlovian defensive stance to strike inflation.

Two separate transformations of the figures, pre- and posttax profits, can be calculated in order to assess price-level relief that might be obtained through draconian measures to lower k: we leave aside the overriding question of how—or whether—the economy would function. Thus suppose all profits were obliterated and prices were reduced correspondingly. The markup would be:

$$kx = (Y - \text{Profits})/wN$$

Thus kx assumes that *all* pretax profits redounded in price reductions; undoubtedly wage earner tax bills would have to be inflated to replace the treasury revenue loss. Sample—simple-minded—calculations appear in Table 11.2.

Table 11.2

The k-Markup and the Wage Share ($1/k$) in the
Corporate Nonfinancial Sector

	k	$1/k$	kx	$1/kx$
1950	1.60	62.5	1.20	83.3
1960	1.53	65.4	1.31	76.2
1974	1.49	67.1	1.34	74.6
1975	1.51	66.2	1.34	74.6

Examination of Table 11.2 suggests that inflation can hardly be attributed to hikes in k for, compared to 1950, the k-decline should have pulled prices in 1975 below 1950! Likewise, since 1960 the markup hardly vacillated significantly during the recent period of extreme price upheaval. On kx, which abolishes profits by a stroke of the pen, the price level would have been lower, substantially so in 1950. But since 1960 the price course would hardly have been deflected. Profits, either pre- or posttax, have had little part in the recent inflation. The wage share, of course, would be elevated (before new income tax imposts). The share would have trended slightly downward more recently. But the stuff of inflation is not discernible in the k-measures, actual or artificial. At best, a sharp cut in k, subsequently maintained, would yield a once-

---

* In net income (thereby excluding depreciation and indirect taxes), the wage bill would constitute 75.6, 81.6, 84.8, and 83.2 percent of the net value added in the corporate sector over the respective years.

over P-descent after which, with $\Delta k \approx 0$, as $(\Delta w/\Delta A)$ tracked skyward, the inflation flight would resume.*

Obviously, the implicit *ceteris paribus* constitutes an ignoble evasion. Among the gigantic ill-concealed monuments are: (1) What to do for an encore—to enhance the wage share or to cut P after profits fell to zero, as in kx? (2) How would the system operate without profits? How would capital formation be fostered? (Socialism, too, would entail $k > 1$). Likewise, (3) with kx there would be a need for a higher personal income tax bite to replace the profit component under higher product prices.

All in all, while a little surcease from inflation might be squeezed out of lower *workable* k-values, it is frivolous to imagine that w/A vigilance would thereafter be superfluous.† The inflation storm will not pass by irate denunciation of typical markups.

Confusing monopoly resource allocation deficiencies with inflation

The monopoly probe can only paddle in muddy waters if it is focused on inflation rather than on resource allocation, income distribution, output composition, and the dynamics of capitalism. On inflation, the gain would be at most a *once-over* price-level downturn effect by some compression of k-magnitudes.‡ Yet the constancy of k over the historic trend requires some answer

---

* Cf. the analysis of oligopoly in inflation by Stephen A. Ross and Michael L. Wachter, "Wage Determination, Inflation, and the Industrial Structure," *American Economic Review* (Sept. 1973). Their analysis may be more germane to the theory of relative prices than to inflation *per se*.

† Under the Labour party nationalization in the United Kingdom, and amid its slumpflation disasters including a 25 percent 1975–1976 price rise, profits in the "company" sector fell from 27.6 to 19.6 percent of the value of output between 1960 and 1971. Again, *falling* prices should have been reported on "profiteering" theses. See Wiles, p. 381.

‡ Almost 40 years ago, in a pioneering essay, Michal Kalecki developed a markup equation, concluding (perhaps with the experience of the 1920s in mind) that because of productivity advances the price level was trending down, aborted by enlarged monopoly power of countervailing size. See his *Theory of Economic Fluctuations* (London: Allen Unwin, 1939), Chapter 1. A more direct markup formula is provided in his *Theory of Economic Dynamics* (London: Allen Unwin, 1954), Essay 1. This refers to the industrial sector, and includes raw materials, in a markup of "prime" costs. For an evaluation of the achievements of this gifted economist, whose reputation has been sustained mainly by the tributes of Joan Robinson and Nicholas Kaldor, see the welcome study by George R. Feiwel, *The Intellectual Capital of Michal Kalecki* (Knoxville: University of Tennessee, 1975).

As a personal note, my own WCM equation was derived independently of Kalecki's work though the latter was known to me from school days in London. It was only after my k-computations emerged as "constant" that I recalled Kalecki on the wage share, to which I then referred. The WCM is, I think, more general and more amenable to measurement than Kalecki's equation. But the substantial priority is his, even though it is more cost-oriented than my own version of demand-and-costs in price level determination, especially in consumer markets. As noted, some

on the operations of the enterprise economy from those who blithely assume that merely political muscle is required to dissolve the magnitude.

The trouble surfaces when, after a long and vexatious strike, as in steel, autos, or transportation, a wage agreement ignites a price spiral. Unions vehemently protest the price hike as excessive, deploring management irresponsibility. Management routinely replies that the price lift falls short of the wage exactions, mourning the absence of union statesmanship. Copious studies generally scatter inconclusive results after banging against the stone wall of privileged business information.

Despite the ingenuity of statistical processing, the facts will remain obscure until we succeed first in stabilizing the w/A ratio. Once the labor-cost balance was maintained it would be possible to determine the extent to which particular profit margins are behaving suspiciously. Clues to monopoly behavior could then be amassed by even amateur sleuths.

Welfare gains in more cars and appliances?

In trotting out the oligopoly industries—autos, steel, and electrical appliances rank near the top of the list—there is more day-to-day evidence of bigness in the enumeration, matching the arms contractors nourished and protected by contracts of the Defense Department (though the lists overlap). For the consumer, the commonplace inference is that lower prices would result after the disintegration of the oligopoly structure—why the result would improve with ten firms rather than four or five is not always clear, especially with the likelihood of concerted actions because of common motivations.

Yet it is possible to view some lower prices more with consternation than jubilation! Lower prices would mean more autos: it seems hard to believe that the number of cars on the road represents a critical and destructive shortage. Likewise, with lower prices, more appliances would be absorbed by householders; also, maybe lower electricity rates and *more* energy use would follow through sterner utility regulation; neither outcome would *relieve* the prospective energy shortage. More aluminum, more steel, would deplete available mineral resources faster, making ecological upsets more devastating.

There is thus some lack of realism attached to the welfare "analysis," despite the seemingly precise Pareto optimal models generally invoked to

---

may claim priority for Keynes and the *Treatise*. Pedersen, too, figures high on the list of claimants.

Otto Eckstein and Gary Fromm have published an equation of $P = (w/A) + (rK)$, where $r =$ "the" profit rate and $K =$ the stock of capital. This is very neat—if only we know K and r. Plugging in either r or K, given P and (w/A), then the residual variable is squeezed out. Mrs. Robinson's dismemberment of K measurement provides the last word—until we find a way of getting into the future without the passage of time. See their "The Price Equation," *American Economic Review* (Dec. 1968).

"prove" monopoly damage. The resource-allocation arguments gratuitously profess a better resource deflection to output unduly checked by monopoly absorption of consumer income: results of maybe more cars, TV in every room, handguns galore, cyclamates, abundant drugs, more tobacco, booze, and more "modern" films—to express some product prudery. The list can obviously be colored by personal bias. But it takes an unwavering commitment to enterprise systems and consumer rationality to take an unadorned perception of well-being after the monopoly-oligopoly dismantlement.

Of course, government could levy excise taxes to pick up the revenue that otherwise swells private monopoly coffers. But this creates problems of execution, with "second-best" implications for Pareto models.

The point is: these matters have hardly entered the discussion in the fervent hand-waving exercises and thoughtless tirades aimed at monopoly which too often equate monopoly to heinous sin whose removal would free us all from insufferable bondage.

Protests are predictable that welfare "value-judgments" are being loosely uttered in this terse evaluation of some monopoly pronouncements. Of course. Yet the very confidence in higher "welfare" in opposing prevailing "monopoly" and its higher *relative* prices also exudes ideological and welfare-value judgments. The Pareto thesis, after all, applies to the *stationary* economy, with rational buyers, without the TV pitch, without product development, without social externalities of private choice. As such, the simple conventional theory is vulnerable to criticism outside of medieval states of stagnancy and in which future socioeconomic directions are independent of price reforms.

This is not a defense of "monopoly"; motherhood, likewise, is a noble institution. But the theory of welfare economics for the changing economy, with product development, TV commercials, and social diseconomies, and the absence of a serious bill of operative particulars on antimonopoly measures for the modern environment, constitutes the missing agenda in theoretical and applied welfare economics.

For inflation control, the monopoly diatribes are usually misdirected. For unemployment, the implicit income distributive shifts through monopoly may entail added I or public sector outlay (G) offsets. But these matters are more in the nature of analytic and policy details, rather than supporting the conclusion that monopoly erects formidable blockages impeding the economy from providing abundant jobs for all who want to work at or about prevailing real wages.*

---

* Many years ago I tried to introduce monopoly pricing into a macro-model, a subject then, as now, notoriously neglected, even by Keynes. The restrictive model elicited some interesting conclusions even though it was built on the limiting hypothesis of constant money income. See "Monopoly Pricing and Unemployment," *Quarterly Journal of Economics* (1946).

Monopoly as a Noninflation Issue

Monopoly practices invite study even in the absence of inflation, or even in an era of price-level deflation. Monopoly has to do with fundamental matters of resource allocation, income distribution, production opportunities, and the quality of life, as affected by production processes and available goods. The relation of antitrust to pernicious business practices can stand on its own, in inflation season and out. But it is a spurious proposition, relieved of fact, to hold "monopoly" as responsible for our pressing inflation disorders.

CHAPTER TWELVE

Government Proflicacy

It is always fashionable to blame government spending, debt, taxation, or deficits for causing inflation. Political "outs" have a handy peg; incumbents can parry by pointing to the spending benefits.

Recently, the litany of grievances concerning government profligacy as the inflation pacemaker has been augmented by lists compiled of costly legislation responsible for low productivity or redundant labor hire, as in rules governing safety, hygiene, packaging, work practices, waste disposal, shipment, and modes of transportation, to name a few. Featherbedding practices, according to the critics, cover a catalogue of about 85 items, many of which involve value-laden judgments about desirable avenues of government intervention and redress.*

In a theory that aims at generality, the comment can be brief: some regulations undoubtedly swell costs, and their removal could lower the w/A ratio—taking the optimistic slant. Cost savings, however, are by nature a one-shot affair. Encores are not self-abetting, and the A-magnitudes are unlikely to be raised by a miraculous touch in efficiency once the new rules prevail. To increase productivity from 3 percent to 4 percent per annum is not a one-point gain, but a $33\frac{1}{3}$-percent improvement—as investment counselors turning compound interest pages confirm. Exhilarating $\Delta A/A$ ascents of this order are not easy.

---

* At President Ford's September 1974 meetings, 24 economists signed a statement agreeing on the elimination of 22 restrictive laws that "inhibit" competition—averaging almost one obnoxious practice per economist.

"Ill-devised" regulations, like other noncontroversial matters, can always be reproached, heroically and courageously: again, this is to stand foursquare for motherhood. Yet for all the attendant noise, the compilation is mostly a vast irrelevancy for grasping the nub of the inflation issue; one beholder's inefficiency is another person's livelihood, for the most part. After the parade of cases starts the conclusion will remain that productivity improvements through time depend mainly on achievements in technology; the most efficient work rules with the technology of 1850 will still mire us in the economy of 1850. The same will be said in the year 2000 about the technology of 1976.

It is easy rhetoric to deride government employees as "unproductive tax-eating bureaucrats." This is of a piece with the Physiocratic veneration of agriculture, or the mystic belief that only farmers "produce," apparently by their going sub-surface to push up wheat, corn, cotton, etc. Reminiscent are Adam Smith's musings of misadventure over "unproductive" labor.* Yet all services whose results are wanted are productive—to the somebody who wants them; the controversies over government must focus on the importance to constituents of communal actions and missions.† Charges of shallow, inefficient, or empty performance can be detailed in private industry as well as government —as the numbers attending afternoon ball games in Chicago, or hacking on golf courses, might certify. "Normal" government operations, like "normal" business practices, reflect the devotion, attitudes, efficiency, and integrity of "normal" people going about their functions with restrained energy and efficiency. In some anomaly, those who denounce practically all government employment as wasteful end up supporting more defense outlays, which are probably the most wasteful of all. Yet, like so many other outlays, they are borne for they are palpably vital in the current precarious and uneasy state of the world strategic balance. Still, as any soldier who has waited—and waited—knows, there is ordinarily more boredom than superhuman efficiency entailed in supporting the mission.

Government expenditure

Flailing government expenditure as the agent of inflation is inherently a disguised Phillips curve theme, or an unintended resurrection and confirmation

---

*   In an excusable and stylistic lapse, Adam Smith castigated as "unproductive labor" those engaged in "the protection, security, and defense . . . some both of the gravest and most important, and some of the most frivolous professions: churchmen, lawyers, physicians, men of letters . . . musicians, opera singers. . . ." (Book II, Chapter III). Smith, of course, was at this point interested only in the output of tangibles as the content of investment and accumulation for growth, disregarding the host of supporting services and activities. It required almost a century before the marginal utility "revolution" would put matters right in its recognition that people and things can only render services, and that so long as the services are wanted, the activities are productive.

†   On the association of wants and productivity, see H. J. Davenport, *The Economics of Enterprise* (New York: Macmillan, 1913).

of Karl Marx's "reserve army of the unemployed" as a discipline on labor, astonishingly invoked by ideological foes. Assessing the WCM elements of w, A, and k, by the puffing up of the government sector only A and w might be influenced. Impacts on A, however, are not always negative. Improved roads enhance industrial productivity, as do fire services and schools, police and sanitation, etc., though the benefits are diffused in time and largely non-quantifiable with any precision. Thus it is mainly w that can be stirred in motion on the inflation trail through G-outlays.

A cutback of G should, directly and indirectly through the multiplier, mean unemployment. Presumably, in weak labor markets, the pace of w would be tempered—the conventional Phillips curve reasoning before the recent pattern of deviations. Nonetheless, the argument is hardly localized to G-sums. Equivalent results would follow any expenditure withdrawal, whether on I or C, as in a slash of consumption outlays on auto, TV, washing machine, or food purchases.

The substantive matter covers the extent to which G can be cut in line with the desired mix of communal and private outlays. Nonetheless, after flaying wasteful G outlays, and after all the fat is trimmed to sate the most ardent advocates of government parsimony, there will still be the need to confront the ubiquitous WCM components, to align w/A to a uniform trend. After the passions subside, the income facts will still obtrude.

As for the consumer price level, recalling the P_c-formula, with G outrunning the C and I outlay the N/N_c ratio will rise. Further, government transfer outlays can elevate θ', denoting the ratio of transfers to the wage bill. Through both channels there can be a prop under P_c. So long as the relative size of G in GNP, and of θ' holds firm, *cumulative* inflation cannot be attributed to G-outlays. Resolution of the "right" amount of G and of θ must come from the democratic consensus, reached with all the electoral imperfections and bureaucratic implementation which can undoubtedly often shortchange the original designs of legislative, constituent, and executive sponsors.

Some relevant facts are collected in Table 12.1, covering some selected years, and not unrepresentative of a continuous series. As a proxy for N/N_c, estimates of GNP/C are used inasmuch as data on N_c would entail some intricate statistical refinement: what is thus assumed is that capital/labor ratios are the same in the C-sector as in GNP generally.

Government expenditures are those of the GNP accounts, excluding the transfers contained in θ. Likewise, military expenditures remain an incomplete category: many other outlays, as for the State Department, international agencies, foreign aid, and space and research support, are not wholly unrelated to our military posture.

The grim picture of civilian bureaucrats appears to be distorted on even a cursory examination of the figures. Military outlays dominate the federal budget and approximate one-fourth of all government outlays at all levels. Considering the lopsided opprobrium reserved for the Washington bureaucracy, they absorb less than half of the military sums, and about one-fifth of

Table 12.1

Ratios of Government Purchases, Personal Consumption, and
Private Investment, Selected Years 1929–1975

Item	1929	1940	1950	1960	1970	1975
GNP	100.0	100.0	100.0	100.0	100.0	100.0
G: Federal	0.0	6.0	6.5	10.6	9.7	8.2
Nonmilitary	. . .	3.8	1.6	1.8	2.2	2.6
Military	. . .	2.2	4.9	8.8	7.5	5.6
G: State and Local	7.0	8.0	6.9	9.2	12.5	13.9
G-total/GNP	7.1	14.0	13.4	19.8	22.2	22.1
GNP/C [for N/N_c]	1.34	1.41	1.49	1.56	1.59	1.56
G/C [for N_g/N_c]	0.11	0.20	0.20	0.31	0.35	0.34
G/I [for N_i/N_c]	0.52	1.07	0.72	1.31	1.55	1.81
θ'	0.02	0.05	0.09	0.09	0.12	0.18

Source: *Council of Economic Advisers*, 1975, 1976. $G =$ combined federal, state, and local outlays. $\theta' =$ Government transfers to persons as a ratio of the wage bill (employee compensation).

total expenditures by state and local incumbents. Local police, education, sanitation, prisons, and road building amass the lion's share of the nonmilitary tax dollar. State and local outlays are just short of 14 percent of GNP; federal outlays come in at about 8.2 percent (in 1975), with the nonmilitary at 2.6 percent.

The GNP/C proxy for N/N_c reveals an enlargement from 1.49 in 1950 to 1.56 in 1975, after a 1.59 figure in 1970. Out of the 150 percent CPI move since 1950, only about 5 percent can be tied to relative resource shifts from C. To be sure, G-outlays were about 20 percent of C in 1940 and 1950, and have jumped to about 35 percent. In a more detailed study, programs like medicare and food stamps containing sums formerly entering C are now submerged (in part) in G (and θ). As a multiplier phenomenon (as we continue to neglect tax aspects) G has become about 80 percent larger than I. This figure ordinarily shows flux as I outlays are sensitive to cyclical fluctuation.

The big balloon is θ', of welfare transfers from the federal government compared to the wage bill. From 2 and 5 percent in the prewar days, to 9 percent as late as 1960, they have mushroomed to about 18 percent of the wage aggregate. Partly, this reflects the high unemployment in 1975. It is this ratio that holds some support for the popular appeal of "welfare hand-outs" as the inflation-maker. Yet it does not follow that if these outlays were cut drastically the "true" θ' would descend dramatically: the aged receiving Social Security payments, the unemployed receiving relief stipends, and the hard core of other welfare recipients would have to draw on what other assets they have, or borrow if possible, or depend on private charity for outlays. Nonetheless the θ' computation is indicative of a growing P_c magnitude. In considering income tax inroads, the elevation in θ' is partly neutralized as an inflation-maker by higher effective average tax rates during inflation in our progressive income tax structure, operating thereby to cut the c-ratios of average C-outlay.

Taxation

On taxes, there are the polar opinions, that taxes raise prices and that they tend to lower them. The former visualizes taxes entering into business costs: it was noted earlier that if the corporate sector profit taxes were abolished, and k fell to reflect this fact, the price level would be lower.* Again, this symbolizes a once-over turn of the crank, rather than a cumulative deceleration of the inflation trend.

Fiscal Keynesianism has argued that taxes are price-*deflationary*. Imposed on the business firm, taxes compel a lowering of the marginal efficiency of investment, less multiplier output and employment, and, on Phillips curve doctrine, deflationary pressure on w. Imposed on individuals, the tax bite cuts into purchasing power, depressing c_w and c_r in the P_c formula.

Unfortunately, the Keynesian analysis is irreparably stationary in character. It assumes that when personal income tax rates climb, either through new tax tables or through the new layering of average money wages and salaries in a progressive tax structure, individuals remain placid. This kind of analysis formed the sawdust pillar in Lyndon Johnson's surtax in mid-1968. Keynesian advisers exuded confidence that the extraction of "real" purchasing power would arrest the "demand-inflation." Releases, reminiscent of Herbert Hoover, that "we have turned the corner on inflation" emanated as late as October 1968. Unfortunately, wage earners upset the static plan: noting the thinned pay envelopes, some bitter demands for higher money wages erupted, demolishing the static Keynesian propositions. The most obdurate inflation in our modern history followed.

The analysis thus cannot be approached from the static standpoint insofar as $w = w(T, \ldots)$, where $T =$ the average tax bite on wage earners, with $(\Delta w/\Delta T) > 0$. Obviously, the money wage sequel reenforces WCM doctrine.

So far as taxes in the corporate sector go, Table 12.2 contains what business firms regard as the gory tax details.

Including indirect taxes (such as property taxes, sales taxes, and the variety of corporate levies by state and local government) swells the corporate tax imposts to about 20 percent. Most of these tax sums, however, are in lieu of direct personal levies: the choice involves administrative convenience and

---

* John Hotson has particularly emphasized taxes (and interest rates) in inflation in, e.g., "Adverse Effects of Interest and Tax Hikes As Strengthening the Case for Income Policies," *Canadian Journal of Economics* (May 1971). Higher interest rates are especially potent in the public utility sector where regulated firms gain rate hikes as interest rates climb. Cf. earlier remarks on banks' rationalization of higher interest rates to "fight" inflation, above, Chapter 9.

Table 12.2

Employee Compensation and Business Taxes As Ratios of Gross
Nonfinancial Corporate Product, Selected Years 1950–1975

Item	1950	1960	1970	1975
Gross Nonfinancial				
Corporate Product	100.0	100.0	100.0	100.0
Corporate Profits Tax	11.1	6.9	4.9	9.3
Indirect Business Taxes*	9.3	10.2	11.0	10.7
Tax Total	20.4	17.1	15.9	20.0
Employee Compensation	62.3	65.3	67.3	68.6

Source: *Council of Economic Advisers* (1976).
*   Also includes transfer payments minus subsidies.

public conceptions of equity. Any lower prices induced by corporate tax relief
would largely be matched by lower, after-tax wage and salary, rent, and
dividend incomes. Little of significance, it might be surmised, will be accomplished to avert the cumulative inflation blight.

Personal taxes, at all government levels, amounted to about 14.4 and 13.6
percent of personal incomes in 1970 and 1975, respectively. Maybe, at a guess,
the c-terms denoting the average propensity to spend were depressed by about
8 or 9 percent as a result of the taxes, operating thereby to neutralize, in part,
the rising θ' figure.

There is a surrealistic quality to pondering the figures and then conjecturing what would happen if taxes dropped to zero, as if government could
somehow vanish, as if its functions are utterly superfluous. Perhaps the only
useful conclusion is that so long as the relative size of government operations
is not enlarged, and the relative onerousness of the tax imposition stays fairly
flat, then any inflation onus would dissolve. Further, insofar as θ' grows, while
the c-propensities are not curtailed, a tauter w/A alignment would have to be
engineered to hold the P_c or CPI line. Unless some sharp trend-breaks in G
and T (tax rates) are in store, despite the impressionistic qualms over absolute
sums which conveniently suppress the enormity of GNP and the w ascent,
government outlays do not figure prominently as an inflation-maker despite the
plethora of scary stories. Too, most of the invective converges on Washington
in almost inverse proportion to state and local government facts.

Deficits

Deficits are sometimes flogged for being the inflation villain. Yet deficits are
solely the arithmetical gap between government outlays (including transfers
of all sorts) and tax and nontax revenues.

The one new item to add is the manner of financing the deficit. The excess
outlays can be financed either: (1) by printing money, (2) by borrowing from
banks, and thus "monetizing the debt," thereby creating bank deposits, or

(3) by borrowing from individuals and nonbank corporations, such as insurance companies, pension funds, or savings banks.

Ruling out printing press money, bank financing—"monetization"—enlarges M. Inflation through this channel of deficit finance is thus a thinly disguised QTM inflation theory.

Alternative lenders consist of individuals and noncommercial bank corporations. In absorbing funds from these sources the government appears as a competitor on loan markets and, unless the central bank smooths the way, there can be some upward pressures on interest rates. Once again, a discussion cannot go far without introducing M-aspects. Some upward interest rate pressure from government borrowing can be to some degree depressing, "crowding out," in the modern phrase, private borrowing and some I-magnitudes.

For the CPI, "large" deficits would entail a rise in the N/N_c ratio, and in recent years in θ', without full offsets in the c-terms. Thus *some* inflation can be attributed to deficits. This part of the ground has already been traversed in the analysis of G-outlays when they are divorced from taxes.

Actually, the federal government has reported only 9 years of surplus in the 46 final budget submissions covering 1929 through 1976, with about 4 of the plusses running at fairly piddling amounts. Yet, over most of the period, and certainly by the gross standards of the last 8 years, P behaved reasonably well, displaying only moderate annual increases. In 1932 and 1933 the deficits approached 50 percent of expenditures—yet the price level fell! Palpably, large deficits do not inexorably spell inflation. This buttresses the WCM tale as against the obsession with deficits as the inflation demon.

Experience in other countries reenforces this inference. In Canada, the National Accounts report sizable government deficits from 1957 to 1963, with P climbing by only 8 percent over the 7-year interval, or just over 1 percent per annum. Budget surpluses have been reported consistently (except for 1972) in the years since 1964. Nonetheless, this has been the period of inflation shock.

A tax cut to fight inflation?

A constant thread running through this analysis of inflation has been the importance of engaging the WCM elements; even an analysis of government fiscal actions must show effects on its components. It is thus conceivable that a tax cut might be an antiinflation antidote so long as it tempered increases in $\Delta w/w$.

The Keynesian attempt to stifle inflation in 1968 has been criticized for its stationary framework in assuming that $\Delta w/w$ would be sticky as tax rates mounted. It is possible to purge the static model by tying tax *cuts* to wage restraint, say offering unions an income tax rebate, in the tax ranges occupied by their membership, in return for a pledge for restraint at the bargaining table. A plan of this nature, to buy off union wage militancy culminating in

the inflation disaster, guided the United Kingdom inflation strategy in 1976.*
(Analytically it is presumed that the partial derivative $[(\partial w/\partial T) > 0]$.)

The national debt

More for completeness than importance, the place of the national debt in the
inflation saga compels discussion. The powerful fear-mystique of debt contains
some ancient confusions on individual versus government debt, and supersti-
tions on a day of reckoning and even the immorality of nonrepayment of debt.
Adam Smith lent credence to the illogic when writing: "What is prudence in
the conduct of every private family, can scarce be folly in that of a great
kingdom."†

Surely, consumers using a car for five years, or a piano or a house for a
prospective lifetime, have every economic reason to finance by borrowing,
within their income limitations, on a repayment basis akin to a rent for continuous use, as TV sets are rented (in other countries) or cars are leased, or
houses and apartments are commonly rented. In borrowing to finance long-
lived goods the differences reside in the extent of ownership versus rental
rights.

Adam Smith's maxim notwithstanding, it is necessary to look beyond the
individual family to the national family, to consider the wider repercussions
on others. Involved is "the fallacy of composition." One person can declare
correctly that there is room for one more on the bus, but it is futile for one
million people to act on the same premise. In a converse analogy, on the other
side of debt, owing, there are offsetting credits, of owning. The capitalist
system generates its dynamism in borrowing and lending—despite the wisdom of Polonius. The mechanics and vitality of capitalism repose in the
transfer of funds from those reluctant to employ their current surplus to those
eager to exploit lucrative opportunities in entrepreneurial uses, and willing to
pay an interest price.

The national debt total is a legacy of past deficits, mainly contracted
during war periods and in recessions as fiscal policy levers are applied. Control
over the debt as an absolute magnitude obviously involves generating surpluses to redeem outstanding bonds, or balancing the future books to avoid
augmented totals. As government bonds held as assets by individuals are part
of private net wealth, the "wealth effect" is argued as tending to enlarge
consumption outlays even as bondholders bemoan the taxes to cover the

---

* Many months before the Ford economic "summit," and about ten months before
the Ford reversal from tax raising to tax cutting, I suggested this policy. See "A Tax
Cut to Avert Stagflation," *Challenge* (Jan. 1974). Late in the day (1975) the tax
cut was passed, without extracting the wage pledge as the administration persisted in
its unemployment and "slow recovery" remedy. The *quid pro quo* ideas have been
taken up in the United Kingdom.

† *Wealth of Nations*, Book IV, Chapter II.

interest payments received by them or others as a millstone. Plusses and minuses must be toted, however, for a really accurate accounting.

Often the fear of bankruptcy intrudes as the ominous cloud over government debt, as in personal or corporate debt, per Adam Smith's strictures. Yet this is to spawn a red herring: bankruptcy is a legal state whereby creditors legally assume control of the available assets under court auspices for *pro rata* repayment. Despite many revolutions in which the powers of the state have been savagely transferred, a creditor *coup d'etat* has not as yet transpired. Governments can be described as bankrupt, in some play on words to denounce futile policies, but transferring the seat of power to a bondholders' committee of regents is not in our future.

The legitimate issues concern the certainty of the government paying interest and principal when due, and whether it should plan to reduce the debt. On the latter, there is involved a two-sided analysis of lower outlays on public services, and higher taxes, with implications for Q, N, and GNP composition of private goods and communal outputs. As debt is redeemed, in a pure case an individual owning $10,000 in government bonds must first pay tax sums to the Treasury and then receive a check from the Treasury to cancel the bondholdings; one is unlikely to feel enriched at the result despite cheery editorial columns on how the nation's moral fiber has been enhanced by the sacrificial act. Where the bonds are held by the commercial banking system, repayment would entail an equivalent deflation of demand deposits until the government bonds were replaced by new bank assets. Government obligations held by the banks amount to $90 billion, with another $95 billion owned by the Federal Reserve (mid-1976). Following the script inherent in the strident pitch of uninformed "experts" would usher in a catastrophic money deflation and a depression to undermine the enterprise system. In matters where more than zealous fears are involved, the enterprise system will have to be saved from its "friends."

Figures show that the national debt has been dwindling relative to GNP or national income; the annual interest charges make only a fairly meager 2+ percent claim—meager relative to the commotion—on incomes and 5.5 percent on tax revenues. Analytically, there is *always* enough income in the economy to meet interest charges, by virtue of the two-way relation: interest payments constitute income subject to tax so that, at a minimum, taxable income equals debt-service interest charges. Also, on fears concerning the selling of new bonds for cash to redeem old bonds, the only substantive aspect is the interest rate: if bonds cannot be floated at 7 percent, then 8 or 9 percent must be offered: in the stable economies buyers will be forthcoming at an attractive price. Maturing bonds are usually paid off, for the most part, by being "rolled over," with holders of old issues subscribing at redemption dates to new offerings.

In Table 12.3 government debt refers to *interest-bearing* debt: currency is also a debt form, but noninterest bearing. Too, government agencies, such

Table 12.3

National Debt, Corporate Debt, and Government Interest
Payments as a Percentage of National Income,
Selected Years 1929–1975

	National income	National debt (publicly held)	Corporate debt	Interest on national debt
1929	100.0	19.0	102.4	0.7
1940	100.0	55.2	93.2	1.3
1946	100.0	128.7	52.4	2.0
1950	100.0	92.0	60.1	1.9
1960	100.0	58.2	73.5	1.7
1970	100.0	30.1	99.9	1.8
1975	100.0	29.8	120.9	1.9

Source: *Council of Economic Advisers*, 1976

as the Federal Reserve, or the Social Security Fund, or the Railroad Survivors Fund, own government bonds for investment or to accomplish their mission, as does the Fed. Their holdings are excluded from the totals. For completeness, private debt figures are also included, for some revelation of the facts rather than to provoke fears.

The figures testify to vocal puffery on the national debt: there has been a steady decline in its relative importance since the war years. Corporate debt has become the larger sky-borne turkey—attesting to the vigor of the enterprise system despite drivel on the "drift to socialism." The inroads of interest payments on the debt as a percentage of income are also displayed. This is not injected to cheer their manageable size—which would be strange behavior for a taxpayer—but to acknowledge the evidence.

Future generations will undoubtedly marvel in some awe at the *small* absolute debt totals of our day, even as we behold with equanimity the sums of the past which were regarded by earlier generations as formidable and oppressive. This is a prediction, not a prescription for bigger debt: calling the winner in a horse race does not constitute enamorment with the horse.*

---

*   With the exception of the last few years, and what now seems a small adventure in prodigality by President Roosevelt in the Great Depression, the far greater portion of the debt was contracted in the war years of World War I, II, Korea, Vietnam, and the "cold war" defense posture. There are some who argue vehemently that debt transfers "burdens on to the future." If there are tax burdens, there are interest benefits. Likewise, those inheriting bonds seldom feel "poor" or "burdened." War-time sacrifices are borne by war-time victims. If past generations were smart enough to transfer "burdens," the future generations should also possess commensurate sagacity and acumen. Some distributive shifts in income, of course, occur as the debt grows. But . . . the past is past. We can always tax ourselves to cut debt, if this is deemed the best policy. Blaming the past is a wasteful exercise in hostility.

Acquittal or Probation?

Many grievances can be nailed on the government's door: inefficiency, imperfect reflection of constituent wishes, cumbrousness, lack of candor, corruption, to name a few shortcomings. But these are "people faults" that we have to endure. Concerning inflation, however, the government budget elicits the Scotch verdict: "Not Proven." Welfare outlays, to be sure, have been a mounting category with *some* effect on the consumer price level. But after the campaigns cease, and government reins pass from incumbents originally "consecrated" to economy to successors "dedicated" to eliminate waste, the inflation sequel will proceed until there is a proper w/A alignment.

A surgical cut in federal outlays by $100 billion (a projection of 25 percent, approximately) in 1977 will amount to about 10 percent of the wage bill. An annual 10 percent plus rise in money wages and salaries would overwhelm the herculean government withdrawal. A 10 percent slice in G would restore maybe $40 billion to taxpayers; a 10 percent wage hike would add $100 billion of personal income. On top of the respective demand impacts, money wages also inflate the cost side of the pricing decision.

Though Mark Twain would, in the best legal tradition, arise to say a few words in defense of Satan, it would strain the best judicial mind to weave a persuasive brief for budget surpluses as the key to inflation control. On deficits in creating inflation, considering our long experience and the Canadian surpluses, the jury might be "underwhelmed" enough to excise the charge from the bill of particulars. Other counts of economic mischief would abound.

Index

Albeck, Hermann, 158n
Alchian, Armen A., 25n
Aliber, Robert, 82n
Andersen, Leonall C., 186n
Antiinflation, not antilabor, 123–124
Arab oil embargo, 14n
Archimedes, 43
Aristotle, 216
Asimakopulos, A., 200n

Banana republics, 8
Banking principle, 77
Banks, and interest rates, 231n
Bastiat, Frédéric, 5
Bentham, Jeremy, 15n
Beveridge, Sir William, 17n
Bishop, Robert L., 203n
"Bite-the-bullet," 15
Bloomfield, Arthur, 169n
Bodin, Jean, 83, 216n
Boom-bust cycles, 7–9
Bowley, A. L., 46n, 98n
Branson, W. H., 102n
Brazil, 158, 181
Brechling, F. P., 81n
Bresciani-Turroni, C., 16n
Bronfenbrenner, Martin, 85n, 97n
Brunner, Karl, 82n, 84n, 88, 185n, 192n
Budgets, government, 23–24
Burns, Arthur, 11
Business taxes, 232

Cagan, Phillip, 172n, 187
Cairncross, Alec, 152n
Callaghan, James, 161n
Calmfors, Lars, 62
Cambridge cash-balance equation, 72, 78n
Cantillon, Richard, 83
CAP, a deflated AP, 130–131
Capitalism, and collectivism on inflation, 114–115
Capitalists "save all," 50–51
Cargill, Thomas F., 182n
Carter administration, 20n, 119n
Cassel, Gustav, 103
Catch-up theories, 106–108, 182–183; and Catch 22, 106
Central bankers: a maligned lot, 89–90; dismemberment, 89
Chamberlin, E. H., 219
Chatterjee, M., 214n
Churchill, Winston, 11
Circular-flow economy, 52n, 66
Clark, J. B., 100
Class struggle, misplaced, 110–112; Marxian themes, 110
Clower, Robert W., 81n, 94n
Cobb-Douglas functions, 46n, 101
Coercive economies, 122
Collective bargaining, 138
Connally, John, 12
Consumer price level, 48–50

Consumption outlay, and employee compensation, 51
Corrections, and indexation, 27–28
Cost-price ratios, 122–123
Cost-push, 43
Cournot, Augustin, 160
Currency principle, 78

Darby, Michael R., 82n, 88
Davenport, H. J., 228n
Davidson, Paul, 35n, 65n, 81n, 88n, 179n, 191, 192n, 212n, 213n
Davis, Richard M., 190n
Debt burden, 235–236
Deficits, 232–233
Deflationary gap, 202–203
Demand management, 7
Demand-pull, 43
Derived-demand theory, 97–99; *ceteris paribus*, 98; marginal productivity and, 99
Dernburg, T. F., 102n
Destroy-to-revive, 20
Dialogue, Keynesians and Monetarists, 7–10
Domar, Evsey, 7
Domino effects, in credit crunch, 192
Downing Street summit, 77n

Eatwell, John, 199n
Eckstein, Otto, 224n
Economist (London), 142n
Egalitarian prospects, 48
Eichner, Afred S., 200n
Eisenhower, Dwight D., 13n
Equation of Exchange, 71
Excess supply, 97
Exogenous-endogenous dialogue, 92–94; autonomous variations, 93; induced variations, 93; spontaneous variations, 93
Expectational theories, 106–108

Falsisms, 45
Fand, David, 181
Federal Reserve, 9–10; Fed and MA, 67n
Feiwel, George R., 223n
Fellner, William, 184n, 187n
Fisher, Franklin M., 47–48n
Fisher, Irving, 58n, 71, 103
Fleming, Miles, 212n
Fogarty, Michael, 114n, 121n, 138n
Francis, Darryl R., 82n

Friedman, Milton, 65, 66n, 67n, 70n, 72n, 78–81, 82n, 83n, 84, 85, 88, 89, 98n, 103, 104, 159n, 172n, 179–181, 184n, 185, 186n, 187, 188, 191, 192n, 210n
Fromm, Gary, 224n
Full employment, and monetary policy, 175–176
Full-time equivalents, 126, 143; and consultants, 143

Galbraith, John K., 15, 83n, 168n, 200–201n, 209n, 210, 217–218n, 219n
Game plan, 11; gradualism, 12; mid-wife vigil, 14; Nixon-Ford, 12–15; WIN buttons, 14
General equilibrium theory, 102–104
Geometry of 45-degree model, 202; misgivings, 203–205
Gibson, William E., 82n, 178n, 181n
Gilbert and Sullivan, 26
Gold standard, 168–170; and money wage standard, 170–172
Government expenditure, 229–231; taxation, 231–232
Graham, Frank D., 16n
Grant, General U. S., 11
Greenspan, Alan, 14
Gresham's law, 155
Gross Business Product, 44
Gross National Product, 44
Guillebaud, C. W., 17n

Habibagahi, Hamid, 80n
Hahn, F. H., 81n
Hansen, Alvin H., 40, 197n, 200, 201n, 215n
Harrod, Sir Roy, 7, 8n, 169n, 179n, 191, 192
Hayek, Friedrich, 84n, 92n, 117n, 175, 178
Helicopter, and money supplies, 103
Heller, Walter, 16, 195n, 209n, 212n
Hicks, Sir John, 40, 80n 97n, 165, 171, 188n, 194, 205, 206n, 215n
Higgs, Henry, 83n
Hines, A. G., 208n
Ho, D. C. C., 86n
Holbrook, R. S., 183n
Hoover, Herbert, 14n, 231
Horwich, George, 71n, 190n
Hotson, John, 47n, 194n, 231n
Hume, David, 83–84; and money dynamics, 83

Humphrey, Hubert H., 10
Hyperinflation, 33

Iceland, 158
Ideological debate, 10
Ignore-inflation Keynesians, 209
Incentive economies, 122
Indexation, 157–160; Keynesians, 209
Inflation: anticipated, 35–37; brain
  drain of, 37–38; compound rates
  of, 19; consequences, 29–33;
  expectations of, 183–184; mischievous
  potency, 33–34; redistributive effects,
  29–30; resource allocation aspects of,
  223
Inflationary gap, 202–203
Institutional reforms, 1
Inventions, and consumer price level, 61
Isard, Peter, 121n, 138n
IS-LM model, 205–207

Jevons, William Stanley, 93
Johnson, Harry G., 82n, 178n
Johnson, Ivan C., 194n, 205n
Johnson, Lyndon B., 12; surtax, 231

Kahn, Lord Richard F., 53n, 71n, 179n,
  191, 192
Kaldor, Lord Nicholas, 52n, 92n, 179n,
  192n, 199n, 208n, 223n
Kalecki, Michal, 46n, 223n
Kaufman, George, 82n, 178n, 181n
Kennedy, John F., 16; Guidepost policy,
  16–17
Keynes, Lord J. M., 7, 9, 17, 25n, 53n,
  54n, 63, 69n, 78n, 87, 99, 102, 103,
  111, 157n, 165, 169n, 179n, 183n,
  184n, 185n, 187, 188, 189, 191,
  194, 195, 206n, 210, 212, 225n
Klein, L. R., 47n
Knight, F. H., 183n
Kosobud, R. F., 47n
Kotowitz, Y., 121n, 138n
Kregel, Jan A., 81n, 199n, 200n
Kuh, Edwin, 208n
Kuhn, T. S., 40n

Labor markets: competitive, 105–106;
  monopoly, 105–106
Labour party, 10, 11n
Lags, 94, 178–179, and wages, 182–183
Laidler, D. E. W., 40n, 57n, 82n, 89n,
  107n, 191n

Laissez faire, 6
Lancaster, K., 191n
Laursen, Karsten, 19n
Lavington, F., 183n
Leijonhufvud, Axel, 195n
Lenin, I., 124n
Lerner, A. P., 14n, 128n, 152n, 211,
  212n
Levhari, David, 158n
Lincoln, Abraham, 11–12
Lindahl, E., 183n
Liquidity function, 203
Liviatan, Nissan, 158n
"Living-with-inflation," 27–28
Litvack, J. M., 102n
Locke, John, 83

MA and Fed, 67n
Macesich, George, 72n, 73n
Madison Avenue, 20
Malthus, T. R., 93
Marget, Arthur, 72n, 78n
Marginal productivity theory, 99–101;
  and marginal costs, 100
Market economy, foes, 1; salvaging, 6
Markups, near constancy, 46–47; and
  money velocity, 173
Marshall, Alfred, 94, 97, 98n, 159, 160,
  183n
Marshall, General George, 13
Marx, Karl, 2, 26, 33, 93n, 123, 184n,
  197n
Maynard, Geoffrey, 16n
McCulloch, J. Huston, 82n, 88, 89n
McDougall, D. M., 102n
McKinley, William, 14
Meade, James, 142n
Means, Gardiner C., 219n
Meiselman, David, 72n
Meltzer, Allan H., 84n., 88
Menger, Carl, 97
Mill, John Stuart, 64n, 66, 87n, 117
Miller, Ervin, 87n
Minsky, Hyman, 31n, 87n, 179n, 191, 192
Mints, Lloyd, 78n
Mitchell, Wesley C., 182n, 192n
Modigliani, Franco, 85n
Monetarism, 2, 10, 77–78; puzzle and
  indeterminateness, 77–84; WCM rap-
  prochement, 86
Monetary policy, classification, 75; prob-
  lem, not solution, 77

Money: accommodating, 77–78; causal, 77–78; does money matter? 87–88

Money demand, 185–190; alternative theory, 187–190; precautionary demand, 191–192; speculative demand, 203; supply-demand interdependence, 190–191; transactions demand, 185–190

Money supplies, potency of, 69–71; in time context, 73–75

Money wages: and expectations, 88–89 and real wages, 101; exogeneity and indeterminacy, 170–171; in time setting, 53–54; standard, 170–172

Monopoly: bilateral, 108; implications, 218–219; in labor markets, 105–106; trilateral, 108

Monroe, A. E., 46n, 83n

Mulvey, Charles, 167n

Myrdal, Gunnar, 183n

National debt, and inflation, 234–236

Natural unemployment, 179–180

Nazis, 17

Neoclassical wage theory, 95–96

Neutral money, 87

New Deal, 13n

Newcomb, Simon, 71n

New Quantity Theory, 71

Nixon, Richard M., 11, 212; control phases, 13

Nonfinancial corporations, 221–222

Nordhaus, William D., 163

Noton, Maxwell, 86n

Ohlin, Bertil, 183n

Oil prices and inflation, 52

Okun, Arthur M., 22n, 23

Open economy: consumer price level, 61–62; general price level, 57–62; money policy, 176–177

Open market operations, 74

Opie, Redvers, 53n

Oresme, Nicole, 46n

Orthodox economics, 6

P and Q matrix, 76

Palmer, Arnold, 12

Pareto optimum, 224–225

Parkin, J. M., 40n, 57n, 82n, 89n

Passell, Peter, 27n

Patinkin, Don, 67n, 100n, 103, 178n, 195n

Patterson, S. Howard, 15n

Payroll taxes, and wage restraint, 152–153

Peanuts, and prices, 104

Pedersen, Jørgen, 19n, 170–171

Peera, N., 100n

Pen, J., 108n

Petty, Sir William, 78n, 83

Pfleider, Otto, 158n

Phelps, E. S., 5, 25n, 35n, 208n, 209n

Phillips, Almarin, 203n

Phillips, A. W., 96n

Phillips curves, 69, 70n, 96–97, 181; Phillips curve Keynesians, 207–209; shifting Phillips curves, 208–209; trade-offs, 207–208

Pigou, Arthur C., 8n, 99, 100, 103, 183n, 195n

Pins, and prices, 104

Policing TIP, 124

Poole, William, 158n

Portes, Richard, 121n, 138n

Price controls, 154–156; black markets, 156; lawyers and, 154

Price-cost ratios, 122–123

Price index, consumer, 19

Princes and paupers, in labor, 111–112

Profit inflation, 54–55

Profit margins, and price, 145–146; and tax rebates, 146

Profits, and wage increases, 134–135

Queeg, Captain, 156

Rasche, Robert H., 183n

Real wages and money wages, 101

Relativities, 111; Keynes and, 111

Resource allocation and inflation, 223

Return, laws of, 70; dynamic change and, 70; productivity and, 70

Ricardo, David, 197n, 201n

Ritter, Lawrence S., 81n

Robbins, Lord Lionel, 92n

Robertson, Dennis H., 35n, 78n, 84n, 183n, 188, 201

Robinson, Joan, 3n, 16n, 46n, 63, 65n, 93n, 103n, 195n, 199n, 219, 223n

Roosevelt, Franklin D., 13n, 236n

Ross, Leonard, 27n, 29n, 35n

Ross, Stephen A., 223n

Rotwein, Eugene, 84n

Rule-of-the road, 118

Ryckeghem, W. van, 16n

Samuelson, Paul A., 40, 96n, 200, 201, 215n

Sargent, Thomas J., 86n

Sayers, Millicent, 16n

Schips, Bernd, 182n

Schultz, George, 13, 82n

Schulz, Henry, 98n

Schumpeter, Joseph A., 52n, 67

Sectoral price levels, 52–53

Seidman, Lawrence S., 121n, 128, 135n, 136n, 138n, 153n

Selden, Richard T., 84n, 178n, 185n

Shackle, G. L. S., 184n

Shell, Karl, 200n

Simon, William, 14

Simons, Henry, 84n, 217n

Skills, upgrading, 131–132

"Slows," 11–15

Slumpflation, 7–9; defined, 76

Smith, Adam, 106, 197n, 228

Smith, W. L., 68n

Smolensky, Eugene, 212n

Social compact, 118

Social contract, 118n

Social Security, 30

Solow, Robert M., 96n

Speculative motive, 201

Sraffa, Piero, 197n

Stagflation, 7–9; defined, 76

Steady-money rule, 84–86; and unsteady economy, 86–87

Stein, Herbert, 13

Stein, Jerome L., 65n

Stiffening wage resistance, 124

Stock market, 32n

Strigl, R., 92n

Supreme Court, 169n

Tabular standard, 159

Tax cuts, as antiinflation, 233–234

Tax rebates, and profit margins, 146

Teigen, Ronald, 183n

Thorn, Richard S., 178n

Thünen, Johann von, 201n

Tinbergen, Jan, 11, 77

TIP, administrative feasibility, 143; collective bargaining and, 137–138; computational steps, 132–133; flexibility of, 139; omissions, 140–141; principle, 126; safety-valve aspects, 139; salaries and, 139–140; supplements, 141–142; technological change and, 131

TIP-P, abnormal pay increases, 150; averaging, 149; irregular incomes, 150; new employees, 149; promotions, 150; self-employment, 150–151; stumbling blocks, 148

TNEC, 219n

Tobin, James, 27n, 28n, 29n, 68n, 188n, 203n

Tolstoy, Leo, 93

Transmission mechanism, Monetarist, 181–182

Trevithick, J. A., 167n

Truisms, 45

Turkey, 3

Twain, Mark, 113, 237

Unemployment, costs of, 21–26; excess amount, 22–23; individual losses, 24–26; rates of, 19

Union busting, 124

Union wage bill sharing, 152

Value added per employee, 129

Vickers, Douglas, 83n, 192n

Wachter, Michael L., 223n

Wage controls, 154–156

Wage earners spend all, 50–51

Wage function, endogenous, 95; and normalcy, 95

Wage increases, and profits, 134–135

Wage-lag hypothesis, 182–183

Wage-price spiral, 89n

Wage-salary norms, 125

Wage unit, 196–197

Wages, simply another price, 104–105

Wallich, Henry, 87n, 121n

Walras, Léon, 97, 102–103

Walrasian equations, 49–50n; general equilibrium, 88n, 91

WCM, and Monetarism, 86; and monetary policy, 69–72, 75–77

Weighted job classification, 127–128

Weimar Republic, 17

Weintraub, E. Roy, 108n

Welfare gains, from more cars, 224–225

Wells, Paul, 212n

Wicksell, Knut, 71n, 175, 178

Wiles, Peter, 46n, 121n

Williams, Harry T., 11n

Williamson, Oliver E., 203n

Wilson, Charles, 13n

Wilson, Harold, 161

Wright, David McCord, 88n

Yeager, Leland B., 98n

0 6 1 6

12